The Elephant in the ADHD Room

of related interest

Can I tell you about ADHD?
A guide for friends, family and professionals
Susan Yarney
Illustrated by Chris Martin
Part of the Can I tell you about…? series
ISBN 978 1 84905 359 4
eISBN 978 0 85700 708 7

AD/HD Homework Challenges Transformed!
Creative Ways to Achieve Focus and Attention by Building on AD/HD Traits
Harriet Hope Green
ISBN 978 1 84905 880 3
eISBN 978 0 85700 601 1

ADHD – Living without Brakes
Martin L. Kutscher MD
Illustrated by Douglas Puder MD
Hardback ISBN 978 1 84310 873 3
Paperback ISBN 978 1 84905 816 2
eISBN 978 1 84642 769 5

Helping Kids and Teens with ADHD in School
A Workbook for Classroom Support and Managing Transitions
Joanne Steer and Kate Horstmann
Illustrated by Jason Edwards
ISBN 978 1 84310 663 0
eISBN 978 1 84642 923 1

All Dogs Have ADHD
Kathy Hoopmann
ISBN 978 1 84310 651 7
eISBN 978 1 84642 840 1

Organize Your ADD/ADHD Child
A Practical Guide for Parents
Cheryl R. Carter
ISBN 978 1 84905 839 1
eISBN 978 0 84700 343 0

Step by Step Help for Children with ADHD
A Self-Help Manual for Parents
Cathy Laver-Bradbury, Margaret Thompson, Anne Weeks, David Daley and Edmund J. S. Sonuga-Barke
ISBN 978 1 84905 070 8
eISBN 978 0 85700 235 8

The Elephant in the ADHD Room

Beating Boredom as the Secret to Managing ADHD

LETITIA SWEITZER

Jessica Kingsley *Publishers*
London and Philadelphia

First published in 2014
by Jessica Kingsley Publishers
73 Collier Street
London N1 9BE, UK
and
400 Market Street, Suite 400
Philadelphia, PA 19106, USA

www.jkp.com

Library of Congress Cataloging in Publication Data
A CIP catalog record for this book is available from the Library of Congress

British Library Cataloguing in Publication Data
A CIP catalogue record for this book is available from the British Library

ISBN 978 1 84905 965 7
eISBN 978 0 85700 910 4

Printed and bound in Great Britain

To Lyndon D. Waugh, M.D., whose concept of the central role of boredom in ADHD led me to write this book, in gratitude for his personal and professional encouragement.

DISCLAIMER

This book is based on the author's experience with individuals with and without a diagnosis of ADHD. Some of the individuals in this book have been given fictitious names and identifying details to protect their privacy. The material in this book is intended to provide helpful information and awareness of the roles of interest and boredom in general and ADHD in particular. The book is solely the opinion of the author based on her interpretation of sources listed, interviews, and personal experience.

The book serves only as a supplement to, not a substitute for the thorough and professional care of a licensed physician, psychologist, therapist, or psychiatrist. It is not meant to be used, nor should it be used, to diagnose or treat any medical condition. Neither the author nor the publisher is liable for any damages or negative consequences from any treatment, action, or application to any person reading or following the information in this book.

References are provided for informational purposes only and do not constitute endorsement of any websites or other sources. Readers should be aware that the websites listed in this book may change.

CONTENTS

PART 1

Boredom, ADHD, and the Elements of Interest

CHAPTER ONE

The Premise

Psychiatrists and other clinicians, counselors, teachers, and parents encounter boredom from time to time, their own and the boredom of their patients, clients, students, and children. Perhaps more often they encounter the behavior designed, knowingly or not, to provide an escape from boredom. The behavior of escape may be brilliant, useful, humorous, original, and desirable, especially so when the avoider has attention deficit hyperactivity disorder (ADHD). The boredom avoidance can just as often be hyperactive, risk-taking, rule-breaking, novelty-seeking, and disruptive, especially when the avoider has ADHD. Boredom and escape from boredom are thus key elements of ADHD—its diagnosis, understanding, and management.

Children are born into a world where everything is novel and challenging, and their interest is abundant. Our efforts to keep the natural ability of children to interest themselves flowing throughout a lifetime require interest-seeking skills as less and less experience is novel and a great many restrictions apply. This book provides insights into the boredom–interest continuum, interest-seeking behavior in ADHD, and examples applying Elements of Interest to otherwise boring situations age by age, from infancy on. We begin with a story.

A lifetime of untreated ADHD

Rob has retired from a job in a big city to live on a farm on the edge of a small town. As Rob and I talk, I notice that he frequently stops mid-sentence and says, "That reminds me…" And he goes off on an entirely different topic without finishing or returning to his thought on the first topic. Some idea or word he himself had used set him off on a new course without regard for the unfinished thought. A lot of people habitually interrupt others and get off track, but Rob's abrupt switches in the middle of his own thoughts seem unusual.

I mention to him that I have noticed this habit, and he acknowledges, "I get bored with what I'm saying and I think of something more interesting."

That statement encapsulates the premise of this book; boredom is the elephant in the ADHD room. When any of us becomes bored with what we're thinking, saying, or doing, we begin to look around for something more interesting to think, say, or do. People with ADHD become bored more often and more intensely, and they find boredom more intolerable than those without ADHD. Reflexively they seek something more interesting. That mental response to boredom parallels the diagnostic events of inattention and impulsivity that characterize ADHD, while the physical need to escape boredom drives hyperactivity, the third diagnostic criterion.

Rob's history shows early signs of ADHD, although he was not diagnosed until much later. He was dismissed from two nursery schools for not doing as he was told and causing trouble, he says. His mother was frequently called into school to discuss Rob's fighting.

Rob succeeded in school, though not to his potential, in a very structured independent school. Writing was emphasized at this school at considerable emotional cost for Rob. I learned that a typical evening scene involved his mother standing over him as he struggled to write a short paper for school. He twiddled his pencil and jiggled his leg while his mother warned, "I'm going downstairs to do some laundry. When I get back I want you to have written three sentences." When she returned, Rob had written nothing at all, and a tirade began: "Why haven't you done anything? Just three sentences! You haven't written even one. I told you…" Rob just couldn't write; he didn't know why. The more pressure that was put on him, the more impossible writing became.

Rob finally refused to go back to that school and graduated from a less demanding school that more often required short answer assignments. His high scores on university entrance exams got him into a prestigious university where, he says, "I learned a lot and read a lot of books but not the ones the professors assigned." The assigned books did not give Rob what he needed: a high level of stimulation. Other books did, so he turned to them.

No wonder. Boredom is the feeling of too little stimulation, a discomfort that ADHD expert and author Edward M. Hallowell, M.D., describes from his own experience as "like being asphyxiated."[1] Similarly, ADHD is characterized largely by a lack of stimulation caused by under-activation of the neurotransmitter dopamine across the synapses of the brain. The parallel between the disruption of stimulation that characterizes both boredom and ADHD is highlighted by the fact that stimulants are often a successful treatment for ADHD, just as the experience of stimulation relieves boredom.

Dopamine is linked to focus, curiosity, seeking, excitement, hope, and "the idea of starting again."[2] Without sufficient stimulation of the dopamine system there is little neurological reward, which results in a poorly defined irritation, like an itch needing to be scratched, and so the bored person, with or without ADHD, is always looking for something different from what he is experiencing now. People with ADHD seek stimulation more than those without that condition and thereby often experience satisfaction, but often only by difficult trial and error.

Rob didn't make it through the first year in the university and, having already enrolled in the Naval Reserves, he lost his deferment status and was called to active duty. Based on results of Navy testing, he was chosen to learn some cutting-edge technology—computers were in their infancy then. The work excited him, and, when he'd finished his service, he began a career in the space industry doing computer work that mostly university graduates were hired to do. He still jiggled his leg to provide kinesthetic stimulation, but the characteristics of this work—challenge, novelty, problem-solving, and few rules about work habits, for example—allowed him to succeed. He had found a way to satisfy or circumvent his hyperactivity, impulsivity, and inattention.

Finding his way has mostly meant finding a way to escape anything boring for the next several decades of his career and on into retirement. Boredom-driven, interest-seeking behavior often means being unconventional and breaking rules. Conventional is boring. Rules lock in boredom.

Moreover, being unconventional often has charm. When an old friend comes to town, Rob takes the day off from work and shows her around the city. He drives the wrong way up a one-way alley, taking a short cut to his favorite lunch place. He orders his favorite dessert and he and his visitor share the sumptuous confection before the lunch menu arrives. Then they order sandwiches. He has rather deliberately taken the power out of all the silly rules so that he can follow his impulses. He has also canceled all the rules that pertain to things not at hand: he doesn't write thank-you notes, he doesn't respond to invitations, he doesn't answer e-mails that he doesn't feel like answering, he doesn't waste time with boring pleasantries like "How have you been?" A visitor to his house he may not have seen for years arrives to find him in the kitchen engrossed in deftly pouring pancake batter onto a griddle. Rob barely glances at the newcomer as he says cheerfully, "Do you want blueberries in your pancakes or pecans?" There's no, "It's good to see you, it's been a long time." Responding mainly to the immediacy of face-to-face stimulation is Rob's style but it's more than a style. It's a way of life.

Meeting children he has not seen in years, he avoids the boring adult remark, "My, how you've grown." He simply sees the child and a Lego set; he picks up a Lego® brick and says, "How about if we put one there?" The child is enchanted to be immediately in sync with Rob without any embarrassing greeting. Rob and the child play with Lego® until one of them loses interest, which takes some time.

The charming side of ADHD got him a marriage partner. A lot of requirements came with her. There is almost always a downside to counter the upside as people seek and find stimulation. ADHD behavior often leads to conflict as the one with ADHD doesn't meet a spouse's expectations. Rob was used to disappointing people. "I just expected to be yelled at for the rest of my life," he says.

Now divorced, remarried, and still seeking stimulation in retirement, there is little downside to his current way of life. Rob is busy all day, every day. Something catches his eye that needs to be done or he wants to do, and he's on it. When he arrived in this small town, he impulsively accepted volunteer jobs that interested him without considering if he would have time to perform them all well. He accepted invitations to work on committees and soon became an officer for several civic organizations, eventually running for public office. If it's there in front of him, he engages it. At home he starts things, promises things, abandons things, and never returns to them. If someone mentions an unfinished project, he says, "Yeah, I need to get back to that." But he doesn't. He knows he won't. He heads for something else that will engage him with its newness until it's not new anymore. Rob treats his boredom from morning to night; he has not treated his ADHD.

Almost every move Rob makes can be explained by his remark, "I get bored…and I think of something more interesting." A kid's version of this statement is remarkably similar. In the following conversation, ten-year-old Harry has just explained to me that he loves a challenge. Then, quite out of the blue, it seemed, he startled me with a statement:

HARRY: *I'm crazy, too.*

LETITIA: *What do you mean by "crazy"?*

HARRY: *I'm kind of crazy. I'm not responsible. I also do stupid things.*

LETITIA: *Stupid things? You seem smart to me. I can't imagine you do stupid things. Do you mean silly things?*

HARRY: *Yes. Sometimes I'll be responsible, but a lot of the time I'm stupid and silly. Me and my friends will be talking and I'll automatically change the subject completely and I'll say something nobody is talking about. Then I'll go back to what we were talking about.*

LETITIA: *So you go off topic sometimes.*

HARRY: *Like we were eating breakfast this morning and I said, "…"*

(What he said sounded like nonsense syllables to me even when I asked to have it repeated.)

> HARRY: *They said, "What?" And then we went on talking about what we were talking about before.*

Perhaps someone has pointed out Harry's digressions to him as I had done with Rob, or perhaps he has noticed them himself. I want to tell him and all those with ADHD, both adults and children, that any of us would go off topic if we saw the specter of boredom coming and felt compelled to jump out of the way. Rob's off-the-cuff explanation for his digressions, that he was bored with what he was saying, corroborates in simple words the premise that boredom is a major force that drives the behavior of people with ADHD.

The idea that boredom is key to the understanding and treatment of ADHD came to me originally from my work with child, adolescent, and family psychiatrist Lyndon D. Waugh, a mentor and author with whom I had collaborated on *Tired of Yelling: Teaching Our Children to Resolve Conflict* (1999).[3] Dr. Waugh feels so strongly that boredom proneness and especially boredom intolerance are such important factors in ADHD that he believes those boredom factors, the emotional part of the disorder, should be worked into the diagnostic criteria.

Dr. Waugh tells this story:

> A 14-year-old boy I'd been treating for ADHD since he was very young came in for a follow-up appointment. He had been away at boarding school so I hadn't seen him in a while. Years before, he had wandered around the room and explored things and was hard to engage in conversation. Now he was trying to be more cooperative, focused and mature. He was sitting still, but I saw his eyes roll upward frequently during our conversation. After a while, with a knowing smile, I asked, "How many are there?" He said, "54." "How did you do it?" "Both ways." We both knew he meant counting the tiles on the ceiling and that he had arrived at the number 54 both by counting every tile and by counting the vertical and horizontal rows and multiplying. He was not alone. Even the buttons in my office have been counted.
>
> When he was caught, the boy was embarrassed that I realized his attention was wandering. I said, "That's okay. I don't mind. I understand how hard it is to sit still and focus without anything else to do. You need to have a busy mind and probably

> often do several things at the same time." I reminded him how he used to get up and run around and explore my office when he was a little kid, and I was pleased to see he had achieved control over that, but I understood the pain associated with limiting his attention to one required activity. My understanding relieved him, and we talked about how his mind worked. He said he and a schoolmate competed to see how many things each could pay attention to at one time. He was the winner.
>
> I then asked him what percentage of his mind was paying attention to our conversation while he was counting the tiles. He said it was about 50 percent. I said if he could work on giving 80 percent of his attention to our talking, he could understand and retain more of our conversation. I knew he had trouble remembering people's names so I asked him how much of his attention he gives to names when he sees people. He said, "The part of my brain that holds the names is this big," and with the space between his thumb and index finger he showed a narrow sliver.
>
> "How much attention do you pay to their faces?" I asked. He showed me a slightly larger sliver. "How much of your mind pays attention to math?" Not much, he indicated. "How much to history?" He smiled and showed me a bigger portion. "How much to your favorite video game?" He grinned and said, "As big as that chair." "How much to anxiety and worry?" I asked. "Not too much," he said. "How about boredom?" His face fell and he appeared sad. "That's about as big as this room," he said. I actually got a tear in my eye hearing how huge boredom was in his brain and watching how demoralized he looked just thinking about it.[4]

Hearing Dr. Waugh's story, I imagined this teenaged patient's boredom as being the proverbial elephant that filled the room, the huge emotion that drives the diagnostic criteria of inattention, hyperactivity, and impulsivity but which is not usually listed by developmental psychologists as an emotion and was rarely talked about as a key to understanding and relieving the challenges of ADHD. And so I began to pull together material for this book.

First, I found a quotation from Patricia Meyer Spacks' book *Boredom: The Literary History of a State of Mind* that aptly expresses how universal the power of boredom is: "...all endeavor of every kind takes place in the context of boredom impending or boredom repudiated, and can be understood as impelled by the effort to understand boredom's threat. I am not the first to say so."[5] While the threat of boredom is indeed universal, it is especially prevalent, intense, problematic, and often unbearable for individuals with ADHD. In a 2002 article Colorado psychiatrist William W. Dodson wrote a clear statement of that premise, which had led to my work with building interest. Dodson, a specialist in adult ADHD, wrote:

> *TAKE HOME MESSAGE #1:* For persons with ADHD, the ability to maintain attention and impulse control is determined by one factor—if the task is interesting, desired, or challenging, the individual with ADHD has no problem with distractibility or impulsivity. If, on the other hand, the task is boring, it is a neurologic impossibility to stay on task. Interest and challenge only determine the ability to function, not importance. This "interest based performance" is coming to be the hallmark diagnostic symptom of the disorder and the key to successful management once medication treatment has been established.[6]

People who are bored not only suffer feelings that range from vague discomfort to something akin to pain, they also endure the judgment of others—if not their own—that boredom is laziness, moral lapse, or lack of caring. And so they feel like failures for being unable to rescue themselves from boredom. Especially when their generalized boredom is related to ADHD, it's an added pound—or even a ton—on top of an already heavy burden of excessive striving and disappointment.

Many people with ADHD seek relief from boredom before they fully realize what they are seeking relief from. They may jump from activity to activity like Rob or nap or daydream. Students with ADHD may be diligent, even frantic to perform well in class, but they lack sufficient ability to choose what to focus on, so they inadvertently or purposely scan the environment for something more interesting than what's going on in class.

If a bored student scans for something interesting and finds nothing, she might begin to daydream because she can imagine things far more stimulating than the class she's in. If not, she naps. She soon learns to skip the step of scanning the environment and intentionally sets this class time aside to daydream or nap. She might be diagnosed with ADHD, predominately inattentive. However, lacking symptoms of hyperactivity and impulsivity, she is less likely to be diagnosed at all. A bright girl with mediocre grades, she may be called lazy, "The girl who sits in the back of the room and daydreams," an underachiever, or simply a poor student.

Another student with ADHD may doodle on paper or even his desk. He may swing his leg and repeatedly kick the seat in front of him or build a clever catapult for spitballs out of pencils and rubber bands. The urges of hyperactivity set his hands in relentless motion.

For the impulsive person, a walk down the street brings ample opportunity for a break from boredom. A wall cries out for graffiti, a stone wants to be thrown, or an obstacle begs to be jumped. Some people with ADHD readily break through boredom by impulsive action, risky behavior, or "poor choices." They suffer consequences from unwise actions or words, often not realizing those behaviors were an escape from boredom. Without taking time even to recognize boredom, they do not resist the hijacking of their attention; they invite it.

On the other hand, many with ADHD have designed activities that fit their interests so well that they reach personal satisfaction and high levels of achievement in school and beyond. Facilitating this process and these outcomes is the purpose of this book. If boredom is the "elephant in the ADHD room," my purpose is to bring it out in the open, care for it, and train it to serve as a motivator for realizing all the charm, energy, intelligence, creativity, divergent thinking, and humor that people with ADHD often have in abundance.

CHAPTER TWO

Boredom and ADHD Through the Centuries

Boredom gets no respect. When children say they're bored, they're often told by parents and teachers, "Only boring people are bored," or "How could you be bored? Don't you have homework?" or "I never want to hear that word in this house again." Through such callous responses, people are taught from childhood not to say they are bored. By the time they are adults, they are not only discouraged from expressing boredom but also from examining it.

At the same time, a diagnosis of ADHD similarly gets no respect in some quarters; ADHD-related behavior is often blamed on parental failure to discipline or other external factors. When the hyperactivity, impulsivity, and inattention of ADHD are expressed as overt boredom or as boredom-escaping behavior, ADHD is too often interpreted as disrespect, laziness, obstinacy, disobedience, not caring, or the ubiquitous "not applying himself."

Novelty-seeking and evolution

The characteristics of ADHD may serve a positive evolutionary purpose. ADHD, like boredom, was named and renamed only in recent centuries. Boredom and ADHD symptoms can be significantly relieved by being physically active, seeking novelty, risk-taking, rule-breaking, exploring, experimenting, and other forms of adaptive "seeking" thoughts and behaviors. Thus boredom intolerance could have made a valuable contribution to the survival of a tribe or community. Scanning for new or different phenomena as well as hyperfocusing on what is crucial are necessary modes of attention for the survival of a group; both attention modes can be typical characteristics of ADHD. The discomfort of boredom may be an evolutionary adaptation as the need for relief serves as motivation to overcome anxiety or fear-based hesitancy in order to explore and experiment. If distinctively different levels of sensitivity to boredom have been useful to the survival of a tribe in the past millennia, the tendency to boredom associated with ADHD may be a natural variation as a type, not a disorder.

When we humans were hunter-gatherers, the type of human with ADHD characteristics was at the forefront of the hunt. These were the ones energized by uncertainty, intrigued by novelty, lured by risk-taking, and driven by increased flow of relevant neurotransmitters and spurts of adrenaline at the sight or sound of a desired prey. They were eager to accept challenge whether figuring out how to get home when their canoe had been lost in the rapids or facing attack from outside tribes. They were not so good at sitting around shelling a pile of nuts; they tended to get bored and wander off, leaving others to finish the job. Far from being disparaged as "irresponsible" or "immature" for not doing the sedentary work, they were admired for their strengths as explorers, hunters, and warriors. Mankind flourished with the ADHD activists who, while prone to boredom in sedentary, rote activities and periods of waiting for action, rose to physical challenges, were at their best in crises, and were motivated by anticipation and gratified by the thrill of the "pay-off" of the hunt or skirmish with outsiders. They were assets, not misfits.

When agriculture became more prominent and hunting and exploring less critical to survival, more people were farmers tied to the land, doing steady, backbreaking work. Survival proved they were good at sticking to this type of labor repeatedly through endless seasons. Hunters still pursued game and explored new hunting grounds; newness and the unknown were strong motivators even beyond necessity. They defended their territory against invaders—or became invaders—because farming required possession of land. The individuals best suited for hunting, exploring, and battle met the description of what we now call ADHD, but they were now less critical to the survival of an increasingly agricultural society.

A related issue was featured in the January 2013 issue of *National Geographic* in an article written by David Dobbs entitled "Restless genes."

> If an urge to explore rises in us innately, perhaps its foundation lies within our genome. In fact there is a mutation that pops up frequently in such discussions: a variant of a gene called DRD4, which helps control dopamine, a chemical brain messenger important in learning and reward. Researchers have repeatedly tied the variant, known as DRD4-7R and carried by roughly 20 per cent of all humans, to curiosity and restlessness.[1]

Curiosity is the pleasant anticipation of something less boring and not yet known. Restlessness is the result of discontent with one's present state, leading to the search for newness.

Dobbs goes on to say:

> Dozens of human studies have found that 7R makes people more likely to take risks; explore new ideas, places, foods, relationships, drugs, or sexual opportunities; and generally embrace movement, change, and adventure. Studies in animals simulating 7R's actions suggest it increases their taste for both movement and novelty. (Not incidentally, it is also closely associated with ADHD.)[2]

Another study and possible conclusion, cited by Dobbs, suggests this risk-taking type of human thrives better in some societal circumstances than others:

> Among Ariaal tribesmen in Africa, those who carry 7R tend to be stronger and better fed than their non-7R peers if they live in nomadic tribes, possibly reflecting better fitness for a nomadic life and perhaps higher status as well. However, 7R carriers tend to be less well-nourished if they live as settled villagers. The variant's value, then, like that of many genes and traits, may depend on the surroundings. A restless person may thrive in a changeable environment but wither in a stable one; likewise with any genes that help produce the restlessness.[2]

Similarly, individuals with ADHD thrive today in a changeable environment and wither in a more settled one.

In his *National Geographic* overview, Dobbs does not shy away from noting other researchers' disagreement with what they consider overreaching conclusions from the 7R studies. He acknowledges that the evolutionary and population geneticist Kenneth Kidd, the very researcher who discovered 7R, points out findings of other studies that weigh against the suggestion of hardwiring in the case of the tendency to explore. Dobbs quotes Kidd, "You can't just reduce something as complex as human exploration to a single gene."[3]

"More likely," Dobbs summarizes, "different groups of genes contribute to multiple traits, some allowing us to explore, and others, 7R quite possibly among them, pressing us to do so."[3]

Whether or not you accept the power of a gene or group of genes to drive exploration and related novelty-seeking, it is well known that the characteristic differences inherent in ADHD that may have favored exploration 200,000 years ago have in modern times led inventors, artists, entrepreneurs, soldiers in battle, first responders, and others driven from boredom to discover new places, new ideas, new products, and new methods, as well as to seek intense action and the thrill of the hunt. In the same issue of *National Geographic*, individual explorers and risk-takers are highlighted. While many of them have done extreme physical feats, also included are two inventors who explored new ideas and in doing so faced fierce opposition and even ridicule until their ideas won acceptance.[4] This kind of fight for new ideas and willingness to break rules—social risk—is as valid as physical feats in describing a risk-taker.

As a long succession of civilizations eventually paraded through history, many people suffered boredom working relatively safely at benches or sweating behind ploughshares for a living. Some individuals ran off to a precarious life at sea. Throughout history, while people have always worked in boring situations for survival, new frontiers offered escape for the daring.

The developed societies of the world currently require an increasing percentage of people who are willing to sit quietly in chairs. Schools and the workplace remain havens for boredom to flourish and ADHD, whether a "type" or a disorder, to be severely problematic. It follows that in the modern chair-sitting culture misfits are more obvious.

Chris Chandler, Principal Lecturer in Psychobiology at London Metropolitan University, in his book *The Science of ADHD* even-handedly weighs the arguments for and against ADHD being an adaptive type. He concludes:

> Whilst the knowledge that the behaviors associated with ADHD were once of some benefit is neither here nor there, the important point is how best to accommodate the needs of those with ADHD and reduce any suffering that they have. However, I think it is necessary to highlight the positive aspects of ADHD, as this may help individuals maximize their potentials—even in the twenty-first century.[5]

Misfits

ADHD is generally accepted by most physicians and other diagnosticians as a physical difference in the brain that is genetic. Those with ADHD have more trouble adapting, at least to today's world, than those without this type of brain function, and that difference increasingly defines it as a disorder. Some of the pathology of ADHD is evident in crime statistics.

An article by Joel L. Young, M.D., supported by an independent educational grant from Shire and published online by Medscape.com, draws from studies of crime and ADHD, summarizing the overlap between ADHD and crime:

> People with ADHD commit crimes for many of the same reasons as those without ADHD: Some want money or property that belongs to others and have little motivation to acquire the loot honestly. Those with ADHD also have other triggers for crimes; adolescents and adults with untreated ADHD are often bored, sensation-seeking, or simply impulsive, and this combination of attributes leads them to react with poor judgment.[6]

I want to highlight the mention of "bored" and the attributes of sensation-seeking and impulsivity, which are means of escaping boredom. Dr. Young continues:

> A desired item appears, they want it, so they take it. It also appears that when individuals with ADHD commit violent crimes, these acts are more likely to be crimes of spontaneous and "reactive" aggression rather than carefully plotted out offenses. Such crimes are generally impulsive acts driven by a provocation or conflict that triggers an outburst. Research with adult male offenders seems to bear out this hypothesis.[7]

While most people with ADHD do not commit violent crimes, of course, a disproportionate number of violent crimes committed are done by those with ADHD. The statistics suggest the importance of treating ADHD not only with medication but also with education on the boredom factor and the means of seeking interest. Instilling in youth their responsibility for escaping or shaping their boredom in positive ways should be a goal for parents, educators, and clinicians.

The brilliant side of the ADHD coin

While the connection between crime and ADHD is troubling, the same characteristics of ADHD that often foster crime, thinking differently, rule-breaking, taking risks, seeking novelty, and especially unwillingness to suffer from boredom very often produce another kind of "misfit," the kind that throws off mundane and outworn norms to create inventions, art, humor, and initiatives that benefit society and to thrill the world with record-breaking sports achievements and performances in arts and entertainment.

Generally, people begin new projects with enthusiasm and focus intently for a while. At the point when the fun of innovation and discovery runs out, some degree of boredom sets in. For many researchers, having new ideas is more fun than doing proofs of something they already believe will work. New concepts are exciting; the details of research projects are tedious. Most people strive on to reach the pay-off. People with ADHD cannot overcome that lowering of stimulation and often quit before the pay-off to seek the readier stimulation of starting something new.

ADHD-type creative giants escape boredom through daydreaming, plunge impulsively into experimentation, drop old projects, and initiate new projects with excitement and curiosity, all of which have been seen as disruptive to their progress.

Biographer Neil Baldwin tells a tale of American inventor Thomas Edison impulsively publicizing a new kind of electric phenomenon he'd discovered before he took the time to understand it, test it, or prove it himself. Public opinion turned against him, at least in this instance. "Edison later regretted the decision to move on so precipitously; but, being irrepressible, the *idea* of penetrating new territory always captivated him, and after the often premature announcement of innovation had been made, the struggle to sustain his crusade invariably bored him."[8] Baldwin italicized "idea" because that is what drove Edison more than the follow-through, which was boring. The follow-through is the giant hurdle facing the entrepreneur, the ADHDer's mountain to climb.

These ADHDers were eventually saved from being troublemakers forever by their brilliance and the utility or quality of their inventions. Those with similar intolerance of boredom who did not succeed in inventing or creating things of outstanding importance had to find other ways to satisfy the demands of their ADHD.

Modern winners and creative geniuses

The energy and incessant need for physical action characterizing hyperactivity in ADHD has propelled many athletes to greatness. Typically they feel scattered, inattentive, and bored during long periods without physical action, such as school.

Some of the biggest names in Olympic history have used extreme exercise as treatment for ADHD.

By the time Michael Phelps left London after the 2012 Summer Olympics he had racked up a record-setting 19 gold medals. Swimming isn't just a winning sport for Phelps; it has always been a way for him to cope with his ADHD. Phelps' Mom Debbie described her son's exhibition of classic ADHD symptoms as not sitting still or being able to focus. However, he channeled that into swimming, and with "continuous praise and positive reinforcement" Phelps had the encouragement he needed to win his golds.[9]

Achievements in other areas of society have been boosted by characteristics of ADHD. For example, James Carville, a political consultant and commentator, is best known for leading campaigns for U.S. President Bill Clinton and Britain's Prime Minister Tony Blair. Carville frequently speaks about his ADHD with organizations such as CHADD. Political competition, like battle for the warrior, offers challenge, unpredictability, risk, drama, conflict, public acclaim, and other stimulating elements ADHDers use to avoid settling into boredom.[10]

Psychology Today has published an educated guess that people with ADHD are 300 percent more likely to start their own business.[10] In any case, people with ADHD are overrepresented in the ranks of entrepreneurs. The motivation provided by new ideas and the dislike of restraints makes many business people with boredom intolerance forge out on their own. Serial entrepreneurs start another business when they get bored with the previous one.

Sir Richard Branson, English adventurer, is an ADHDer who dropped out of school at age 16 and soon published a successful youth culture magazine titled *Student.* Virgin Records, Virgin Atlantic airlines, space tourism company Virgin Galactic, and hundreds more followed, making Branson a billionaire entrepreneur.[11]

Another entrepreneur in the field of aviation, David Neeleman was quoted in *ADDitude Magazine* saying he has trouble dealing with details and completing routine tasks. "I have an easier time planning a 20-aircraft fleet than I do paying the light bill," he said. Of course, a fleet of airplanes is more interesting than the light bill, and designing one lifts a person out of tedium. Neeleman also notes that creativity and thinking outside the box are ADHD traits that have helped him. The inside of the proverbial box is boring; escaping it is the exciting challenge of the unknown.[9]

Most of us cannot reach such dizzying heights as these celebrated examples of ADHD success. Lacking the talent, flamboyance, determination, opportunity, or just plain luck, many of us settle for more mundane lives. Whether fascinating or tedious, all our occupations, like our lives, entail some degree of boring tasks. In recognizing the power of boredom, we can devise our individual responses.

Games people play

Boredom is a concept rampant in our culture: comics, news, crime reports, everyday discourse, blogs, search engine words, all reflecting the prevalence and power of boredom. Nobody understands boredom and the principles of dispelling it better than video game designers, surprisingly serious people who study the difference between boredom and interest. Game designer Chris Bateman, perhaps best known for his design work on *Discworld Noir* and *Ghost Master*, has also written books on game design and studied the neurobiology and aesthetics of play. While pursuing research into the neurology of gaming, Bateman developed a player model, BrainHex, based on neurobiological principles published in the paper *The Neurobiology of Play* (with Dr. Lennart Nacke); the BrainHex test has been taken by more than 80,000 people.[12]

The test identifies test-takers according to which type of stimulation they seek and identifies types of gaming personalities somewhat like those personality types identified by the Myers–Briggs Type Indicator.[13] Games can then be designed for each type of player.[12]

For example, the reward schedules or leveling mechanics of games "work because when we win or attain something, the pleasure center in the brain (the nucleus accumbens) releases a neurotransmitter called dopamine, which is chemically similar to cocaine," explains Bateman. He describes additional sources of gaming interest as neurological mechanisms "in which a player can trip the pleasure center and derive enjoyment from a game."[12] Integrating systems described by such researchers as B.F. Skinner and more recent work by brain researchers Irving Biederman and Edward Vessel using MRI scans, Bateman connects these mechanisms to different parts of the brain and different neurotransmitters. For example, one neurological mechanism for interest (or curiosity) involves "the visual cortex, a part of the brain where memory is coordinated known as the association area (hippocampus) and a neurotransmitter called endomorphin, which is chemically similar to opium."[12] He also connects the excitement of what he calls "rushgames," including the elements of speed, time pressure, and fight or flight responses, with the release of adrenaline, more recently called epinephrine. Strategy and puzzle-solving for those with skill and patience increase the pay-off of dopamine when success is achieved. Playing games with trusted friends even in a temporary situation increases the flow of the neurotransmitter oxytocin, associated with the warm feeling of socialization.[12] Thus Bateman names elements of interest that are common to the gaming market and which we recognize as particular needs of those with ADHD. Moreover, he connects these sources of stimulation with the same neurotransmitters, those feel-good chemicals that flow through the reward circuitry too little too late in individuals with ADHD. No wonder ADHDers are especially drawn, often addicted, to video games.

School daze

With all the recognition of boredom as a yardstick by which to measure an amazing array of facets of society, what could be more important than making freedom from boredom a significant measure of good teaching as well? Then students with ADHD would not be so likely to fall far below their potential in school with long-term negative consequences. How could we apply to education the energy and ideas that game designers have applied to video games?

The results of the 2009 High School Survey of Student Engagement (HSSSE)[14] conducted annually by the Indiana University Center for Evaluation and Education Policy "closely resemble past findings, reflecting bored students who say they are not connected to their school." Ethan Yazzie-Mintz, HSSSE project director, said, as quoted in a press release, "…about 49 percent of the kids are bored every day, 17 percent every class. That's two-thirds of the kids who are bored at least every day."[15] Moreover, "42 percent said they thought of dropping out because they didn't see the value in the work they were asked to do."[15]

School in general takes eager young people and designs a process by which many of their Elements of Interest are thwarted. At an age when young people want and need and are designed to be most physically active, they are required to sit for six hours a day in a straight-backed chair. When they need to be proceeding at their own pace, they are required to follow the pace of the 30 other people in the class. Just when they need adventure, they are given routine. When they want to be interactive, they must work alone. When they need a personal relationship, one-on-one, with a role model, they have instead an authority whose main job is often to keep order. Because of the complexity of modern society, when young people are eager and ready for independence, they are kept dependent until they get a diploma or degree or certification sufficient to earn a living, which is a really long time.

In the typical classroom, students are denied these Elements of Interest: frequent physical activity, the right amount of challenge, variety, interaction, and independence. The result is boredom; which is incidentally the chief reason given by high school students for initially using drugs and for dropping out of school. For students with ADHD these unmet needs are doubly problematic. And so without understanding the nature and power of boredom, we raise another generation that doesn't understand their own interests, doesn't develop their productive passions, and instead seek the easy, instant fixes of video games and constant chat on electronic devices which do not require long periods of concentration or contemplation.

For all its power, few counselors, coaches, teachers, or parents deal head on with boredom by teaching boredom awareness and avoidance. Many fail to recognize the power of boredom, sometimes seeming to feel that the discipline of enduring boredom is an educational goal in itself. A better educational goal is to teach the concept that it's the individual's responsibility to recognize boredom and "Escape It or Shape It". Likewise it's wise for clinicians and parents to offer to their charges the direction, flexibility, and freedom to pursue the Elements of Interest that are the keys to individual motivation.

CHAPTER THREE

Elements of Interest in Spontaneous Expression

A mother complained to me that her eight-year-old son Will told her "I'm bored" an average of eight times a day. Every day he wanted a friend to come over and play but, when the friend came, he wanted his mother to take them to a video arcade because they were bored. The mother felt pressured to provide this entertainment, even guilty if she did not.

Soon after I met him, Will told me, "I'm very, very, very, very, very, very bored in school." Not wanting our time together to seem anything like school, I took Will to a nearby stream along with Callie, my son's border collie. I encouraged Will to throw rocks in the water because Callie liked the splash. She bounded through the water to the spray, snapping at it and yipping in delight. It didn't take much encouragement as boys are born to throw rocks in water. I took this active approach because Will has ADHD and the physical exertion would provide the stimulation he needed to help him pay more attention to our conversation.

I pointed out how Callie waited in the water for the next rock to be thrown, focusing intently on him. The dog didn't seem to be able to go in the water and play by herself. She's a herding dog and is bred to watch for motion, rush to it, and nip it into line. When the motion stops, her job is done. Eager for the pleasure of this job, her eyes begged for a splash. Her vigilant, reproachful eyes often made me feel guilty if I didn't throw a rock, even if I was tired of finding and throwing them, just as Will's mother felt guilty if she didn't provide entertainment for Will.

"Do you think we are responsible for entertaining Callie?" I asked. Will first said, "No," then he changed his mind and said, "Yes." After a thoughtful silence, he said, "Maybe she could learn to entertain herself." I was very pleased at this idea, and told him so. Will then got down on his knees on a rock and demonstrated splashing the water with his hands. Callie was attracted to the splashing. Will tried to coax her to splash for herself, saying, "Splash, Callie, splash!" When she finally started pawing the water and yipping at the splash, Will and I were both delighted. In fact, weeks later, Callie still responded to "Splash, Callie, splash!" by creating a splash with her front paws. Border collies are highly trainable dogs. I used Will's lesson for Callie as a starting point for exploring with him how he, too, could entertain himself when he felt bored. After all, it was his idea!

Professionals who work with boredom-prone individuals, especially those with ADHD, can help patients or clients realize that cultivating interest, as opposed to boredom, is their own responsibility. Will was not too young to learn these skills. Even though he was helped by medication and was attending a special school where his needs could be addressed, he had a need for more stimulation. Not surprisingly, even the most interesting schoolwork is not as stimulating for Will as the video games he craved.

People with ADHD, students in particular, may not see that their behavior—sleeping through classes, avoiding starting a project, daydreaming, off-topic thinking or talking—is boredom related. They may not complain about boredom as Will did, but when I bring it up, they usually agree that the things they find themselves avoiding are boring and they are seeking an escape. Sometimes they are bored with things they enjoyed for a while. When newness wears off or mastery takes over, boredom sets in. Some clients, while not recognizing their boredom as a motivator, readily escape boredom by impulsive action. They don't suffer boredom long enough to identify it because they take quick action and move on.

Acknowledging boredom

The first step for clinicians, coaches, teachers, or parents is to let their clients and students know that their boredom is accepted and understood. Let them know that it is typical for people with ADHD to be bored when they are insufficiently stimulated, and it is normal for anyone to be bored in situations where they are not free to entertain themselves. For example, you may say something like this to a teenager:

> Boredom is really uncomfortable, isn't it? I can remember being bored in a long, pointless meeting, and I could hardly wait to get out. Some people are more easily bored than others and some people hate boredom worse than others, but we're all bored some of the time.

The teen may say:

> My mom doesn't think so. She says, "How could you be bored with all there is to do?" Or she says, "So what if it's boring, you have to do it anyway." Then she tells me all the boring things she has to do. Guilt trip!

You could reply:

> Your mom may experience boredom differently from you. I'd like to know more about how *you* experience boredom.
>
> At this point or later, you might explore his boredom together and guide him to learn to quantify it by severity and cause. You might say:
>
> What's the most boring thing you've had to deal with today?
>
> What's the most boring thing ever?
>
> Suppose we rate your "most boring thing ever" as a 9 on a scale of 1 to 10.

The student might ask:

> Why is the most boring thing ever a 9? What's a 10 for?

You might answer playfully:

> I'm saving the 10 for something even more boring than [the most boring thing he's experienced].

If you elicit a chuckle or a groan, so much the better. Next, ask him something else that will clarify the scale:

> What is the least boring activity you have in a day?

He might name a sport. He may say, "Lunch." Accept that. Ask him what is interesting about lunch. He may mention the friends he eats with or the food or a game of catch they play with the muffins. Any of these answers tells you something useful.

Now that you have established the ends of the scale, you may ask him something practical about the middle of the scale where you can work on improving attention. You could say:

> If a 5 or 6 is bearable, neither boring nor exciting, something you can pay attention to for a while, what would that be?

Suppose he says, "American History class." You could say:

> How so?

He might say something like:

> Mr. Clark doesn't just talk, talk, talk.
>
> He moves around a lot and gives us short little exercises to do. Sometimes they are boring, but sometimes they are pretty cool like the other day he had us act out the roles of the delegates to the Continental Congress. They were arguing how to form the new government. I was John Adams and I argued that the new country should have a king. John Adams really did that. It blew my mind! What if we had a king instead of a president?

You as the coach have already learned from this exchange what aspects of a class interest this teen and what teacher behavior bores him. You have also seen him display, in his last remark, that he has curiosity, an important weapon against boredom. Your goal is to guide him to seek and use such weapons. You could say:

> I wish all your classes were as interesting as Mr. Clark's. How would you feel about exploring with me how to liven up some of your other activities that you now think are very boring?

By asking him to examine his boredom and interest, you are letting your client or student know that you accept and even respect his feelings of boredom. You are giving him a tool to measure it, and you are offering to partner with him in reducing boredom and increasing interest.

From time to time when you are talking to him about difficulties, you may ask him where a particular experience, either past or anticipated, appears on his boredom scale, reinforcing the value of acknowledging the boredom experience and quantifying it as well as noting his role in shaping it.

The next step is to discover your client's true interests, as you will soon be focusing more on building interest and shaping interesting experiences than you will be on what he finds boring.

Elements of Interest

It is important not to assume you know what is interesting to an individual. It is better for your patients, clients, students, or your own children to discover and embrace their own individual interests. Also, while it is obviously good to know their interests such as subjects, sports, or hobbies, it's more important to recognize the portable, lifelong Elements of Interest that favorite activities involve. I use the term to mean the underlying aspects of an activity that interest or excite them versus a complex interest such as history, lacrosse, or model airplane building, which involve many elements of activity and interest.

The person who loves to play soccer may love it because *physical action* and *competition* are among his Elements of Interest, but it may be that the social aspects of *affiliation* and *social interaction* with the team are more important Elements of the game for him. Your job is to help him focus more on the Elements than the activity.

It would be important to know if the person who says she's interested in politics has Elements of Interest that suggest she'd be more satisfied as a volunteer on a campaign, an activist, political reporter, or candidate for office. Or would she just like to talk or blog about it? What aspect of her interest in politics is truly elemental?

Soccer is a sport, not an Element of Interest. Politics is a subject or a whole arena, but it doesn't tell you what Elements turn the person on.

You could, of course, try to identify a client or student's Elements of Interest by asking, "What are your interests?" Typically that question yields useful information but remarkably little of the Elements. It is more important to look for these Elements, for example competition, physical action, and teamwork, than the broader activity of a particular sport. For example, you may work with a student who says he wants to major in history. Would he prefer an internship or career spending time in an archive of primary source material sifting through records to find information about the 16th century people who left their homes in Portugal to colonize the coast of India? Or would he rather be a tour guide leading a group on bicycles through the Old Town of a large city telling them about what happened there long ago? Would he prefer to be digging around in the foundation of an ancient building? Would he like to be a history teacher leading a class? All of these activities concern history but each calls on its own Elements of Interest.

Researching in an archive, for example, involves a great deal of sameness, which could be tedious, with only occasional hope of discovering something new. It involves *problem-solving* and *attention to detail.* It's mostly solitary and sedentary. Scholars are recruited for archival work. On the other hand, leading the bike tour of an historic site involves the Elements of *physical activity, social interaction, performing in public,* and fairly certain *audience approval.* Actors are often hired as tour guides. They are a good fit: actors love *performing,* enjoy *a new audience* every day, often inject *humor* into their spiels, tolerate repetition, and are energized by favorable audience response.

Physical action, competition, affiliation with a group, problem solving, attention to detail, performing, audience approval, humor—all these are Elements of Interest. There are many more to be discovered. The Elements are part of your clients' and students' personalities and are evident from childhood, even as activities change throughout life.

Spontaneous expression of Elements of Interest

Finding the Elements in spontaneous descriptions requires a certain listening mindset. You notice words you might not have noticed before. When you hear a description of an activity or event from a client or student, listen for what gave her joy or satisfaction, use the words that she used, and give them back to her.

There are, of course, standardized personality tests indicating what energizes a person, but I find that observing the language clients use spontaneously and the situations from which they arise is a more valuable source of information. Clients' choice of words provides vocabulary, metaphors, and nuance that can be used for better communication with the client immediately. A shared language also deepens understanding in a long-term professional, parental, personal, or other relationship.

Listening for Elements of Interest becomes second nature once you are aware of their value. You distill them from conversations, not only with those it is your duty to help, but also with friends and strangers. They are often captured most effectively in writing.

"There are moments throughout the day where I get very bored," Elyse Brantingham wrote in a blog post "Boredom is never good." On this particular day, not wanting to do something meaningless, this young woman took an unfinished wooden box she had bought to hold some games, and she put a "scrunchy textured blue finish" on it and turned it into an *objet d'art* as well as a useful container.[1]

"I am pretty proud of my creation," she said. "This makes our games look stylish, and it was really fun to do!...Those are the projects I love the best. Fun, messy, and they have a purpose."[1]

I was first drawn to Elyse's description because of the last line. By characterizing what she liked about the project, she has spontaneously identified her Elements of Interest: Many people would agree that *purpose* would help them to beat boredom; it is a common and strong Element of Interest. However, a lot of them would have balked at "messy." Elyse obviously likes to get her hands into things. Tolerating and even reveling in *hands-on* messiness is an Element of Interest that puts her in the good company of artists, craftsmen, handymen, automobile mechanics, and surgeons. And let's not overlook *style* as an Element Elyse cares about, along with creativity and *skill*, which give her pride, a strong motivator. Through these few phrases we see that Elyse, even though she gets bored fairly often, is aware of boredom, and makes the decision to turn on the Elements of Interest right away.

From Elyse's unsolicited description, I quickly learned about what she needs to be satisfied in life, about what dispels boredom and excites her "feel good" chemicals. I believe I gathered more accurate and immediate information this way than if I'd asked her directly what aspects of life interested her.

As clinicians, coaches, teachers, and parents, we must habitually listen for the language our clients and students use spontaneously to guide our work with them. We listen for the excitement in their voices when they describe their most satisfying experiences to help identify their Elements of Interest so that we may point them out and guide clients to bring interest into their lives.

"Spontaneous" expression doesn't necessarily mean these expressions always arise totally unprompted; it simply means that they haven't been expressed for the purpose of analysis. Ask whatever you ask out of genuine curiosity.

The way you as a clinician, teacher, or parent can elicit expressions of motivating, lifelong Elements of Interest is much the same way the writer Paige Parvin did for an article in *Emory Magazine*, entitled "The Secret Lives of Faculty."[2] Whereas you will be seeking clients' Elements of Interest and helping them find age-appropriate expressions of these interests to weave into their lives and otherwise tedious tasks, Parvin was interviewing only those faculty of Emory University, located in Atlanta, who had already successfully discovered and integrated their Elements of Interest into their lives, usually in forms very different from their career activity. They are good models of how to bring those Elements of Interest into their lives that a career may not fully offer.

Ann E. Rogers, a professor of nursing, is a bassoonist and flutist outside of her professional life at Emory. "When I practice, I can hear the difference in my playing. The immediate gratification is very rewarding, since many things I do involve delayed gratification."[2]

There's one Element of Interest she's named: *immediate gratification*. It's an Element to be considered in sustaining motivation of any client. For those who particularly need it, which would include most of those with ADHD and a tendency to boredom, you will want to give them something they can see as reward quickly as well as steps to long-term goals.

In addition, Rogers says, "I also enjoy ensemble playing and *participating in the creation* of a sound that's greater and more interesting than the individual parts."[2] She enjoys collaboration, whereas you may find others who want to be soloists in their chosen fields. Note that she also used the words "more interesting."

Joel M. LeMon, assistant professor of Old Testament at Candler School of Theology, is also a trumpet player. He says, "When I play a good jazz solo or play a classical piece with no misses or flaws, it is one of the most gratifying experiences I can have."[2] *Mastery* is an obvious Element of Interest for this musician as opposed to those who are happy just messing around with an instrument.

Nadine Kaslow, professor and vice chair for faculty development in Emory's School of Medicine Department of Psychiatry and Behavioral Sciences, describes her secret life as a ballet dancer: "It is a wonderful form of physical exercise… It helps me get away from the demands of work and focus on an activity that combines athleticism with art. Dancing helps me to feel stronger and more in control, both emotionally and physically…"[2] Easy-to-see Elements of Interest in this description are *exercise*, *athleticism*, *art*, *strength*, and *control*.

Jonathan Beitler, professor of radiation oncology, otolaryngology, and hematology/medical oncology at Emory University, enjoys being in the US Army Reserves and Connecticut National Guard as a flight surgeon; he is also an Angel Flight pilot. He says, "As a flight surgeon, I get to combine my love of flying with a bit of patriotism… At my age, it is a great opportunity to continue serving the country. Particularly with an army that has been at war for more than ten years, this activity satisfies the innate drive to do good…"[2] There you have his Elements: *love of flying*, *patriotism*, and *the drive to do good*.

Marcia McDonnell Holstad, associate professor in the Nell Hodgson Woodruff School of Nursing and an assistant director of a section in the Center for AIDS Research, began to compete in swimming a few years ago and has won medals in the Georgia Senior Olympics in several events. She says, "What's most rewarding is the rush you feel when you dive into the pool, surface and take off as fast as you can."[2] While she adds that swimming is great exercise, it's clear that *competition* is also an important Element of Interest along with the sheer joy of *speed.*

Joyce King, assistant professor at Nell Hodgson Woodruff School of Nursing, says of her extracurricular activity as a bicyclist, "There is nothing like coasting at 40 miles per hour down a long hill on a hot summer day… I have also met some fantastic people over the years."[2] It sounds like *speed* and *social interaction* are noteworthy Elements of Interest.

The purpose of quoting the remarks of these university faculty members' extracurricular passions is to show both how people can often reveal very specifically the Elements that interest them or turn them on, and how they have brought these Elements into their lives either as a supplement to their professional lives or as a deliberate change from the form and pace of their jobs. Either way they are living their passions, which the study of Elements of Interest is intended to promote.

These words of the Emory University staff members illustrate how Elements can enrich lives. While as clinicians and teachers you carefully observe spontaneous expressions that reveal Elements, in the case of ADHD and boredom proneness you also need to elicit Elements of Interest from individuals who cannot recognize or state enduring elemental interests or think how to bring these into their lives or activities. The next two chapters explore ways to evoke expression from which to extract these Elements.

CHAPTER FOUR

Top 10 Joys

How do we discover these Elements of Interest, if they don't readily roll out in conversation or written expression?

I often elicit underlying aspects of experience by means of techniques that do not allow the expectations of others or the subject's own critical self to influence them.

One of the most interesting and useful techniques for eliciting a client or student's Elements of Interest is what I call the Top 10 Joys. Listing one's lifetime joys is not a unique exercise, though how I use it may be. The experience provided me with valuable insights, and soon I was asking my clients to make the same list in order to discover those lifelong "Elements of Interest," which everyone would benefit from learning, not just those with ADHD and boredom.

It is important for the clinician or teacher to ask a client or student to write this list without saying you are going to find anything particular in it or analyze it in any special way. You want them to go back in time, feel the joy, and write down enough to remind them of the occasions so you can talk about them. You do not want to make them think of how you will react to their list. If you tell them you are looking for their interests, they may give you items about history or sports or other things they consider are their interests, thus skewing the results. Instead say something like, "Write down the ten occasions, events, or activities in your life that have given you the most joy or the greatest satisfaction or made you the happiest." Note that the use of several alternative words may help; some people may find "joy" over the top but find "satisfaction" more comfortable.

The second step in the use of the Top 10 Joys is to interview the person about the items on their list. For each item, ask the person, "What about this made you joyful?" Here their choice of words as well as the actual reason they felt joy for each experience is very important. Some people will have already written beside each item why it made them joyful. These notes are valuable, but ask again; the responses offer the opportunity to enrich the information as the interview goes on. Take notes on key words, concepts, and metaphors to aid you in interpretation.

The third step is to group the responses into Elements, drawing on all that has been said. After grouping them, you will see that the Top 10 Joys of some people are almost all about only one Element. Those of other people may be about five Elements. Ideally, an Element will be repeated, verifying its importance. You may note that Joy and Interest are not the same thing by definition. However, what brings you joy will interest you, attract your attention, and draw you in. If you can bring a bit of joy into a boring task, job, or life, a spark of Interest will light up. The sources of your joys are your Elements of Interest.

The Top 10 Joys exercise is fun, like having your fortune told. Most people who do this with me say that it lifted their spirits to remember these joys and that they found it interesting to explore the elements involved.

As an illustration, here are the Top 10 Joys of an adult with a varied and rich life.

Susan's Top 10 Joys

1. My brother Alf's wedding.
2. Being a voting observer at the first free elections in Indonesia.
3. Working as an usher for the Atlanta Braves, especially at the "Bark in the Park" game, with my dog Chipper Jones in attendance.
4. Traveling on the island of Bali.
5. Honeymooning with Paul in Turkey.

6. My first year as a trainee/rookie at IBM.
7. Being a cheerleader in high school.
8. Time spent in our beach condo.
9. Giving big parties, especially the one last fall with a house concert.
10. Seeing my former IBM Kazakhstan/Russia employees flourish and succeed.

For the second step, Susan wrote down, at my request, what aspect of each experience made it joyful:

1. At a superficial level, it was beautiful and perfect. As children we had a tough time, and, a year younger than I, he had it even tougher. I knew the wonderful woman he was marrying and felt they would be happy. The wedding symbolized for me that he had made it (emotionally healthy, especially).
2. Top day in my life. The Indonesians had just overthrown 30 years of oppression by dictator Suharto (first EVER election in their history). They voted by pushing a nail through a paper ballot. Right there an official held it to the sun, saw the hole, and counted it. I lived right across the street from the polling place. I saw the joy in their faces. The first person chosen to vote was a journalist who had been tortured and imprisoned by the previous regime. People said, "You mean I get to choose whoever I want?!" They were weeping with joy.
3. Being an Atlanta Braves usher combines two of my great loves, baseball and giving a party. My section was like my party. I got to be myself more than in any other place in my life. I could act crazy and talk to people, free to be me.
4. Bali is a beautiful place with an admirable culture of beauty and kindness. Bali is a happy place. I'll never forget the sun shining over the rice paddies.
5. We'd been married eight months, living in Kazakhstan where Paul was the head of the Peace Corps there. It was a gloomy, Soviet-style existence, bad food, bad everything.

We were allowed to take a break for our honeymoon in just three places. Turkey was the best of the three. In Turkey there was great food, fascinating, beautiful things to see.

6. My first year with IBM was an incredible ego trip. I got to use all of my business and personal skills. It was fully challenging, but it came easy. Perfect. The next year was back to real life.
7. Cheerleading was a young girl's ego trip. It was fun, I got a lot of attention. I enjoyed making sure everyone had a good time.
8. So relaxing, a wonderful view of the beach. Beautiful. I like to putter around and work. I can quit any time and just sit and look at the water. Vegging out. I loved giving parties to our neighbors.
9. Giving parties. Seeing people have a good time. The party with the inhouse band was everything I envisioned it would be.
10. Seeing my Kazakhstan employees flourish and succeed. I'd quit IBM to get married and go with Paul to Kazakhstan. I got a temporary job at the embassy in Kazakhstan. I convinced IBM to open a branch in Kazakhstan and they did. Working there for IBM I got a trip to Moscow where I helped people set up business. We hired people as contractors who had no notion of business; they didn't know what profit meant. A few of them did so well. I was so proud. One woman came to Toronto where she had a joyful wedding; I'd introduced her to the man she married. They lived all over the world.

Letitia's reply to Susan

Your overwhelming Element of Joy is seeing other people joyful and thriving: #1, 2, 3, 7, 9, and 10 (6 out of 10 items).

Another very strong Element is that you are significantly responsible for their joy and thriving as in #3, 7, 9, and 10, where besides teaching employees and encouraging them to learn about business, you said about one woman who married, "I introduced them."

Getting attention and being acknowledged is a strong Element of Joy. #6, 7, and all the parties, acknowledgement as the fun-maker as well as probably acknowledgement in items of accomplishment like #6 and 10. Let's call it pride in accomplishment and also acclaim.

The above three Elements all work together to bring you your greatest joy, then, now, and in the future!

"Fully challenging, but it came easy" and used "all of my business and personal skills" is an approximate definition of "flow," the perfect balance of challenge and skill as described in Mihaly Csikszentmihalyi's famous books on the subject.[1] While defined in just one item on your Top 10 Joys list, I sense it in other items, like #3, 7, 9, and especially 10. Flow will always be a source of joy for you.

And let's not overlook appreciation of beauty as a strong Element of Joy in #4, 5, and 8.

In sum, helping people thrive, succeed, or just have fun and being acknowledged for this is where you will continue to find joy. The "ego trip" that goes with it is a joy, but I see no joy in getting attention without skill and accomplishment. The joy is always a result of your work for others' joy. Deserved acclaim, I call it.

I want to point out the additional Element in #3, which is very important. "Free to be me." Once you find your Elements of Joy, to reproduce them in the future, you need freedom. Financial freedom, good health, and all the other freedoms like freedom of permission, freedom to act, and freedom to be fully yourself. Obtaining this freedom is for many people the personal challenge to experiencing joy.

When working with children, the process is much the same. While I sometimes allow or suggest adults do their Top 10 in writing, it may be more of a chore for children to write; I almost always interview children in person. Below is an interview I did with 12-year-old Riley.

Step One, Riley

LETITIA: *Riley, thinking back on your whole life, the years you can remember, can you tell me what is one of your greatest joys or happy occasions? A time when you really felt happy or very satisfied.*

(I'm using "joy," "happy," and "very satisfied" to try to give him a word he might best relate to. I don't use "fun" because I want to elicit a range of sources of joy and interest that "fun" might not cover.)

RILEY: *Being at the lake with friends, playing games.*

LETITIA: *That sounds like fun. Can you tell me another happy time?*

RILEY: *Spending time with my dad.*

LETITIA: *Nice. I'm glad you enjoy that. Can you give me one more, like an especially happy day?*

By saying "an especially happy day," I'm encouraging him to be more specific. More specific memories usually offer more detail from which to draw Elements of Interest.

RILEY: *On my birthday when I was ten, we had a big game truck come with lots of games I could play with my friends.*

LETITIA: *You're good at this. Can you tell me another super happy time?*

RILEY: *No, that's all I can think of.*

Riley has given me three joys, a typical number that a 12-year-old will come up with at one sitting outside of school.

Step Two, Riley

I go back over Riley's list of three Joys and ask him an important question in several different ways. I'm taking note of his choice of words.

LETITIA: *Let's go back over these three happy times. Being at the lake with friends, what made that so happy?*

RILEY: *Just being with each other. Playing ping-pong and board games. My friends all have houses around ours and I've known them my whole life.*

LETITIA: *How many friends come over at one time?*

RILEY: *Oh, one, two, or three, or maybe five.*

LETITIA: *Tell me about being with your dad. What makes that happy?*

RILEY: *Just being with him is really fun. He is usually out of town three or four days a week, so I like to be with him when he's home. It doesn't matter what we do. Just being with him.*

LETITIA: *Tell me about the birthday party with the game truck.*

RILEY: *It's just really fun to play games with my friends.*

Something interesting to me is that Riley is a very talented musician, who has had lessons and lots of practice. His mother has told me that he won a big talent competition in his school and has been featured on guitar in other performances as well as solos on the bells in the school band. He has received a lot of acclaim for these performances but he doesn't mention them to me as one of his Joys. I conclude that performance, competition, and winning are not as big Elements of Interest to Riley as for some children who are eager to tell of their triumphs.

Step One, Garrett

I did the same exercise with ten-year-old Garrett. He is quick to respond with one Joy:

GARRETT: *On my fourth Christmas, I got a stuffed animal bunny.*

LETITIA: *You're good at remembering so far back. Do you still have the bunny?*

GARRETT: *Yes, I keep it with me on my bed.*

LETITIA: *Can you tell me another happy occasion?*

GARRETT: *Getting my first Pokemon card. My great grandmother gave it to me.*

LETITIA: *Nice. I've heard of Pokemon. Do you remember another happy time?*

GARRETT: *My first laptop. It's a Dell 5. It was my grandma's. It's beat up now and it has loose wires, but it worked then.*

LETITIA: *You have lots of joys to remember. Do you have one more?*

GARRETT: *I play Minecraft a lot. It's really fun.*

LETITIA: *Great. You gave me four Joys or happy activities. Now let's go back over them and I'm going to ask you some questions about them.*

GARRETT: *Okay.*

Step Two, Garrett

LETITIA: *Tell me about getting your bunny? What about that made you so happy?*

GARRETT: *I keep it with me when I go to bed and it helps me sleep. I like it because it's really soft…soft as a bunny, literally.*

LETITIA: *Soft, I like that, too. And "literally" is an interesting word. You have a good vocabulary.*

GARRETT: *Yeah. Thanks.*

LETITIA: *What was joyful about getting your first Pokemon card?*

GARRETT: *I've always wanted to collect Pokemon cards and then I got that. It was the first. It got me into collecting. I play with the cards with my friends. There's this attack…*

He goes into a detailed description of the cards and the characters. As he does he realizes he had a few cards before the one his great grandmother gave him, so he explains:

> GARRETT: *It wasn't really my first card but it* felt *like it was my first.*

> LETITIA: *That's pretty cool. Now tell me about Minecraft.*

> GARRETT: *Do you know what Lego® is? Well, Minecraft is like Lego® on a computer. There's survival mode and creative mode. If you can imagine it, you can build it.*

Perhaps returning to what makes him happy, Garrett adds:

> GARRETT: *I'm really smart. I want to do algebra. I play math games.*

> LETITIA: *What about math games makes you enjoy them?*

> GARRETT: *The challenge. It's fun. I'm in the fourth grade and I do Singapore [math curriculum]. Only four or five of us in the class get to do that.*

I call the Element of Interest revealed in these last remarks *reveling in skill.* It doesn't matter what you name an Element as long as you and your client or student know what you mean. With adults I sometimes call this Element "Damn, I'm good!" Use your client or student's language or metaphor when possible. This Element of reveling in skill leads people to do things that require skill just for the pleasure of observing how well or easily they can do it.

There's also pride in accomplishment in Garrett's Top 10 and maybe some enjoyment of competition shown by telling me only four or five out of 19 classmates do Singapore math.

The biggest differences between the Elements of Interest of the two boys is that Riley's show more that he enjoys the relationship with people, the togetherness of playing games with others, and he expresses little interest in competition. Garrett enjoys the things, the games themselves, along with challenge and reveling in his skills. He likes being special. It's also interesting that Garrett, in a small sample of four Joys, mentions his "firsts" twice, adding that one of them may not have been the first but "it felt like the first." I could label that Element as "firstness," but I think it is the extra thrill that novel experiences bring and can be grouped with *novelty* as an Element of Interest. It's nice that he associates the bunny and collector card with the people who gave them to him, a sign of gratitude.

Just in these two short conversations, I feel I know a lot about what makes these boys tick. The differences in Elements of Interest suggest that the boys would be motivated in different ways.

The Elements suggest that Riley would be more interested, and less likely to be bored, if he were paired with another student or put in a group to do a project. With friends he's happy, no matter what they are doing. Garrett would be more engaged, and less bored, if there were a challenge and some acclaim to go along with his success.

A class of third graders

The Top 10 exercise can be done in groups also. For example, a dozen third graders, asked to draw a picture of their happiest time ever, drew pictures ranging from adult-level drawings of people to minimal stick figures engaging in activities. Instructed to write down their ten happiest times, four of them neatly listed exactly ten joys, and the rest listed from one to 20 joys.

While their teacher recognized how their happiest times reflected well what she knew of their personalities, she was also surprised at what new things she learned about her students, whom she had been teaching all year.

The boy who listed only one joy drew a clear picture of it—his family in a tent, looking out of it through a window covered in mesh.

A girl demonstrated her artistic bent and Elements of Interest by naming craft projects, decorating her room, "making up stories," and teaching. Her drawing was very mature, and her handwriting was beautiful with little circles dotting every lower case "i".

Another girl stated as one of her joys, "The day I learned to draw this flower." Her picture was a drawing of the flower, an intricate stylized blossom, with a pencil drawn beside it labeled with a number 2.

A child whose Top 10 Joys included six that specifically named family members said, "We were rolling down the hill. My parents were going to catch us." Her picture showed three children rolling down a hill and the parents waiting at the bottom to catch them.

One child listed as one of her Top 10 joyous occasions the time when she found out her grandmother "is friends with the prensabul [principal]."

The child who wrote 20 top joys included 11 items that were new experiences—"I caught my first fish," and "I saw my cousin for the first time"—indicating that novelty is an important Element of Interest to him. As ten-year-old Garrett had said, "firsts" had a special feel to them.

The teacher also asked the children what was boring in their lives. Almost all of them said the standardized achievement tests, on which they had just spent a week, were boring. They have to stay at their desks until the end of the allotted time even though they have finished, and they cannot play during that time. Waiting in line was also named as a cause of boredom. Asked what they did when they were bored, one third grader wrote, "I run around," which the teacher heartily confirmed. Another wrote, "I'm patient (on the outside)." One, diagnosed as ADHD hyperactive, escaped his boredom; the other endured it.

With younger children, a more casual approach is useful: Ask a child or a group of children to volunteer to tell just one time they felt joyful or very happy. At any age one joy with enough feeling and detail can tell you a lot about what makes them happily engaged.

A teacher attempting to win over a student of any age may find the Top 10 Joys exercise useful to engage a student one-on-one. The teacher not only learns what motivates that individual but also gives the student a boost in confidence to know that her teacher cares about what makes her tick. Any interpretation she volunteers should be accepted, and any interpretation you offer should not be offered authoritatively but for her consideration. You may say, "How well does that fit with what you think interests you?"

In the few cases when a client has told me she has experienced no joy, I have rephrased the request to "What made you feel the best?" or "What was really satisfying?" Also, I have brought the topic up again when I heard her recall something with excitement or satisfaction. I have said, "That sounds like a joy to me. How did it feel to you?" Even the unfortunate child who, for whatever reason, truly leads a joyless life can learn to notice small pleasures so that she can build on them. More joy in life is the goal and more small satisfactions in the everyday moments of living.

CHAPTER FIVE

Elements of Interest from Childhood Pastimes

Near the beginning of a coaching relationship, no matter what the issue, I usually say something like this:

> Look back at what you did as a child for pleasure in your free time… Think about what you used to do as a child when you were free to do as you wanted… What was the most pleasant way to spend your time? Maybe it's something you could do for hours, as long as your parents would let you.

My goal is to bypass the client's adult analysis of interests and explore the pure memory of childhood pleasure with little influence from others because, when we were children doing what we wanted to do, we were our true selves, enjoying our individual Elements of Interest.

I notice what makes the client's face light up or her voice show excitement. I coach often by phone, so clues in the voice stand out.

When Sallie, a college student for whom I enjoy being an ADHD coach, described one of her favorite childhood pastimes, her face certainly lit up.

> Many of my most vivid childhood memories are memories of play. In one of my favorite games, my best friend and I would go into outer space. A secret cubby [a finished storage closet] off of her playroom was our space ship. We were scientists. We would take off, float around in space for a while, and then land on another planet. We would leave the space ship and venture all the way down to her finished basement, which her dad used as his office. It was dimly lit and sterile with white

> walls and carpet—an alien world. Throughout the course of our exploration, we would pick up odd stuffed animals, friendly extraterrestrials. Then, suddenly, the mission would become a rescue mission. The huge, scary alien that we had feared would appear was going to eat our dear little alien friends...and us, too. We would race back up stairs to the space ship, tripping and falling, adding tension to the chase, and finally making it back to the cubby, slamming the door before launching an emergency takeoff. Whew! We made it!

As I do with the Top 10 Joys exercise, I asked Sallie about each detail of her account. I noticed what each piece meant to her. In our conversation about the words she had used in her story, Sallie revealed which Elements really interest her. For example, to the question "What was it about your playmate that made her your best friend?" Sallie replied, "She's positive and easy to be around. She let me take the lead. She could go with my ideas and be excited about them." The Element of Interest revealed is leadership and a bit of control. If Sallie had not already told me that her friend followed her lead, I would have asked her, "Who was captain of your ship?" Sallie added, "In addition to the plot, I remember flashes of the state I was in while I was playing these games... My friend and I had joined together to create this fantasy world in which we were in control. The appearance of a parent, the authorities in the real world, was a jarring return to our roles as children." Independence from authority correlates well with the Element of control, and often engages ADHDers.

Sallie's choice of a space ship as conveyance and the friends' roles as scientists interested me. I could not have guessed the Elements these images represented for Sallie from the fantasy alone. "It's professionalism," she explained. She and her friend spent a lot of time preparing and supplying their space ship before they took off, and they had plans for making observations and collecting specimens. Organization and preparation are key parts of the fantasy project, which we could call the Element of order, if not her own word, "professionalism." Another aspect of achieving the preparation and order seems to be the Element of control. This was no haphazard jaunt!

It might seem surprising that Sallie, who was diagnosed with ADHD as a very young child, included organization, preparation, and order into her fantasy when these Elements seem to be the opposite of ADHD behavior. We might guess she'd design a playtime fantasy world where such order was not required. We talked about that seeming paradox. Sallie agrees she was disorderly as a child and her room was messy, but "Creating this world, starting from scratch, getting organized was deeply satisfying." She notes that as an adult in her summer jobs and in her new school terms, "When my notebooks are all in order and my supplies are at hand, it feels so good. A fresh start is very satisfying." Sallie craves order although she struggles with it. She loves to have control of her time, space, and things. Order is a strong Element of Interest she fantasized as a child and seeks in her adult life. A related Element I call "time limit," the factor that motivates a person to start a task or project by promising an end fairly soon, is not only an end but a promise of a new beginning, a clean slate, where disorder of the past is wiped away and order once again seems possible. For Sallie, as for many ADHDers, dividing situations into discrete steps, each like a new flight into space, can and should allow time to prepare and organize in a formal or "professional" way, as the captain of the space ship does before each takeoff.

Space and "an alien world" in Sallie's childhood pastime were new and exotic; novelty is an almost universal Element of Interest and a necessity for those with ADHD. The aliens interested Sallie and her friend first as specimens and soon won their hearts. Sallie used the word "nurturing" and explained this Element of Interest by saying they had "made connections" with these aliens and saw them as friends; these feelings inspired the children to rescue and protect them.

Their adventure had risks, and the physical and emotional experience of risk, which might frighten some, gave Sallie's reward circuitry the stimulation it craved; she loved the danger, the chase, and the urgency of the takeoff. Risk-taking, if only imaginary, is clearly exciting to Sallie. "Tension," she called the Element of risk-taking.

When you as clinician, teacher, or parent look at a person's childhood pastimes, look beyond the activities themselves to the Elements of Interest involved. Here are a few out of many questions you might answer by listening to the person's choice of words, whether you are observing spontaneous expression or asking questions:

- How much did he prefer to play alone?
- How much did he like a companion or a best friend to do it with?
- How much did he enjoy a whole crowd?
- How much did she like to take charge of an activity?
- How much did she love the applause?
- How much did she revel in her skill?
- How did she like competition: who could make the most points or run the fastest or collect the most awards?
- How much did she use her hands?
- How much did he imagine that wasn't really there?
- What physical acts did he perform a lot, such as swaying to music, pounding things, running, dodging, and precision work?
- How careful was he about details?
- How original or creative were his activities or products?
- In what areas or ways or senses was he most creative?

Observations and questions about childhood interests help identify how much a person needs companionship, how big an arena she needs, what role she wants to play, what she wants from others when she is doing this, and what form her actions take.

Here are some additional questions to answer about a favorite childhood pastime:

- Who was the boss?

- What did you actually do in this play scenario?
- Who were you when you were doing that?
- Which senses were most involved?
- What sensory pleasure did you get from the activity?
- What were your skills?
- How did you feel about the outcome?
- How often did you drop one activity as soon as you figured out how to do it?
- How much did you care about mastering it?

Whatever questions you ask, do so out of genuine curiosity. Like the Top 10 Joys, the Childhood Pastimes exercise should be fun, not a test.

Childhood elements last a lifetime

You may remember Susan whose Top 10 Joys included introducing two friends to each other and seeing them fall in love and marry, seeing her employees in Kazakhstan flourish in a new business environment under her leadership, seeing people have fun when she was an usher at baseball games, or giving parties and seeing people enjoy themselves. In asking her a question about her childhood pastime, I expected her responses to reflect the Elements of Interest I had extracted from her Top 10 Joys from adulthood because an Element of Interest is a basic part of a person's personality that endures over a lifetime.

Answering my question about what she liked to do in her childhood when she was free to do whatever she wanted, she wrote:

> It's interesting to think about what I liked to do when I was eight or nine, because anyone who knew me then will tell you that I wasn't really childlike. Things were very hard for my family, and I took on a lot of responsibilities far too young. For free time, I liked to do "projects"—decorating my room, making

> something useful, organizing something. I think that's why I'm so irresponsible and silly today!

Even though Susan suggests that her basic demeanor today belies her serious childhood demeanor, I must add that, while Susan loves to have fun now and seeks out fun, as her Top 10 showed, including being silly occasionally, she is by no means irresponsible. Shortly after she wrote this Childhood Pastimes exercise, she organized a highly successful fundraising campaign including a pledge drive for her congregation. In accepting this challenging job, she called on the pastimes of her childhood—projects, something useful, organizing something. She has also added to this job and other aspects of her life some Elements of Interest that she didn't have the opportunity to express in her childhood. Not only did she very intentionally make the campaign fun, she added a theme of leafing out a tree and decorations (as she did to her room as a child) and even a person dressed in a squirrel costume, chattering as she handed out candy acorns in celebration of a successful pledge drive. Even the fun was a "project" that required organizing.

One might question whether such an exercise is a valid way to identify lifelong interests, and of course, the results are anecdotal. Still, from observing my own children for decades, I note that the constancy of spontaneous enthusiasms seems lifelong. Their expression just changes form.

As parents we have the opportunity to observe how childhood engagement plays out in adult life or how they follow a path that is not satisfying long term because it doesn't engage their observed Elements of Interest. But who can wait so long? At my age, I've had the opportunity to observe the lifelong nature of these Elements in my own family, and I would not likely have been able to do so with clients. It is quite amazing how my sons' childhood interests continue in adulthood, but in a different form, to enrich their lives.

One day our second son's teacher came to us for a serious talk. The roof in the classroom had been leaking, rain dripping down into the classroom, and so far the leak had not been remedied. Five years old at the time, our son got excited about his idea of how the rain was getting in, took paper, and drew a picture of the roof, the rafters, the joists, and the likely path of the rain drops to that particular spot on the ceiling. He was eager to show the teacher his analysis. She had been impressed with his ability to represent these unseen parts of the construction on paper as well as his excitement—the sign of an Element of Interest.

When he was a teen, his father and I were recalling something about a house we'd lived in a decade before and were trying to remember a detail about the second bathroom. Our son grabbed some paper and drew the floor plan of that house, which he had left for good at age four and a half, then added three-dimensional walls to the drawing, and placed all the pictures on the walls and the furniture in the rooms just as they had been. It's obvious that he had paid close attention to the physical scheme of structures in his early childhood, and this talent and enthusiasm were important attributes that we now see played out in his adult career.

Today he works for an engineering firm, drawing plans for engineering projects on the computer skillfully and rapidly. What's more, he is enthusiastic about this work and seems to experience real excitement about each project, showing the pages of site plans or electrical circuits to visitors. In hindsight, it's easy to see that his talent and interest would and should lead him to computer drafting as a profession that would hold his interest long term.

Our third son similarly revealed enduring Elements of Interest in childhood. I have photographs of my youngest, just out of diapers, in his first "big boy pants," swinging in the dogwood trees two meters off the ground. Yes, I was a little worried that he might fall, but it was clear he had the skill and the confidence. In fact, later this kind of activity turned out to be a passion. When I look back on the family photos, I also see him climbing on a huge fallen tree at age four, 10 meters up in the pear tree at age seven, and in a tree hanging over a stream at a park when he was about eight.

The second equivalent to the Childhood Pastime exercise was created, when he had to write an essay about himself in his final year of secondary school for English class. He chose to write about climbing trees and asked me for copies of the pictures I just described. He revamped this same essay when he applied for admission to university. I recently looked through this essay for clues to his Elements of Interest.

Below is the analysis I have made of his essay.

Elements of Interest

- Physical exercise and challenge, from "raced around," "had sword fights with leaves," "swing from," and "jump off."
- Reveling in skills, from "I put my climbing skills to good use" in picking pears; "I developed my techniques to the point that I could..."
- Possession: "My own little kingdom to rule"; and "survey my yard."
- Social: "I invited my friends."
- Balance: "...on days when I felt like a challenge I..."; and "perfect combo of challenge and relaxation."
- These could represent several Elements and I wouldn't jump to any conclusions without asking some questions about the phrases: "Anything and everything was possible on a dragon tree"; "awed by the sight of the huge trunk"; "had sword fights with leaves"; and "best of all ride the dragon."

He's still physically active in his mid-thirties, plays soccer, and runs. I haven't seen him climb a tree lately, but I do have photos of him as an adult carrying a full backpack, climbing up a ladder to negotiate a steep hiking trail on the west coast of Vancouver Island. In the photo, taken from above by a hiking companion, he's on the ladder emerging out of a canopy of lush trees. I'd say the tree-climbing adventure is still with him. He is well aware that he needs to keep the Elements of Interest that tree climbing affords as a frequent part of his life. He takes every opportunity he can to seek out physical action, a challenge balanced with relaxation.

Our Elements of Joy are largely abstract, not specific or concrete, although they are revealed in specific experiences like tree climbing or drawing houses or taking care of pets, and they remain with us over our lifetime.

There are, of course, other, better-known, and validated ways of determining personality traits that relate to motivation or interest. Among the best known, the Myers–Briggs Type Indicator[1], –

for example, determines whether social interaction energizes a person, and "energizes" is close kin to "motivates," just as interest also motivates. "Energizes" likely involves "stimulation," the key to interest and lack of which is the basis of both boredom and ADHD. The difference is basically *story*. In standardized tests, you get a number or a label. By doing these exercises to find Elements of Interest, you hear your client's story. You hear his own choice of words that you replay to him as you connect. I've found and been told by teachers and others that you learn more about the person in a shorter time than anything they had done before to learn what makes a client or student tick.

As a parent, I observed some of my children's childhood pastimes, while missing others—the pastimes are supposed to be what the child does when he can do whatever he wants to do and that means parents may not have been supervising. As for the Top 10 Joys, I only learned later in my own children's adult lives and quite piecemeal what experiences had been most joyful for them, when as adults they mentioned how much they had loved an activity as a child that they had not expressed to me at the time.

Best of all, knowing your clients', patients', students', and children's Elements of Interest, derived from the Top 10 Joys and the Childhood Pastimes exercises, guides you to help them bring these satisfying features into their lives, chores, lessons, and any area or time when boredom keeps them from achieving or enjoying life.

Selected Elements of Interest

Listed below are some of the Elements of Interest I have recognized in and outside of my work as coach, teacher, parent, and writer. Many of them overlap; it doesn't matter. I choose the term that seems to best fit what the client, student, or child has told me and in the language they have used or will understand. For example, if a child says he loved it when an audience applauded a play he was in and gave the performance a standing ovation, I use the word "applause" to mean that actual ovation and also as a metaphor to refer to the experience of receiving public credit for performance where no one actually clapped for him. Some might call it simply "credit" or "acclaim."

Similarly, "social interaction" covers all kinds of social engagement, but some people strongly prefer that this interaction be one-on-one while others want to be in a group. It's important to distinguish the two when the client expresses that preference.

"Uncertainty" is sometimes a cause of great stress, but it also holds open the door to "curiosity," a very powerful Element of Interest. Uncertainty is also related to "suspense," an Element that some people seek out and others can't stand. In accommodating all of the possibilities, the list may be endless in practice; this one is limited by necessity:

- Acclaim
- Action
- Advocacy
- Affiliation
- Altruism
- Applause
- Certainty
- Challenge
- Color
- Competition
- Conflict
- Contemplation
- Control
- Credit
- Curiosity
- Danger
- Design
- Drama
- Entrepreneurship
- Exercise
- Face-to-face
- Fostering
- Group participation
- Hands-on interaction
- Humor
- Imagination
- Instant gratification
- Mastery
- Multi-sensory experience
- Nature
- Newness
- Nonconformity
- Novelty

- Nurturing
- One-on-one interaction
- Order
- Originality
- Physical action
- Predictability
- Problem-solving
- Purpose
- Rebellion
- Reveling in skill
- Rhythm
- Risk
- Romance
- Rule-breaking
- Scent
- Sex
- Skill
- Social interaction
- Speed
- Story
- Surprise
- Suspense
- Taste
- Texture
- Time limit
- Uncertainty
- Urgency
- Variety

CHAPTER SIX

Using the Elements of Interest as Tools

Dopamine and norepinephrine are the principal neurotransmitters that serve as "get-up-and-go" stimulants and "feel-good" chemicals as their journey engages the reward center of the brain. Low levels of stimulation because of lower-than-normal flow or shorter duration of flow of neurotransmitters across the synapses of the brain are characteristic of ADHD. The feeling of having too little mental stimulation is close to the definition of boredom. The parallel between the disorder and the state of mind is neurochemical as well as psychological; by either standard there is too little stimulation. When people have an inability to get started on a task they intend to do, it's often because they anticipate and avoid boredom. They lack the get-up-and-go they need to "do it anyway." When they get started but can't seem to finish, they are bored with doing it. People with ADHD can only attend well to things that interest them. Thus boredom accounts for inattention. When they find something more interesting to think, say, or do, they jump to it without regard for consequences; that accounts for impulsivity. When their constant and chief relief from boredom is the stimulation of excessive physical action, they are hyperactive.

This premise, by being an oversimplification, allows an uncomplicated response to boredom: "Escape It or Shape It" by finding individual Elements of Interest, which both stimulate and reward, and by inserting them into the boring situations of life. However simple the premise, the application is an art. Some are better at it than others, but it is teachable. Once you accept the avoidance of boredom as the key to many doors, you as a clinician, teacher, or parent can guide others in the art of aiming for their individual Elements of Interest.

When James and I began coaching, he told me his history. I listened for his spontaneous references to his Elements of Interest. He had no one in his neighborhood near his age to play with, "to build a fort or hide from pirates." He had little social life because his father insisted he go to work at his grandfather's clothing store when he was 12; he worked Monday through Saturday, 60 hours a week, in the summer. "I never had any choice. I never had to think, What do I want to do? I didn't know I was missing anything. I didn't choose to be without friends my age, but I was kept so busy that I was never around other children except in formal situations like school or choir." In that history, I heard little joy.

In the Childhood Pastimes exercise, I asked James what he did as a child in the few moments when he could do whatever he wanted. James replied:

> Being alone in the forest behind our house when growing up—nobody bothered me and I observed and talked to the squirrels, birds, deer, etc. (Except for their normal animal sounds, they did *not* talk to me.) It was my magic realm and I was king over all the plants and animals. When I was nine or ten, I got a book from the library, *How to Do Nothing with Nobody All Alone by Yourself,*[1] and I learned how to never be bored. I always found something to do.

From this memory, I learned of James' affinity for nature and his imagination. I also learned that control was an important Element of Interest. His forest kingdom was an escape—from people bothering or controlling how he used his time—and that he turned to books to help control his situation. Being king over a magic realm must have been very satisfying.

James discovered early on that he had one special talent. "I made a place for myself with my drumming and musical ability. I started with the elementary school band in first grade," he said. In second grade he made first chair, outpacing a seventh grader who previously held that position. In high school he started in last chair and was quickly promoted to first.

From his Top 10 Joys, I also learned that James took pride in bench-pressing 100 pounds greater than his body weight. Another joy was getting his pilot's license for small planes. Clearly achievement is one of his Elements of Interest. He has always enjoyed music, an Element in itself, and rhythm in particular. Of his Top 10 Joys, six were public performances as a percussionist in prestigious places. I noted again the underlying Elements. Asked what he liked about performing in public, he said, only half-jokingly, "Everyone had to sit down and shut up and give me—the band or orchestra—their full attention." A later remark named that Element: control. He said, "I think I liked performing so much because I was in control on stage. I knew what everyone around me was going to do…"

His account of his most joyful moment of the Top 10, the climax to a happy time in his past, was eloquent:

> When our long-time beloved pastor retired, we hired Superman for our new pastor. He brought in his best friend from college as youth minister, and the church hired a dynamic and passionate minister of music.
>
> This ministerial team was magic, and suddenly I was living in a modern-day Camelot. I was 13. My group of about 50 young people idolized the new ministerial team.
>
> We were all in the choir or orchestra and we went on tour in the summers performing at churches all over the southeast, including a performance [at a national convention].
>
> This was the peak. There were almost 13,000…delegates in this gigantic arena and our choir and orchestra were on a big stage looking out over it all. I played the tympani/kettle drums. I was on a riser even above the choir and orchestra—up above and over everyone.
>
> It was my 17th birthday and as I looked out over the crowd I was king of the world.
>
> And I had the first note, a big BOOM and rolling thunder on the tympani—our music director raised his arms. Everything got real quiet. I was so excited that when I came down on that first note I blew the entire trombone section forward two feet.
>
> "For one brief shining moment in time, there was Camelot." And I was lucky enough to be part of it.

With such a strong Element of control, James doesn't much enjoy spontaneity. He likes applause or acclaim very much, but he says, perhaps because of his lack of childhood social life, "Offstage I have always been uncomfortable around people. I hope they don't notice me... Heaven forbid they ask me to join in [their activities]."

Nevertheless, while in college, James worked as a youth minister and assistant minister of music in another church. "Several days a week, on my way home from school, I stopped by my [childhood] church just to say hello to the pastor and minister of music." James may have enjoyed aloneness, but belonging to something, that is, affiliation, was also an Element he relished.

Unfortunately, Camelot came to a painful end in every arena of James' life. The murder of civil rights activist Dr. Martin Luther King and Robert Kennedy, President Jack Kennedy's brother, as well as the Vietnam War and anti-war movements, all affected him greatly. Closer to home, a scandal involving the beloved members of the ministerial team broke his church apart. The split made lifelong enemies of family members and former friends. Inner turmoil and being drafted into the military took him well off his path to become a minister of music in a similar church. James felt betrayed by church, friends, family, and country; his ability to trust was broken.

His military experience was rough, and on his return home things got rougher. One day on a construction job a metal beam fell on his head and instantly made him totally deaf. Along with losing his major avenue to communication, he lost his ability to hear music and to play it with others. The Element of rhythm remained as he drummed silently on his bed at night and on his steering wheel when driving, remembering the music he loved. He was totally deaf for ten years until an early version of a cochlear implant device restored some degree of hearing and some sense of control. Even so, he went through bankruptcy and other losses. Then he was diagnosed with cancer. Loss of the Element of control in his life was overwhelming. He had to have major surgery to survive the cancer, and he remembers that he did not care if he never woke up. In fact, he thought death might be the best option:

> Through the nearly 30 years that I wandered in the pathless land, the truth eluded me. I did not figure out why until I was lying in the VA hospital...after my cancer surgery...
>
> I didn't want to die so much as I just could not see any way forward in my life. I thought I had no options.
>
> The day after my surgery, I was hitting the morphine button every hour or two and I remember thinking, "Oh, darn. I'm still alive." When I found myself working hard to recover, I realized I wanted to go on living but I had no idea why.
>
> I decided I would not die until I found the reason why I wanted to live.

This is where James' Elements of Interest began to come into play, although he had not yet heard that phrase. First, he decided to regain the important Element of control in his life. He asked himself when he had ever been happy. In a process not unlike the Top 10 Joys exercise, he asked himself what had been the sources of his joy.

He recalled his happy time being a part of his old church before the split, performing music, and trusting people. Then, lying in his hospital bed, "I realized I wanted to be a part of something good again," he recalls. He set out to find the Element of affiliation again.

His religious beliefs had changed over the years, and he began to do research that would lead him to a new spiritual home. Two weeks after his discharge from the hospital, he walked fearfully but bravely into a new congregation, a new denomination, whose guiding principles led him to believe he could learn to trust people again. "I came seeking community because intellectually I realized that no one makes much of a success in life alone."

In our coaching sessions, I asked him to evaluate his satisfaction in eight aspects of life, with zero meaning no satisfaction and 100 percent meaning complete satisfaction. His first self-evaluation went like this:

> Work/Avocation 5%, Money 10%, Health 20%, Friends 0%, Family 5%, Fun 0%, Environment 5%, Growth 0%.

His second evaluation two months later showed some improvement:

> Work/Avocation 17%, Money 10%, Health 20%, Friends 20%, Family 15%, Fun 5%, Environment 10%, Growth 15%.

Exactly four years later, long after his coaching experience ended, I asked him to reprise the evaluation, with this result:

> Work/Avocation 60%, Money 40%, Health 50%, Friends 75%, Family 50%, Fun 60%, Environment 50%, Growth 71.3%. (The last statistic reflects James' sense of humor and playfulness more than any need for precision.)

How did this change happen? Being with people with values similar to his fulfilled his need for affiliation, "to belong to something good." Also, good things seemed to happen, some seemingly by chance, but in important ways, by his being open to opportunities that offered his Elements of Interest: From the Veterans Administration he got a new state-of-the-art device for his cochlear implant that, after a period of training, allowed him to follow most conversations and to enjoy music again. A drum circle was formed within his congregation for anyone who wanted to participate. James joined in and drummed cheerfully, although the simple rhythms did not really satisfy his need. The music director soon asked him if he would play percussion to accompany a few hymns in a service. This performance was not challenging, but it was a start. The music director then organized a small band to play regularly at services. James is now performing with other talented musicians, belonging to something good, enjoying the appreciation of an audience, though smaller than in his youth, and the camaraderie of a sort that he says he has never felt before. He has not only become active in more than one service group within the congregation but he has led a monthly discussion group. So much for his declaration, "Heaven forbid they ask me to join in…"

In telling his story before the entire congregation one morning, which was a big step in confidence and trust, he said, "I've been here two years and made lots of mistakes and missteps. But you've all given me the benefit of the doubt, plus a lot of love and support. Just like I had to learn to hear again, I'm having to learn how to be part of a congregation again." Telling his story publicly put James "on stage" and made him feel once more like "king of the world." The response he received from the congregation for his personal reflection amply rewarded him with another long-missing Element of Interest—acclaim.

James has systematically identified and been open to the Elements that had been good for him in his much earlier era of happiness. Moreover, he was brave enough to ask for help.

The Elements of Interest provide a way that you as a clinician can lead the client to look at situations in new ways and to explore interesting possibilities with an open mind. This exploration can lead to a life-changing new direction or to small changes that allow clients to "escape or shape" boring situations.

Physical action

Doing physical action like jogging, cycling, or playing sports gets the "feel-good" chemistry going. Physical action is not only an Element of Interest for many people, it is also a necessity for some, especially those with hyperactive-type ADHD.

Physical action as an Element of Interest, especially for the hyperactive type of ADHD, can be brought into boring situations; for example, a student can enhance the task of memorizing a poem or a list of historical events by bouncing a basketball to the rhythm of the poem or list and taking a shot after each stanza of the poem or each century of historical events. Adults can borrow their kids' balls to practice a presentation or speech they must give; take a shot after making each bullet point to help focus on the next one. The shot is a spurt of action to reward making the talking point. If he makes the shot, it's a little spurt of accomplishment or competition with oneself or a "study" partner that keeps the cycle of motivation going. I sometimes coach clients while walking together to keep their attention going, or I coach them by phone while they walk.

Linda James, "The Lady with the Moves," coaches people to get exercise while doing mundane chores, and it's hard to tell if they are making the chores interesting by the physical exercise or making the exercise less boring by the achievement of the task. It works both ways. In one of James' videos she produces a ginger chicken entrée while stretching and doing squats.[2] To work cooking and exercise into one series of movements is also a mental novelty.

For many people, achievement, physical action, and novelty are all Elements of Interest—you get three in one and a chicken dinner.

I remember a client whose Elements of Interest included strength and speed as well as challenge. When she was laid off and forced to do temp work of a rote nature far below her level of expertise, she had nothing to keep her mind engaged or reward her with good feeling. She mentioned that the sameness and the lack of challenge were not the only reasons she hated the job. The most boring thing was that the computers were very slow and she had to wait too long for the next task to load onto the screen. She had also complained about losing her previous level of fitness during this discouraging period of time. I asked her how she could use the few minutes of down time between tasks on the computer to serve another Element of Interest. She said she would not be at all embarrassed to do exercises with dumbbells or resistance bands in front of all the others in her pool of workers. Think how much fitness she could achieve if she did a regimen of strength exercises during every slowdown of the computer during a workday.

The client didn't care much about the Elements of competition, socializing, or leadership, but this solution could have been expanded, under the right leadership, into a really fit group in that workroom, especially among those for whom competition was an Element of Interest, if they chose to become workout buddies or friendly competitors.

While few studies have been done that show exercise in itself is a successful treatment for ADHD, anecdotal evidence suggests it does. "I hear it every day," said Denver, Colorado, psychiatrist William Dodson, M.D., in an August 2013 webinar for *ADDitude Magazine*. About one-third of his adult patients can treat their ADHD almost as well as with medication by doing an hour of aerobic exercise per day. "These are very fit people," he said. He gets them as patients only "when they tear their ACL [anterior cruciate ligament]" and can't exercise as they did before. They seek medical treatment for their ADHD, he says, only after their exercise regime is curtailed.[3]

Dr. Dodson observed that an hour of aerobic exercise would improve focus ability for about four hours and sometimes serves as well as short-term medication with a stimulant in reducing the symptoms of ADHD. By providing stimulation, the feelings of boredom are diminished and the person has a more positive feeling towards assignments, tasks, and life. Exercise also enhances the positive effect of medication that has been prescribed for ADHD.[3]

Dodson mentioned that champion Olympic swimmer Michael Phelps, who was diagnosed with ADHD when he was a child, later worked out for hours a day in addition to his training in the pool.[3] This level of exercise no doubt contributed greatly to his ability to focus on his other daily tasks without ADHD medication, which is banned in Olympic competition.

Adding Elements of Interest to physical action

Most of us with ADHD can't aspire to Olympic gold and, what's more, some of us for whom physical exercise is not an Element of Interest find physical workouts more boring than the tasks they are supposed to help. That's when it's time to bring in other Elements.

Two of my favorite swimmers, both of whom have ADHD, have faced the repetition of their training and long-term commitment by shaping their swims to include other Elements of Interest.

Harry Briggs, who was the first person to swim across Lake Erie and who is still swimming in his 90s, told me the greatest problem he had in crossing those 32 miles of Lake Erie was boredom, and the length of time he had to be bored was almost 35 hours. Choosing not to give in to boredom, he had to shape his situation. He turned the all-day and all-night swim from one long act of following behind a guide boat to many time-limited achievements. Part way across the lake, bored with the endless strokes in a seemingly infinite body of water without observable accomplishment, he asked his coach in the smaller boat beside him to request of the captain of the larger guide boat to pause every half hour and let him catch up to it, instead of going on at the same distance ahead all the time. This change satisfied his need for an end to each increment of the swim, the Element I call "time limit," as well as his need for accomplishment. The crew added another Element to boost Harry's interest; they came to the stern every half hour and applauded as he approached. "That made all the difference," Harry said. "I couldn't have done it without that."[4] Applause was, of course, one of Harry's Elements and satisfying it with the headlines in the newspaper a day later was not soon enough to keep him going hour by hour.

When he was a quarter mile away from shore, he began to hear loud horns blowing all around him. He found the noise very annoying until someone told him that this was how spectators in the boats on the lake were cheering his approach to success. When he saw the honking noise as applause, he felt a surge of motivation to overcome the hypothermia, fatigue, and boredom that had almost drained him.[4]

Owen, another favorite swimmer, says he shapes the boredom of swimming laps as training for competition by watching the people in the next lane, noticing their strokes, kicks, and turns to see what techniques work for them. He's learned a lot this way that not only helps symptoms of ADHD, but informs the instruction he now gives young people in swimming and water polo. Water polo added additional Elements of Interest to his life: competition, affiliation, reveling in his skill, and social interaction. When he organized and led a co-ed polo league, he was really in his Element, combining all these joys with the entrepreneurial Element he shares with many ADHDers.

Having tasks that are time-limited is a big Element for ADHDers. Runners sometimes use the telephone pole method of turning a long run into a series of time-limited events that end before boredom sets in. They tell themselves that they only have to run to a certain pole or even the next telephone pole. That's it. Then they can walk. A few strides before the target goal is reached, they say to themselves, "I feel fine. I don't have to stop here. I'll run to the next pole and then stop." Just before arriving at the next pole, they ask themselves whether they could run a little further, just to one more telephone pole. They can always go a little bit further because it's time-limited. This can go on for a long time. The distance is doable because it's not one long struggle but shorter, doable achievements.

Another Element that is very effective in making physical fitness training less boring is imagination.

In a rowing machine, you can imagine a real boat and you see the villages pass by as you row; you may see villages you have visited and you enjoy the Element of nostalgia, or they may be villages in a country you have not seen and thereby fulfill your desire for novelty or exotic newness. Or imagine that you are rowing hard to escape pirates off the coast of Somalia or long ago off the fictional Treasure Island, or you are an explorer and you are discovering a new land. Imagination is a chief Element of Interest and invoking it is an important strategy for escaping and shaping boredom.

Imagine

Imagination is an Element of Interest in itself as well as an Element that can help you bring all the others into play in a highly satisfying activity. Imagination is a perfect escape from boredom during long, lazy afternoons of a child's summer vacation or long waits in an examining room before a doctor shows up. Pure imagination without much context is basically daydreaming. While daydreaming is one of the biggest problems of ADHD in the classroom, it plays a valuable role in the right situations.

When my daughter was little, I often looked in the backyard and saw her sitting in a swing, not actually swinging but deep in thought, her lips occasionally moving in conversation with herself. Never bored, she spent hours in an imaginary world. While the distinction between reality and fantasy is more relevant to adults, even they can fill time instead of kill time by losing themselves in the imagined world.

A writer friend of mine tells how she was intrigued by the title of a sermon her clergyman was about to deliver. As the sermon started, she eagerly gave it full attention, but as the sermon progressed, it proved duller than the title promised, and my friend turned her attention elsewhere. Her mind did not drift away, she recalls, so much as she told herself the sermon was boring and intentionally gave herself permission to use her time in the pew to daydream. She pondered the intriguing title of the sermon and let her mind run with it. She played an entire story out in her imagination. When she got home, she wrote it down the way it had come to her. Not long afterward, its stream of consciousness style made her work stand out from the other submissions in a short story contest that had attracted hundreds of entries, winning her the first prize and publication. Countless works of art and invention have been inspired by the collision of boredom and imagination.

Adults and children who don't choose to devote their empty time to fantasy may evade boredom while waiting in the dentist's office by thinking out a useful plan for a project or for the day. Making a plan is equally a process of imagination. We imagine a series of actions that tend to be more practical ones or at least more possible ones than a true fantasy. How many of us have designed a kitchen renovation or our dream job? A plan is a dream you believe in, but the enjoyment of planning is not necessarily lessened when you do not expect to put the plan into action; then it's just called daydreaming, no different from the little girl sitting in a swing talking to herself.

Boredom provides space for imagining. Thoughts bounce around in the head of a bored person, with little attempt to control or bring to order. Inevitably, some collide, connections are made, and new ideas pop into the person's head. In fact, people with ADHD typically make connections more readily than people without ADHD wiring. They are good at putting things together in original ways, though not necessarily what their bosses, teachers, or parents appreciate.

Imagination, pure and simple, can fill empty hours with pleasure, and give time and reason to create, plan, and invent. It can run along with a boring activity, not requiring one's complete attention as in daydreaming, while folding laundry, cutting the grass, and waiting for a draft of a report to print or popcorn to pop. A watched pot never boils—unless you daydream while you're waiting.

Not only can pure imagination wrest the spirit out of the grasp of boredom, but imagination can team up with almost any Element of Interest to make it more powerful and make a boring job more possible. The real magic of imagination comes when you are able to imagine the presence of one or more of your Elements of Interest that by definition brings you pleasure.

Imagination plus

Anna loved to play school. In second and third grade when she had a play date, she immediately insisted she and her friend play school. "You are the child and I am the teacher," she said. Some of her friends really didn't want to play school after a day of sitting in chairs in front of an authority figure. Anna soon became an unpopular playmate. In elementary school Anna had counseling for her social skills and was urged to be less bossy.

Her spontaneous revelation of her main Element of Interest was clear: teaching. While teaching is usually too complex an activity to call an Element, for some people, I believe, teaching could be an Element of Interest in itself. For example, a retired engineer I know has told me several times, "Send me someone to train. Give me a piece of chalk and I'm off and running." Alternatively, teaching can be broken down into Elements of Interest such as control—being in charge—and reveling in skill. Anna enjoyed both; she was a good student and knew things to teach. Analyzing masses of material and distilling it down into teachable concepts is a skill worthy of reveling in. Social interaction was clearly an Element of Interest Anna craved, even though her playing the teacher tended to drive others away. She compensated by conjuring up students to teach and could be heard in her bedroom explaining arithmetic problems to imaginary pupils.

As Anna grew older and the subject matter grew harder, she was required to spend more time studying. She was good at it but didn't find studying—going over lists of dates and learning science terminology—nearly as interesting as teaching. In fact, she was more interested in processes than facts, and secondary and university-level courses required the learning of too many facts that were too boring to hold her attention. At that point, with better social skills, her inner teacher became an asset. Anna reduced her own study time by teaching poorer students who really needed her skills in summarizing, extracting important points, and organizing material. Verbalizing the important points to others made them stick in Anna's mind better than if she studied them alone, and she enjoyed inventing mnemonic devices for her students. She was using her Elements of Interest in an appropriate manner and in a situation where they were appreciated, and as much for her benefit as theirs. The masses of material she was required to learn were no longer boring when she applied her own Elements of Interest to the task.

When Anna did not have students to teach the particular material she needed to learn, she again added the Element of Imagination to her teaching passion as she did in elementary school. While Anna taught in order to study, she had to imagine props or students. As an organizing tool she said out loud, "Okay, this is what we're going to do now. Get out your book and find the section on..." Or "We're going to make an outline now. What's the first main point?" And then she was prompted to answer her own question.

Dr. Lyndon Waugh told me about several patients with ADHD who did imaginary teaching as a means of study. One young woman lined up dolls and stuffed animals to teach, even adding teacher-like scolding for misbehavior and admonitions to pay attention. Dr. Waugh was retelling an older patient this description he'd heard, when the patient confessed, "That's the only way I got through college!" She had joined an organization, volunteered for an office, and in that role had a key to an isolated room. She went to that room frequently so she could more deeply learn by lecturing out loud.

By bringing imagination into boring situations, you can add drama, nurturing, altruism, purpose, social interaction, a limited time period, sensory stimulation, rhythm, or any other Element of Interest. Those for whom competition is important score a goal for every task or step of a task completed. Those who seek applause imagine an appreciative audience for every piece of work completed and an Academy Award or a medal for the whole stack. On the last few pieces of work, they can start composing their acceptance speech.

Imagining a scenario that satisfies strong Elements of Interest in an intense way is a great use of imagination.

CHAPTER SEVEN

Freedom and Boredom

While the first roadblock to developing interest in activities and situations is not knowing how, the next most likely and pervasive roadblock is likely to be lack of freedom. Thus coaching, counseling, and advising those with ADHD and boredom proneness is often chiefly about shaping situations to allow or create freedom.

We are not free. We are continuously contained, directed, limited, required, forbidden, prevented, and restrained. We are thereby productive, appropriate, out of trouble, safe from harm, polite, employed, and sometimes paid.

We are not always free to be ourselves. We are sometimes bored. If we have ADHD, we are often bored, restless, dissatisfied, frustrated, and very often not our true selves. Dealing with boredom is much easier when we are free to do whatever we want.

Seven-year-old Ryan is bored while waiting with his grandfather to be seated at a table in a restaurant. He sits briefly in a stuffed chair beside the door. Soon he kneels on the seat of the chair and looks up at a picture on the wall behind the chair. It's a landscape, the same boring landscape that is outside the restaurant. He butts his head against the back of the chair. His grandfather says, "Ryan, turn around." He turns around and swings his legs. Then he turns around in the chair and inches his legs up on the chair back, letting his head drop off the front of the chair. His grandfather admonishes Ryan to sit up "properly." "Properly" is the by-word of boredom.

Compare that scene with one at home in which Ryan has been interrupted while building a bridge for dinosaurs out of Lego®. His mother has asked about his homework. He says he hasn't done it and he doesn't remember what it is. His mother looks in his backpack and finds an assignment to write six sentences about his pets. "I can't think of anything to say," he says. His mother says, "It's hard to think of things when that's not what you are thinking about right now. And especially I bet you couldn't think of six things to say about your pets if you were upside down on the sofa."

Ryan gets a twinkle in his eye. It's the first time his mother has said anything like this. He immediately drops the Lego®, flops on the sofa, and lets his head drop off the front all the way down to the floor. He says nothing, just enjoying the new position. His mother repeats, "See, you can't think of even one thing to say about your pets when you are upside down."

"I can too," he says, "Darth is black and Vader is black with white on his chest. That's how I can tell them apart. They aren't exactly afraid of Winston [the dog], but they sneak around the side of the room when he's lying in the middle. He's not mean. He doesn't pay any attention to them. He mostly just wants to eat and go outside. He chases squirrels, not cats."

"That's amazing," his mother says. "You *can* think of things while you are upside down." She pauses until she gets a twinkle in her eye. "I know one thing you could *never* do."

"What?" he wants to know. He is curious about what his mother is thinking.

"I bet you could *never* write down those things you just said on a piece of paper *while* you were upside down."

He jumps up and gets his pad of paper from his backpack. He lies on his stomach on the sofa again with his head and arms hanging off. The paper is on the floor. "I have to kinda hold myself up with my elbow," he says, maneuvering.

"Ha!" says his mother. "I knew you couldn't write *and* think at the same time *and* be upside down."

"It's easy!" he says, beginning to write on the paper.

You can see where this is going. What Ryan wrote was not as fluent and complete as what he had said about his pets, and the handwriting was not great, but he got a whole paragraph about his two cats and one dog written. He drops the pencil and lets the paper drift under the chair. He is grinning. But then his mood changes.

"It's not very good."

His mother glances at it and says, "It's pretty darn good for someone who wrote it while upside down. I bet nobody in your whole classroom could do that but you. Your teacher is going to be surprised… Of course, she'll have to look under the sofa to find it… Bet she can't find it while she's upside down."

Ryan grins and thinks for a few seconds. He flips off the sofa, pulls the paper out from under it, and puts the paper in his backpack, where with luck—and a grin—it will arrive at school the next morning.

Ryan and his mother both know what has just happened here. The mom knows just a little bit more about what has happened. She has given Ryan a half dozen of his Elements of Interest: novelty, physical action, humor, curiosity, challenge, and surprise. She also threw in one strategy she learned from Kirk Martin, author of ADHD University instructional materials, who gives science-based training to educators, parents, and children. In an *ADDitude Magazine* webinar in September 2013, he said, among a great many other strategies, that being upside down allows a rush of blood to a child's head that actually stimulates the ADHD brain.[1] That's one reason kids like to do that.

The difference between that scene and the scene in the restaurant was basically the freedom to be upside down in a chair. How often is a child really free? How much less often is a child free in school or in a restaurant? What could the grandfather have done with Ryan in the restaurant? What freedom could he have given him? I actually don't think a seven-year-old upside down in a chair is something that must be forbidden. If it is disturbing others, if people are kicked or things are knocked over, or loud noises are made then, yes, it must be stopped. If a quiet upside-down child is just something unusual, he might actually keep the others waiting in the restaurant from being bored.

Customers, however, sometimes complain about the behavior of children in restaurants. As an alternative, this grandfather could have asked Ryan to walk quietly down the hall like a giraffe and come back like a squirrel. He could have given him a task to do: Go over to the bulletin board and see what's on it and come back and tell me about it. Go see what kind of desserts are in that display case and come back and tell me what looks good. He could plant a penny or two in a magazine on the table and say, "See if you can find a penny in this magazine, I have a feeling someone might have left one or two inside it." Most grandfathers have a few tricks up their sleeves. But first a grandfather has to understand that waiting in a chair for dinner is boring for anyone, that Ryan, being a child with ADHD, is especially boredom prone, and that he needs a few tricks, not a scolding. Helping a grandfather understand ADHD is an important undertaking for a family counselor or teacher.

Many of us are bored if we have to be still for too long. Freedom to seek interest is what we all need—and a few tricks. Ryan has ADHD but it doesn't really matter if he does or not. What's good for ADHD is good for everybody who is stuck in a boring situation.

"How could anyone be bored?"

While I was engaged in writing this book, people often asked what I was writing about and I had to say, "Boredom." I dreaded this frequent rejoinder: "I don't understand how anyone could be bored with all there is to do in the world. There are museums to visit and books to read and…" They proceed to name all the interesting things a person could be doing.

"Only the boring are bored" is a too well-known adage repeated by those who think that bored people are too dull witted or lacking in creativity to entertain themselves. People who are chronically or occasionally bored are not dull witted and lacking in creativity. In fact, the dull witted and lacking in creativity are not so easily bored; they are more likely to be content doing tasks they long ago mastered, enjoying the security of not having to learn something new. The people who are chronically or occasionally bored are more likely to be lacking in freedom than creativity.

Being free to do what interests us is crucial to escaping or shaping boredom. I have frequently asked interesting people what they find boring. Ellen, a long-time schoolteacher, replied, "Sitting in math and science classes and later in faculty meetings. Thank goodness they are all behind me now!! I'm retired now with all this time on my hands and I'm never bored."

When Ellen says "with all this time on my hands…I'm never bored," she means, "With all this freedom on my hands, I'm never bored." In retirement, Ellen has a full life with children and grandchildren and friends; moreover she goes to events like plays, festivals, reunions, picnics, or lunch with friends or family several times a week. When in the past she was confined for an hour or two in required classes and faculty meetings where topics irrelevant to her needs were being discussed—then she was bored. She tried to pay attention and, if that failed, she zoned out. Free at last, she is now almost never zoned out. She actively engages her Elements of Interest in her retirement and avoids what used to bore her.

Freedom to act is a critical factor in bringing Elements of Interest into otherwise boring activity and into life in general. Limitations on freedom include lack of permission, space, or funds. Age—both old and young—poor health, disability, and many other factors interfere with freedom. Many necessities and demands compete with freedom to seek interest on any given day or in any given decade. Without freedom, the resulting irritation, anger, and negative behavior of those with ADHD (or without) come from intolerance of boredom. The task of clinicians, teachers, and parents is often more about coaching to overcome obstacles to freedom than about directly addressing boredom itself. Partnering with the person suffering from boredom in necessary tasks is a problem-solving situation. You are in luck if problem-solving is one of that individual's Elements of Interest. It often is.

Never bored, often irritated

A high-energy entrepreneur, Mel sees himself as never bored. He has so many projects going, how could he be bored? However, when encountering a slowdown of any significance on an expressway, he barks (unheard outside of his car) for people to move out of his way until he can dart off at the next exit, where he performs cleverly intricate maneuvers to get where he is going. Problem-solving and speed are two of Mel's Elements of Interest. With the traffic lights and left-hand turns, it ultimately takes him longer and burns more gas than waiting in the stop-and-go clog on the freeway, but at least he is doing something besides sitting there. He is never bored;

he is just often irritated. He doesn't realize that his irritation is a reaction to impending boredom where he lacks freedom to escape.

Those who endure boredom the most easily suffer boredom the longest; those who cannot endure boredom do something even if it's the wrong thing. Harry Briggs' retrospective description of himself in high school, from his memoir, reflects many of the themes of this book:

> ...academics weren't really a love but a major occupation. If I liked a class, I'd get an A. If I didn't like it, I'd get a C. I got good grades in what interested me. My parents were always getting after me to do my assignments. In the end I did discover a field of study that really turned me on for a lifetime. In the meantime, I was a thorn in the side of my teachers... I remember feeling that people were saying and thinking, "You will never be as smart as your sister."
>
> ...so I decided to be bad. I did all kinds of tricks. I'd bang a book on the floor just when a teacher was about to make a good point, or I'd fall asleep and snore. Why I wasn't expelled I don't know...
>
> ...One day I started to ride Mr. Whitney. I'd ask him a question and I didn't like his answer so I got the whole class laughing. I thought, I can destroy this guy and I'll see what he's made of. I have people like that in the classes I teach now; I call them sharpshooters. Once I was wising off and Mr. Whitney grabbed me by my shirt and held me up in the air, so we were eyeball to eyeball until he let me go. I thought, Man, how'd he do that to me?...
>
> Yes, I was a wild kid in high school. I got into a lot of trouble. I was belligerent and always wising off, mostly in a humorous vein. I was named Class Wit, and I was always showing off...[2]

You will be happy to know that Harry ran into Mr. Whitney in another city a decade later and asked his former teacher if he remembered him. Mr. Whitney had not forgotten. Harry said, "Good, because I want to apologize."[2] Harry, the same Harry Briggs whose marathon swim across Lake Erie is mentioned in an earlier chapter, went on to get a PhD and become a professor himself. At every step of the way his ADHD characteristics played a major role as he made his swims, took ten years to get his doctorate degree, started several businesses of his own, taught, coached, promoted events, and managed sports facilities—all at the same time.

If you can relate to Ryan, Mel, or Harry and their sense of being trapped, you may understand how your patient, client, student, or child with ADHD often feels. With deficient activation of dopamine and other neurotransmitters, he is boredom prone. Only those things that truly interest him can satisfy his need for stimulation and yield to him the neurochemical reward other people feel more readily. Without interest he is unable to focus his attention and he feels uncomfortable. He must choose then between trying to control his irritation over this discomfort and creating some action, drama, danger, suspense, or other more stimulating Element to relieve this discomfort.

Among those with ADHD and often boredom prone, those whom I call Zoned Out are more likely to be ADHD inattentive, and those whom I call Riled Up are more likely to be ADHD impulsive and/or hyperactive. The responses of the Riled Up are more likely to be problematic and lead to conflict; the responses of the Zoned Out are more likely to go unnoticed, undiagnosed, and untreated.

Clinicians may be helpful in relationship counseling by exploring with couples and families their experiences with boredom and their various ways of avoiding and responding to it, especially when ADHD is a factor.

"I couldn't just walk away..."

People are often locked into a state of boredom by internal restrictions such as lack of skills, fear, and the tyranny of politeness. Most of these obstacles can be reduced by understanding the effect of boredom as a neurochemical lack of stimulation and by knowing how to bring Elements of Interest into potentially boring situations. Equally important is finding or creating more freedom to seek interest, an area where teaching, counseling, and coaching can be very helpful, opening up exploration of new possibilities.

Asked "What is boring to you?" Kirsten replied, "Receiving quite lengthy, unwanted, and unnecessary instructions on how to do something when I have been doing the task longer and more efficiently than they ever have done or will do. They were in a position of authority, so I couldn't just walk away or tell them they were wasting my time and theirs."

While Kirsten had freedom in certain aspects of her job, when her condescending supervisor came to tell her how to do something she had been doing for years, she did not feel free to cut the instruction short. She was trapped by authority, and she was bored.

It's possible that Kirsten would have felt equally trapped if the person instructing her were not an authority over her, but a nice, helpful person Kirsten didn't want to offend. In fact, next to authority, politeness seems to be the biggest enemy to freedom many of us experience. We tend to think of people in prison as having lost their freedom. Yes, but they are at least free to be impolite!

Whether trapped by authority or a desire to be polite, escaping this kind of imposed boredom means giving yourself permission to set a boundary. When Kirsten said, "They were in a position of authority, so I couldn't just walk away or tell them they were wasting my time and theirs," in fact, she could walk and she could talk. What she couldn't do was give herself permission to stop her supervisor from giving her instructions because of her fear of consequences. Probably the struggle between desire and fear made the discomfort of boredom more intense. Without that internal struggle, she could perhaps have comfortably zoned out until the ordeal was over.

Was there a tactful way for Kirsten, the veteran office worker, to tell her boss that she was familiar with his instructions and he didn't need to repeat them to her? Probably. I have observed many people successfully do something similar without provoking a negative reaction, although that does depend on the person.

Professionals can work with clients to overcome unnecessary fear and to increase skill. A coach might ask Kirsten, "If you did stop him, how would you do it?" "What could you say that would not make him defensive?" "What's the worst that could happen if you held up your hand to stop him and told him pleasantly that you were already familiar with this process?" and "Let's role play that conversation to see how it feels."

Such an approach at least opens the door for your client to seek freedom instead of enduring boredom and the anger or frustration of being trapped.

It could be that if Kirsten asked innocently "So it's the same as last time?" her boss would have to say, "Yes." Then she could say quickly, "Okay, I got it. I'll have it done by the end of the day." He might get the point painlessly that his directions were not needed. Or she might go one step further and pleasantly hold up her hand to stop him mid-sentence, before saying, "So it's the same as last time?"

Kirsten may fear she would lose control and, if she opened her mouth, she would let the sarcasm she was thinking pop out. She might be afraid that, in getting up a head of steam, she would allow herself to go over the line and say, "So it's the same as last time…and the last 250 times I've done it?" Or "Okay, I got it… just like I got it in 1995." Once sarcasm is in the mix, everything goes downhill.

If Kirsten felt so irritated by imposed boredom that she feared losing control and jeopardizing her job, she might be harboring unexpressed resentment of another sort. On the other hand, it could be that the unexpressed resentment is a sign the whole job is boring, that in spite of her competence the job has not changed in decades, and it offers little challenge or other Elements of Interest that Kirsten craves. That suggests the pursuit of another level of freedom.

Coaching to achieve freedom

Kathy was near the end of her junior year in high school when I began to coach her. Along with good grades in courses that interested her, she had two Ds; a C or better was required for her to receive credit for those courses. Without those two credits, she could not graduate the next year as expected. We had six weeks left in the spring quarter to turn things around.

When asked to do the Top 10 Joys exercise, Kathy told me she'd never experienced joy. Nevertheless, when encouraged further to recall a happy time, she came up with one vivid experience of intense joy that revealed several strong Elements of Interest: a feeling of closeness within a group, achievement, applause/acclaim, and reveling in her skill. While it was helpful to get from Kathy's single description of joy such strong indications of her Elements of Interest, one experience of joy in life is sad.

Early in our coaching relationship Kathy told me she now had a boyfriend at school. "Don't tell my parents," she said, and of course I didn't. Before long, however, it was time for Junior/Senior prom. She was going to the dance with her boyfriend, and, because of her need for a prom gown, her secret was out. Her mother then told me about the boyfriend, lamenting, "Another distraction!" She limited Kathy's time with the boy to one meeting on the weekend and one during the week, usually dinner at each other's homes under watchful parental eyes. To me this new "distraction" was an appropriate and badly needed additional joy that signaled the Element of closeness or romantic attachment.

The coaching model I was using with Kathy in order for her to meet her goals of better grades included a contract between me and her and the possibility of a reward from her parents for taking observable actions to improve her grades. While a reward is less effective with children with ADHD because they simply *are unable to* focus on uninteresting tasks regardless of the promise of a reward (or a consequence), offering a quick reward for specific immediate actions can be helpful. Kathy's actions included getting to class on time, doing her homework, completing school projects on time, and remembering to turn them in. We worked on strategies to promote these actions, and her grades began to rise. The improved grades themselves were actually the best reward possible for Kathy because she was eager to graduate on time and go to college. Moreover, in the shorter term she got her parents off her back; when she got home from school and the questions began about her day's accomplishments and grades, she had something to say that satisfied them. As for the reward to be provided by her parents, she had never chosen one.

I had suggested we wait before choosing the reward until I at least knew more about her Elements of Interest. What she wanted and needed was freedom to pursue an Element that she had never experienced before. She had relatively little freedom for her age. So I coached her on how to ask her mother—not easy—to give her, as a reward for one week with all assignments completed and turned in, one additional time she could spend with her boyfriend the following week and the same arrangement for subsequent weeks. Her mother was not thrilled with the idea, but she had to admit that the restrictions had been designed to get Kathy to concentrate on her studies better. If she did her work well and turned it in, there was no reason not to allow her this joy one additional time per week. Kathy raised her two Ds to Cs in the six weeks remaining in that spring term, thereby receiving credit for the courses, and in summer school she got As. Kathy earned the freedom to spend more time with her boyfriend and enjoy a close relationship appropriate for her age. It took just a bit of support for Kathy to find the courage to ask for more freedom as an incentive to do all the actions necessary to earn it.

Kathy's story is one example of how coaches and other professionals can help a young person and her family shape a situation so that her Elements of Interest can be more fully expressed.

Extreme barriers

Freedom for a high school student to have time with her boyfriend may seem trivial compared to the extreme lack of freedom some people have in extraordinary circumstances. In addition to occasional or short-term lack of freedom to seek interest, intractable obstacles to freedom include dire ones like imprisonment, poverty, poor health, disability, and isolation. Job requirements and confining duties as caregivers for children or the infirm are common obstacles to engaging in one's Elements of Interest.

In a most extreme case of a severely impaired nine-year-old child with a mental age of a young infant, a treatment was designed to be one that would be stimulating to a young infant. The unfortunate child, who earlier whimpered and cried a lot, calmed down when receiving a light massage of his limbs, being turned over to a new position or moved to a new view, hearing music, the human voice, and the rhythm of a heartbeat, or having a colorful mobile turning above his face in his crib. Newness and sensory stimulation were assumed to be his main Elements of Interest just as for an infant, and change offered through many sensory pathways was a reasonable and desirable way to make his restricted life comfortable. Returning to the Elements remains a way to start and to judge the interest level of experience in any condition.

In my work for Recovery Outfitters Inc. (ROI), a treatment center in Georgia for young men addicted to drugs and alcohol, I have had the pleasure of writing dozens of success stories. A majority of ROI clients have ADHD. Some ROI alumni who are now in recovery have spent time in prison for dealing drugs or driving under the influence of drugs and causing injuries. In the cases of serving prison time with which I am familiar, these young men and boys have found significant ways to lessen boredom while incarcerated. They have pored over legal reference books to write convincing appeals for parole or sentence reduction in order to seek treatment, which satisfies the Element of purpose as well as makes them ponder the question of why in fact they deserve to be released. They have educated themselves on other topics useful in leading better lives after their sentence was fulfilled or participated in a program to tell their story to at-risk young people on the outside in hopes that these kids can go straight before they get into serious trouble.[3]

While prisoners in general are well known to thwart boredom by escape strategies, violence, and flagrant rule-breaking, some prisoners have tutored or ministered to others in incarceration. They have trained dogs to serve the disabled or veterans of Iraq and Afghanistan who are wounded or suffering post-traumatic stress disorder.[4] They have written books, poetry, and dissertations.

A little over 50 years ago, Martin Luther King Jr. penned a masterpiece now called "Letter from a Birmingham Jail," about which King said, "...what else is there to do when you are alone for days in the dull monotony of a narrow jail cell other than write long letters, think strange thoughts, and pray long prayers?"

That was enough for him to do; that beautifully constructed and convincing document inspired many Americans to join the side of human rights.[5]

As 17th century English poet Richard Lovelace wrote, "Stone walls do not a prison make nor iron bars a cage." With effort and inspiration, boredom can be allayed almost anywhere. While incarceration is an extreme example of being trapped in a boring situation, those who refuse to be bored find a way.[6]

Freedom and resources

Freedom to seek interest is limited by many forces including poverty or lack of resources. I once coached a woman I'll call Jillian, who, through a traumatic event no fault of her own, had no job, was running out of money, and had a child to support who had also suffered through the same trauma. She had little time or resources to provide herself and her child with interesting experiences. Among her Top 10 Joys this mother listed horseback riding; she'd once owned her own horse. When I asked what about riding horses made her happy, Jillian said speed, her strength, and control. I was not surprised that control was an Element of Interest for her, and I was aware she had little control of anything at this time. The simple answer to her mood of discouragement, if she had money, would be to resume horseback riding. That cost money she didn't have, of course.

I asked her how much she knew about the need for volunteers at horseback therapy programs, people who would walk with children and adults on horseback, leading them safely and with encouragement. She said she did not even want to touch a horse because it would bring back the pain of her loss. Even so, she began to volunteer in the organization in other ways than handling horses and soon found her daughter was qualified for the free horseback therapy because of her post-traumatic stress disorder (PTSD). Soon through the networking aspect of her volunteering, Jillian ended up being invited to ride herself without charge in this program, based on her own diagnosis of PTSD. The horseback riding did not entail the same level of speed and strength as she had experienced before she lost everything, but it did offer the Elements of physical action and control, which she had missed.

There are other less elaborate ways that people without adequate resources can access sources of interest at little cost. There are books on having fun for free and articles on free resources in local newspapers and online resources. Clinicians and coaches can brainstorm with clients for creative ways to gain access or assistance that will allow the expression of Elements of Interest for those with limited resources.

CHAPTER EIGHT

Attention, Focus, Hyperfocus, and Flow

A staff meeting at a counseling program for at-risk youth was being held to discuss the nonprofit organization's lack of funds and to decide if they could even continue operation. As they had done many times before, they discussed ways to cut costs or raise funds. They also discussed how they would manage a shutdown if they were unable to keep their doors open. The jobs of everyone there were at stake as well as the welfare of clients; most of the staff worked there because they were passionate about helping their clients. The meeting was of critical importance to all.

During a lull in the discussion, as they considered the possibilities of the situation, one counselor I'll call Jacob gestured to a few empty chairs at the conference table and said, "Did you ever notice that the spindles on those chairs are not exactly the same? See, that one has bigger rings around it and that one is skinnier at the top."

Eyes rolled and someone muttered, "That's ADHD for you."

The others at the table were very familiar with ADHD. They knew that the importance of the meeting didn't matter to the ADHD brain as long as it was a boring meeting with the same old questions and few new ideas. The discovery that the chair spindles were not all the same had no importance to anyone but was new to Jacob. His interest in them would soon pass, but for the moment they engaged his attention and satisfied his brain more than the meeting did.

While Jacob is an inattentive participant in a meeting, he is an excellent counselor. He's in charge of the outdoor recreation, and he organizes adventures meticulously, paying close attention to the details of logistics, and leads with inspiration. He is the first up the mountain and at the front of the first raft to hit the rapids. He knows the lore of the forest and the best fishing places. He also is aware of learning opportunities for the young people and sometimes has life-changing conversations with clients on horseback or around the campfire. Back at the counseling center, he is more aware of impending trouble or available opportunity than most people because his eyes and ears are always open and scanning for anything unusual. Nothing happens without him knowing. His vigilance is useful.

At day's end, do you think Jacob sits down and writes out his clinical notes for the day's adventures, insights, and conversations? Not at all. He lives for action and doing something new; he doesn't want to sit down to write or to revisit past encounters. Regardless of the importance of clinical notes, he puts them in that spot on the calendar called "some other time."

As William Dodson, M.D., discussed in a 2013 webinar for *ADDitude Magazine*, importance is not a motivating entity for the person with ADHD; only what's interesting. And especially boring is what he calls "second hand importance," that is, what's important only to someone else,[1] like the administrator who insists on collecting clinical notes from counselors, at the very least, to satisfy legal requirements.

Attention

Our main but not our only avenues of attention are vision and hearing. Vision has a periphery and a focal point and several areas in between. A quick dart of the eye can leave one focal point and find another that a moment before was only peripheral. The brain allows or directs vision to the new focal point. The brain also allows other senses to divert attention. An itch can insist that you scratch or a remark can make you listen more than you watch.

Hearing takes in the whole surroundings and yet it can be focused. While we sit at a table with a friend in a café engaging in pleasant conversation, we may pick up an intriguing remark made at an adjacent table and begin listening to that conversation instead. None of us has perfect control of our eavesdropping tendencies, and those with ADHD have even less because our ADHD brain is always open to something more interesting. This quality is what made Jacob more aware of needs and danger signs in the counseling center than his coworkers who were often more narrowly focused on particular tasks or one-on-one conversations.

Attention can be almost automatic in everyday activities such as when driving a car through the countryside on an expressway. The driver can follow another car at a steady distance behind without thinking about that car. She is aware of the car in front of her but is not focusing on it. She can deliberately pay attention to the scenery at the same time. Her visual attention is divided. She may also comment to her companion about the funny sign she sees on the side of a barn off to one side of the road, engaging other parts of her brain like language and hearing. When a red brake light on the car in front of her suddenly brightens in the periphery of her vision, the scenery drops from her attention; she focuses in front of her again, puts on her brakes, or makes a quick glance in the next lane to see if it is clear for her to swing around the car in front.

While her attention is often snagged by something interesting, alarming, or useful, the driving behavior just described to a large extent reflects an intention, a choice of where to put focus. Attention is a very mobile and busy entity.

The ADHD mind in particular is looking for something interesting, new, and even dangerous. The person with ADHD would likely have no problem responding quickly to the brake light of the car in front. She switches attention to the brake light ahead and goes into action. Her mind craves the chemical stimulation epinephrine (often called adrenaline) we all feel when a brake light goes on in front of us on a fast-moving highway.

On the other hand, her ADHD mind, seeking interest instead of the boring sameness of the car in front of us, might become so engrossed in conversation or the sign on the barn that she breezes on past her intended exit. She might not even notice her mistake until she finds herself approaching a high bridge over a river. The bridge is interesting, different, new to the scene, and, she suddenly realizes, not on the way to her destination. She's not absent minded; she's just mindful of things unrelated to reaching her goal.

ADHD is not so much a problem of inability to give attention, but an inability to choose and control where to give attention in a world of so many possibilities.

Multitasking

Attention, some level of directed awareness, is at the heart of the issue of ADHD, as the name Attention Deficit implies, and yet "attention excess," as Dr. Dodson calls it,[1] is equally or even more of a problem in the disorder. The world is full of innumerable internal and external objects that, for better or for worse, draw our attention.

Switching from one thought or activity, which is often impulsive rather than thought out, is a way of snatching anything of interest from the less interesting background in order to gain stimulation for the brain deprived of sufficient dopamine and thus easily bored. The ADHD brain loves multitasking because two or three things of even low-level interest are more stimulating than a single task of low-level interest.

Some people with ADHD pride themselves on the virtue of multitasking. While there are times when we have to juggle things and multitasking is necessary, the objects of shifting attention do not get full attention, by definition, and multiple tasks are not carried out as well as if they were a sole focus. The multitasker gets by; many things are not worth full attention, but focus is needed to do certain things well.

While ADHDers delight in unbridled multitasking or "multithinking," this process is likely not as fluid as it may seem. An American Psychological Association review of research (on normal subjects) published from 1995 through 2003 on multitasking versus focusing on one task for a long time revealed that multitasking is just not as efficient as sustained focus on one task:

> According to Meyer, Evans and Rubinstein, converging evidence suggests that the human "executive control" processes have two distinct, complementary stages. They call one stage "goal shifting" ("I want to do this now instead of that") and the other stage "rule activation" ("I'm turning off the rules for that

> and turning on the rules for this"). Both of these stages help people to, without awareness, switch between tasks...
>
> Although switch costs may be relatively small, sometimes just a few tenths of a second per switch, they can add up to large amounts when people switch repeatedly back and forth between tasks. Thus, multitasking may seem efficient on the surface but may actually take more time in the end and involve more error. Meyer has said that even brief mental blocks created by shifting between tasks can cost as much as 40 percent of someone's productive time.[2]

The APA review noted research by Robert Rogers and Stephen Monsell, as follows:

> ...where there appears to be two parts to the switch cost—one attributable to the time taken to adjust the mental control settings (which can be done in advance if there is time), and another part due to competition due to carry-over of the control settings from the previous trial (apparently immune to preparation).
>
> In experiments published in 2001, Joshua Rubinstein, PhD, Jeffrey Evans, PhD, and David Meyer, PhD, conducted four experiments in which young adults switched between different tasks. The subjects took significantly longer to switch between more complex tasks.
>
> In a 2003 paper [by] Nick Yeung, PhD, and Monsell... The results revealed just some of the complexities involved in understanding the cognitive load imposed by real-life multitasking, when in addition to reconfiguring control settings for a new task, there is often the need to remember where you got to in the task to which you are returning and to decide which task to change to, when.[2]

There is a use for the talent of multitasking, and ADHDers need to find careers where it's most valuable. Unfortunately for them, in most jobs focus is needed often and for long periods of time on tasks that are not especially interesting in order to achieve goals.

Focus

Focus by definition narrows the range of attention to make one area clearer while what is in the periphery stays in a lower level of consciousness. In her book *Rapt: Attention and the Focused Life*, Winifred Gallagher has written a particularly clear description of what attention does:

> Neuroscience's truly groundbreaking insight into attention is the discovery that its basic mechanism is a process of selection. This two-part neurological sorting operation allows you to focus by enhancing the most compelling, or "salient," physical object or "high-value" mental subject in your ken and suppressing the rest…
>
> As the expression paying attention suggests, when you focus, you're spending limited cognitive currency that should be wisely invested, because the stakes are high. At any one moment, your world contains too much information, whether objects, subjects, or both, for your brain to "represent," or depict clearly for you. Your attentional system selects a certain chunk of what's there, which gets valuable real estate and, therefore, the chance to affect your behavior. Moreover, this thin slice of life becomes part of your reality, and the rest is consigned to the shadows or oblivion.[3]

For many of us and especially those with ADHD, the "high-value" mental subject is the most interesting one, and, not always being the best investment of our "limited cognitive currency," it sometimes negatively affects our behavior.

Focus is choosing a point of attention and holding it there for as long as our executive functioning or rational part of our brain requires. Sustained focus on what we *deliberately* choose for a chosen length of time is often necessary or ideal. Notice that "deliberate" means "fully considered; not impulsive: done or acting in a careful and unhurried way."[4] Acting deliberately, by that definition, is not exactly the ADHD way.

The ADHD brain, however, has a weaker executive function when there is a lower-than-normal dopamine activation, especially in the frontal lobes where we make deliberate, thought-out choices.

The more exciting stimulation of impulsive, careless actions overrides the executive function. This creates a disconcerting effect like an airplane making an unscheduled stop or going somewhere not on the ticket. The result is confusion and anxiety along with missed connections and late arrivals.

Hyperfocus

Seven-year-old Reed and his older sister were at the zoo with their grandmother; they'd been quite a few times before so the novelty had worn off. At the elephant pen, they stood by the fence and watched the elephant eat hay. Reed had stood on the bottom board of the fence and thrown his arms over the top, but the elephant with its familiar swaying trunk and hay-stuffing did not attract his attention. Something on one of the fence posts caught his eye. Some wood had broken away from the post, revealing the metal bolts that had been drilled inside the post before it split. Reed began to examine the bolts. Whether it was the construction that interested him—construction is one of his Elements of Interest—or whether it was some insects or moss or rust in these components of a fence that drew his attention, he became more and more deeply engrossed. He poked his fingers in the split and felt around, furrowed his brow, and found a stick to plumb the depths of the split in the post.

His sister had also glanced at the elephant and took no further interest as it had been a long day. If you've seen one elephant you've seen them all, she seemed to think. She wanted to move on, but Reed seemed to be mesmerized by the post. Their grandmother said, "Come on Reed, let's go look at the primates." They started walking. Reed stayed behind. They called back to him, "We're going." Reed stayed.

Their grandmother walked back to him. "We're going on to see the monkeys and orangutans, Reed. Let's go." She turned and walked back to her granddaughter. "Let's go," she said to the girl, using an age-old parental trick for moving children on. "He'll come on when he sees we're gone."

His big sister said protectively, "He doesn't like us to go on without him."

"I know. That's why he'll come when he sees us going. He'll stay there as long as we'll stay with him, so the only way to get him to come is for us to go on."

Sure enough, as his sister and grandmother paused in the distance, Reed came running, crying forlornly, "Don't leave me."

His sister repeated, "You can't do that with Reed. He gets upset."

Back home his mother further explained that Reed is unable to tear himself away from something he's focusing on as easily as other children. He's truly distressed at being left. "He's not being disobedient. He doesn't even hear you. You have to go back to him and disengage him first, by touching him or putting your face down in front of his to be sure he's listening to you, and then take him with you."

Reed's mother also says he sees things the rest of us don't see, in our goal-oriented way. He thinks thoughts that we, in our prosaic, literal way, don't think. He has made his family laugh at his quirky remarks. His way is charming and whimsical, and sometimes incomprehensible and inconvenient. The ordinary way of perceiving things is boring to him. Insisting that he see things our way discourages his thought and encroaches on his creativity.

Reed's deep attention to the inside of a rotting post is called hyperfocus, the opposite of scanning, the other side of the ADHD coin. It's not just reluctance to change focus; it's inability to change until interest wanes. People with or without ADHD have intense interest that engages them to the point that it's almost painful to let go because that stimulation boosts the activation of dopamine, creating reinforcement from the reward circuitry for the duration of that interest. If boredom is painful and we have found a source of intense interest, why would we let it go? People with ADHD experience hyperfocus even more keenly than others because the stimulation of interest is so precious.

People with ADHD do not necessarily pay too little attention. They may pay the same amount as anyone else; it's just allocated differently, sometimes inappropriately, and it's harder to shift their attention from one thing to another. While people with ADHD focus too little on necessary tasks they find boring, they may focus their attention too much when they can't tear themselves away from something they find extremely interesting even when they know it's time to leave it. Shifting focus is difficult, especially "down shifting" from a more stimulating activity to a less interesting one.

Hyperfocus on a current activity also makes it hard to "see" or "feel" rewards possible in the future. Sometimes Reed is invited on the spur of the moment to go somewhere with a friend to do something he really enjoys like watch a movie or a swim in a friend's pool. He turns down the invitation because at the present moment he is fully engaged, hyperfocused on building a structure with Lego®, something he loves. In his hyperfocus, he doesn't think about the movie or the swim. He only knows he's happy now. His mom sometimes insists that he go to the movie or pool with his friend anyway because she knows he will have a lot of fun and the Lego® will be there when he comes back. Reed grumbles, but he comes home glad he went to the movie or the swim, a choice he didn't—and couldn't—make for himself.

Hyperfocus on the present object of interest, which makes it hard to foresee bigger rewards for different choices in the future, is often considered a need for "instant gratification." Willingness to wait or work for longer-term rewards is a major predictor of overall success in life. Preferring the "present reward" over the more distant one is natural and more predominant the younger or less mature a child is. Why would a kid give up feeling good right now? Why would he expect feeling good later would be better?

We cannot know the value of Reed's hyperfocus on the broken fence post. If we say choosing to work on the Lego® structure, which he could do any time, is shortsighted and choosing the more exciting invitation to a movie or a pool with a friend is more mature by taking a long view, we are making a value judgment of his activities based on our values. We don't realize how totally satisfying what he's doing now is to him or what it may mean to him later.

Judging the value of intense, narrowed focus by whether it serves the person's goals is one way of appreciating focus or hyperfocus. Often, however, another person's choice of focus is judged by the goals of the parent, teacher, employer, or partner in a relationship. The parent wants a neat bedroom and living room floor. The teacher wants 25 math problems worked correctly. The employer wants progress reports on time. The spouse or partner wants the backdoor fixed because its sagging condition bothers her. The person with ADHD has serious trouble converting other individuals' wishes into his own Elements of Interest and he is truly unable to focus on what is not interesting to him: unable, not selfish or immature. Not careless, but *care more*.

If Reed is able to turn his interest in construction into a career, it will be clear that the hyperfocus of his childhood on the construction of fences and Lego® towers served not only as an Element of Interest but as preparation for a satisfying life.

Having the capability of sustained hyperfocus is a requirement of many emergencies and other high-risk situations. For example, an airline pilot may have the most boring job in the word on long uneventful flights, but he must be able to attend well to a great many things during takeoff and landing, and he must be able to summon a sustained concentration on complex systems during emergencies. The action, risk, skill, challenge, urgency, and other Elements of Interest called on during emergencies obviously get the pilot's attention.

Military operations often require similar prolonged and intense periods of concentration. People with ADHD, while not performing well in boring situations, are often at their best in the intensely exciting points of battle. For example, having ADHD is not always a deterrent in a mission of the Army's Special Operations. People who can turn on a high degree of sustained focus in an emergency also make good first responders such as police, firefighters, and emergency room staff.

Many of us enjoy reading books or watching television shows or movies about such moments of hyperfocus. We are riveted on the situation and the task. We become vigilant. We find ourselves bringing that plane down to safety against all odds or escaping the bad guys by racing through the jungle. We are experiencing the hero's hyperfocus vicariously. The suspense is "killing us," we say, but really it is thrilling us.

Flow

A special kind of hyperfocus is a psychological state Mihaly Csikszentmihalyi famously called "flow" in his first book describing his research on that state. That 1975 title gave boredom its due: *Beyond Boredom and Anxiety: Experiencing Flow in Work and Play.*

Flow is that ideal level of focus about which Csikszentmihalyi says:

> It is not boring, as life outside the activity often is. At the same time, it does not produce anxiety, which often intrudes itself on awareness in "normal" life. Poised between boredom and worry, the autotelic experience is one of complete involvement of the actor with his activity. The activity presents constant challenges. There is no time to get bored or to worry about what may or may not happen. A person in such a situation can make full use of whatever skills are required and receives clear feedback to his actions...[5]

From then on, he referred to "this peculiar dynamic state—the holistic sensation that people feel when they act with total involvement—as *flow*."[6]

By "autotelic experience" Csikszentmihalyi means a point where the activity is being carried out without need for awareness of purpose or outcome. That doesn't mean it has no purpose or desired outcome but that the person in the state of flow is not aware of anything but the process of using his skills and energy in the sweet spot of perfect or near-perfect challenge between boredom and fear. Flow is a satisfying state but to notice it or internally verbalize that satisfaction is to fall out of flow.

Csikszentmihalyi researched flow in work and play rather than in emergency. It's hard to say if the experience of the airplane pilot who brings his plane to safety when power has been lost in its engine is in flow by Csikszentmihalyi's definition. Surely, there is anxiety and concern for the outcome, which are not part of the famed researcher's flow model; however, the pilot *puts aside fear* to do his work and he has to *let go of the outcome* in order to concentrate on actions that would result in the best possible outcome. To my mind, this is optimal performance, if not the "optimal experience" about which Csikszentmihalyi wrote.

When seven-year-old Reed became captivated by a fence post that was falling apart and revealing the fence's inner construction, his hyperfocus did not seem to involve constant challenge as Czikszentmihalyi's definition of flow requires. His was more contemplative, although perhaps his thoughts were addressing mental challenges. He was not bored but engrossed, fascinated, lost in his observations, and unconcerned with time or the wishes or words of others.

It seems to me that flow is the upside of hyperfocus. The difference between hyperfocus and flow seems largely subjective. Flow is the medium in which delicate surgeries have been performed, great discoveries and inventions have been born, new businesses have been hatched, poems have been written, Lincoln Log towns have been built, and skateboard rides around obstacles have been completed without tripping. When flow lasts too long or happens at problematic times, when it destroys balance in life or gets a person into trouble, it becomes hyperfocus, as hyper simply means too much. When Thomas Edison spent hours and hours working into the night on his inventions, he no doubt experienced long periods of flow. His thousands of innovations offered many benefits to society, but his marriage suffered. The distinction between flow and hyperfocus may be a judgmental one. When a parent can't get a child's attention away from an elaborate tower he is building or he is lying on the ground in his best clothes while pushing toy cars through the mud, the state she's interrupting may be flow to the child and hyperfocus to the parent.

I believe I have experienced flow many times during the writing of this book. At these times my skills have been perfectly matched with the challenges, and I have worked for hours at a time without thinking of time or hunger or results, without boredom or anxiety, just enjoying the process and reveling in my skills. I have also many times reached the edges of experience far outside of flow. I have been bored with putting references into the proper format, and I have been anxious about my deadline. I have sometimes found the challenges too great for my skills, and the unchallenging parts too tedious.

Being in flow is something we only recognize as we come out of it, as we become aware of our feeling and think, "Damn, that was good!" These are times we would be wise to note what we were doing when we entered flow, of what made up the components and the environment at the beginning of this magical state. As clinicians, teachers, and other professionals, you can encourage your charges with ADHD and a tendency to hyperfocus to evaluate the times, reasons, and appropriateness of each occasion of hyperfocus and to see it and seek it as flow experience when it is helpful and positive in reaching their goals. Likewise you can help those you counsel to devise strategies for coming out of hyperfocus when appropriate. The more we know about our own focus, the more likely we are to be able to use it intentionally.

CHAPTER NINE

Boredom in Addiction, Recovery, and Relapse

Boredom is not lack of something to do but lack of something active, interactive, new, bold, and meaningful to do—and the freedom to do it. Young people or those without the skills or opportunity to find what interests them, people in midlife who are trapped in routine, unchallenging jobs because of the need for income, and older people who have retired from or are unable to continue in something meaningful or novel are all likely to be bored.

A common solution to relentless boredom is the use of mind-altering substances. Boredom, as a major contributor to experimenting with drugs and alcohol, is therefore a factor in drug dependence and addiction.

"Edward," telling his recovery story on the website of COPAC, a treatment center in Mississippi, recalls: "There was a lot I wanted to escape. I wanted to escape the mundane; I wanted to escape the small town; I wanted to escape this feeling of general boredom. But I wanted to escape also this feeling of not being at ease in my own skin."[1]

Health writer Carl Sherman, PhD, quotes a special education teacher speaking of her college years when her ADHD had been undiagnosed: "The boredom was impossible. I could be sitting in an interesting lecture and be totally bored. When I drank, I didn't care that I was bored."[2]

Sources that list reasons why people first use mind-altering substances usually put boredom or curiosity high on the list. The two go together. Curiosity is interest-seeking, the motivation for escaping boredom, and so first-timers try drugs and alcohol to "see what it feels like." It's something to do when they have nothing going on inside their brains to give pleasure, that is, novelty-seeking, when they are bored. It follows that those under-stimulated by low levels of dopamine and other neurotransmitters because of ADHD are overrepresented among problematic users of drugs and alcohol.

Thrill-seeking and rebelling or rule-breaking, both characteristics of ADHD, are also listed. Escaping problems is on almost all lists of causes of substance abuse. Given that young people with ADHD often have the problem of striving but not succeeding and their behavior being called "not trying hard enough," a desire to escape those feelings of failure or criticism drives them to mind-altering substances. Peer pressure or fitting in socially, assumed by many to be top motivators, make many lists but not as often as one might think.

While experimentation with drugs does not necessarily lead to dependence and addiction, it certainly is a first step. A U.S. National Survey on Drug Use and Health (NSDUH) surveyed persons aged 12 or older who first used a particular mind-altering substance 13 to 24 months prior to the survey interview. Of those who had first used alcohol, 3.2 percent were dependent on alcohol in the 12 months before the survey, 5.8 percent for marijuana, 9.2 percent for crack cocaine, and 13.4 percent for heroin. Though those percentages for first-time users are lower than those who may eventually become dependent or addicted, the NSDUH study[3] shows that the first use, the experimentation that so often takes place as "something to do" during boredom, is a factor in addiction.

According to an article at ADD & ADHD Health Center on WebMD.com:

> It is also more common for children with ADHD to start abusing alcohol during their teenage years. In one study, 14 percent of children ages 15–17 with ADHD had problems with alcohol abuse or dependence as adults, compared to peers without ADHD. Another study found that at a mean age of 14.9 years, 40 percent of children with ADHD began using alcohol, compared to 22 percent of children without an

> ADHD diagnosis—strong predictor of alcohol and substance abuse in adulthood. Young adults (mean age of 25), on the other hand, were just as likely to use alcohol whether or not they had an ADHD diagnosis, but those with ADHD were likelier to use alcohol excessively.[4]

Numerous sources agree with the susceptibility of those with ADHD to substance abuse. A long-term study in Sweden tested three dimensions of childhood personality variations. Children were tested at age 11 years and then evaluated for alcohol abuse at age 27. The results linked the prevalence of substance abuse to all three personality traits and found novelty-seeking and low harm avoidance, another word for risk-taking, as the most predictive of early-onset alcohol abuse.[5] Novelty-seeking and risk-taking are, of course, characteristics of both ADHD and boredom avoidance. Indeed, in my terminology, they are Elements of Interest.

It's no surprise that boredom is one of the top reasons people, especially young people, give for trying and using alcohol and illicit drugs in the first place. Boredom comes into play during that first decision to use and it doesn't go away during treatment or recovery.

Using and abusing

That "seeing what it feels like" stage can last through experimentation with all manner of drugs. "Pot did nothing for me so I tried cocaine," said one heavy user who later was diagnosed with ADHD. Another young man in recovery in spite of multiple relapses once told me that when he had considered staying sober he would ask himself, "Is there a drug I haven't tried?" The answer was always, "Yes." The curiosity, novelty-seeking, and risk-taking that relieve boredom continue to drive users to maintain their addictive behavior.

There are, of course, many causes of addiction besides boredom, and, in fact, saying boredom "causes" addiction is not a completely accurate way of looking at the boredom/addiction connection or the connection between addiction and any other of its "causes." American psychotherapist Albert Ellis developed a form of cognitive behavior therapy (CBT) called rational emotive behavior therapy (REBT). As one construct of REBT, A stands for activating event, B for beliefs, and C for consequences. Applying that construct to addiction, substance abuse is the consequence (C) of beliefs (B) about boredom (A).[6]

A belief about boredom seems to be something like "I can't stand boredom" or "If this goes on any longer, I feel like sticking a pencil in my eye," statements I've heard spoken by boredom sufferers. What I call the "riled up" type of boredom-intolerant person is more likely to express such extreme thoughts than the "zoned out" type. The premise that, for people with ADHD, boredom is indeed more painful than it is for others must be fully recognized. Moreover, the anticipation of boredom, the belief that an upcoming experience will be boring, contributes to the discomfort attributed to boredom. Both the experience of boredom and the anticipation of boredom contribute to an inadequacy of dopamine and the shortening of the time it spends in the synapses between neurons. Too little activation of the dopamine system results in a failure to deliver a neurochemical reward required for an individual to be comfortable. Nevertheless, believing boredom is intolerable pain is not as helpful as believing it is a call for problem-solving just as being intolerably cold, a genuine feeling about a dangerous condition, is a call for finding shelter or sources of heat. The goal of solving the problem is an equally important part of my premise.

"Why are they doing this to me? I deserve to be entertained" is a belief behind the "Mom, I'm bored" complaint. I'm reminded of a *New Yorker* cartoon in which two children, riding with their parents in the back of their canoe-topped station wagon, are obviously headed for a fine vacation; nevertheless, they are holding up signs in view of passers-by, saying, "Help! Our parents are boring us to death."[7] The attitude of entitlement to entertainment is something that should be discouraged from an early age.

"This is so boring, she is so boring, school is so boring" could be replaced with the I-statement, "I feel intensely bored," and "This boredom I feel is a problem for me to solve." The belief that it's the fault of others that I am bored is less helpful than the idea that this activity doesn't match my interest at this time and I need to figure out how to "Escape It or Shape It."

F. Michler Bishop, in his book *Managing Addictions*, presents a list of "irrational" or unhelpful beliefs. "I need the excitement" is one reason clients give for continuing addictive behavior. "The client may know that what he is doing is frowned on by society and may have negative consequences for him, but he loves the excitement too much to give it up. Perhaps his nine to five life is fairly boring."[6] Or perhaps he has ADHD.

Bishop continues, "...he may be exaggerating the negative, boring aspects of his job, and there are ways he can make his job less boring." Also, "The therapist may be able to help the client find legal ways to fulfill his need for excitement even as he works at a boring job."[8] My book is aimed at helping the therapist and other clinicians and parents do that.

Bishop does not deal with the special prevalence of boredom in the lives of those with ADHD, but he does recognize the power of boredom in addiction. The addict, Bishop says, "uses addictive behaviors to escape (or to avoid in advance) boredom. He may not have realized that boredom is the problem. He may engage in an addictive behavior so quickly, in order to...stop being bored or to prevent being bored, that he rarely experiences what he is avoiding. In fact, he avoids it so effectively that he does not know what it is that he is avoiding."[9]

I am especially pleased at Bishop's statement, "He does not know what it is that he is avoiding."[9] So many people who have asked me what I'm writing about, and to whom I have replied "Boredom," quickly respond, "I'm never bored. I don't understand how anyone can be bored." Most of these people have the freedom and resources to readily find interest or stimulation because their careers not only suit their Elements of Interest but their jobs allow flexibility. Their finances may allow them to travel easily, take lessons, hire people to do boring tasks, seek entertainment, or buy new things. Just buying the latest digital innovation or upgrade and exploring how to use it seems to keep a large portion of my friends engaged until the next one comes out! Take away their freedom and resources and they may come to know how someone can be bored.

Links between ADHD and addiction

Health writer Carl Sherman, Ph.D., reported in 2007 that "Intoxicants are risky business if you have attention deficit disorder (ADD). A recent survey found that more than 15 percent of adults with the disorder had abused or were dependent upon alcohol or drugs during the previous year. That's nearly triple the rate for adults without ADHD."[2]

Put another way: Half of all adults with untreated ADHD will develop a substance use disorder at some point in their lives.[2] "Untreated" is an important word in Sherman's statement.

Because most medications prescribed for ADHD are controlled substances, stimulants, and abusable, many doctors are reluctant to prescribe them and patients and families are reluctant to take them. "Because of this, some people assume that it's risky to take these drugs. In truth, it's the opposite: ADDers who take these medications as prescribed are *less* likely than untreated ADDers to drink or abuse drugs. Put another way, treating ADHD effectively is powerful protection against substance abuse."[2]

Among my coaching clients, those who take stimulant medications for ADHD tell me they do so as prescribed because it helps with symptoms; they do not like the feeling of taking too high a dose and prefer the lowest effective dose. If those prescribed stimulants or other ADHD medication were prone to become addicted to them, it's curious that so many of them forget to take their meds or choose to use them more sparingly than the prescribed frequency.

There are, however, other people without ADHD who acquire ADHD meds illicitly, for example students without ADHD who want to stay up all night cramming for tests. Such use should not be confused with legitimate use by those with ADHD.

Not all of those who self-medicate with alcohol or illicit drugs become addicted. However, sooner or later, with regular use, the body tends to adapt to many drugs, whether legal or illegal, even prescribed drugs such as painkillers used as directed. As the body adapts, it requires more of the drug or a stronger alternative to achieve the same effect. Withdrawal may require stepping down in the dosage gradually to avoid uncomfortable or dangerous withdrawal symptoms. Naturally giving up a palliative effect or facing withdrawal symptoms is a deterrent to stopping the use of a drug. Still, many people do discontinue the use of such drugs. These people are dependent but not addicted.

Addiction, on the other hand, is an unwillingness or inability to stop taking a mind-altering substance (or activity) even when the user's life is severely affected. He may be aware he'll lose his job, his license, his marriage, his children, or even his life because of his substance abuse, but he cannot stop using, at least not on his own. It is characterized by unhealthy thinking such as denial of the problem, as well as antisocial behavior like lying and stealing. Addiction, like dependence, has a physical effect on the brain chemistry that makes it unable to turn off craving and addiction just as a person with ADHD seems to have a physical anomaly in the brain that makes it crave more stimulation.

In a chapter of his book *The Science of ADHD*, titled "Addiction, Reward, and ADHD," Chris Chandler, Principal Lecturer in Psychobiology at London Metropolitan University, says of ADHD, "...the Reward Deficiency hypothesis has a direct application to the disorder. Reward deficiency is where there is reduced efficacy of the reward pathways in the brain. The reward pathways ensure our survival as individuals and a species. In ADHD and addiction they are argued not to be optimal. Thus addiction and ADHD have some underlying similarities."[10]

Chandler has reviewed research extensively and cites reviews of the literature on ADHD and addiction by other sources. These investigators "have reviewed the data of reward function in ADHD and suggest that the reward system is indeed dysfunctional and treatment with methylphenidate corrects this dysfunction."[11] Methylphenidate, often called by the brand name Ritalin, increases dopamine levels in the synapses of the brain.[12]

This genetic deficiency is associated with a reduction of receptors for dopamine, that chemical that is released during stimulating (that is, rewarding) experiences and even in anticipation of these experiences. Dopamine is reduced during lack of stimulation and in anticipation of no such reward.[13]

In my opinion, this phenomenon explains the dread clients say they feel before starting tasks they expect to be boring as well as tasks that they are experiencing as boring in the present. It's the reason people with ADHD have difficulty starting projects. They are not only deficient in the ability to receive a reward via the stimulation of interest but also the anticipation of no reward, that is, the anticipation of boredom kills their motivation.

Also, people with ADHD respond better to small, frequent rewards than to larger, later rewards. So a large project and its associated reward, like a good grade, is not so motivating, and a thesis with its reward of achieving a university degree is just not near enough to raise the feel-good chemicals at the outset. Addiction and ADHD have similarities: Impulsivity and unwillingness to put off reward make an addict with ADHD less able to give up the drug and more likely to relapse.

Moreover, when addicts use illicit drugs or abuse legal ones, they begin a game as mentally challenging as chess, as demanding of bluff as poker, and as exciting as cops and robbers. They must acquire the drug, often by fooling people into giving them access. The habit demands strategy, nerves of steel and a poker face, planning skills, sales pitch, and the know-how to evade authority, whether that is concerned or over-controlling parents, the drug squad, or the local dealer. People spend hours playing video games with all these aspects; the addict plays the Real Game. What others might feel as fear, boredom-prone people with ADHD often feel as excitement. It's fun. It becomes a comfort zone. Getting high works—until it doesn't.

At some point, using the drug no longer provides the thrills or escape from problems. It no longer satisfies the curiosity. It becomes a physical need. Sooner or later the level required to provide a tolerable level of comfort escalates till there is no such thing as a "high." The amount required for a high is so close to fatal that seeking it means death. Too many addicts take the next step, more or less knowingly; there's a thin line between overdose and suicide.

The more fortunate ones, either by a wakeup call like nonfatal overdose, intervention, arrest, or their own still small voice within, choose to try sobriety.

Sobriety

Boredom, that prevalent state that is much more painful and much more powerful than "having nothing to do," is a major contributor to relapse. It is the emptiness that opens the mind to cravings, reliving of trauma, and enumeration of discontents. It is a discomfort particularly problematic in the first three months of recovery especially if the addict has to do menial jobs below her skill level and can see no activity as a stepping stone to a goal. It is a particularly critical force for the boredom prone, especially those with ADHD.

Detox takes the mind-altering substance out of the addict, and to the addict it feels as if it has taken the substance out of life. Curiosity is sated, and The Game is gone. For addicts attempting sobriety, their using buddies, their only friends, are off limits. The Comfort Zone is gone. Life is empty. Addicts sometimes call their drug of choice their "friend," and they have lost their best friend. Boredom overtakes them.

Yet the typical addict has no skills to entertain himself or, more important, to take on more interesting challenges. He tries things and doesn't like them because he's not good at them, maybe having ceased to develop skills outside of The Game when he began abusing substances in his early teens. He has little experience with thrills outside of drugs. He can't even imagine the pride in achievement, the thrill of acclaim, the satisfaction of creativity, or the comfort of a healthy relationship—joys experienced through Elements of Interest that many of his sober peers have come to know and seek.

Addicts with ADHD must be treated for ADHD as well as addiction from the very beginning of treatment or as soon as the dual diagnosis is possible. Carl Sherman, in an article section with the subhead, "Double trouble, double treatment," quotes a woman who had been in rehab and many 12-step meetings without success before she was diagnosed with ADHD. She said:

> In meetings, my mind was on anything but what they were talking about. How ugly the walls were. How annoying the speaker's voice was. I'd think, "How long are they going to talk? The coffee is getting cold. I have to meet so-and-so at the mall."[2]

It is the job of addiction professionals and ADHD specialists to guide if not insist that the addict in early recovery stays busy, while realizing that "busy" is not a long-term interest but a temporary way to stay out of trouble. New admissions may be watched carefully by treatment center staff or they will seek the only easy way out of boredom that they know. While they are observed to see what kinds of experiences they gravitate towards and with whom they bond, seeking true interest—the opposite of boredom—in early recovery is often impossible.

As a writer, I have learned a lot from the program of Recovery Outfitters Inc. (ROI), a long-term treatment center for young male addicts near Atlanta, Georgia. ROI provides its clients a range of experiences with high-intensity adventure like white water rafting, horseback riding, and deep sea fishing in order to show these young men, many of whom have ADHD, that they can feel good while sober. Clients also are offered calmer encounters with arts and music so that they may experience the natural satisfaction of creativity. These and other activities are all aimed at helping these boys and young men find the Elements of Interest that make them feel alive without the influence of mind-altering substances that have been their sole interest for too many years.

Soon they are ready for ROI's on-site high school or jobs nearby. For their stay of up to a year, most addicts are doing menial jobs far beneath their capacity because they can't get other jobs or they lack skills. It becomes increasingly important to discover and hone interests that motivate naturally and stimulate the dopamine-deprived brain of those with ADHD, who are overrepresented in the world of addiction.

Relapse and recovery

While sobriety means being free from mind-altering substances, sobriety is not recovery. Nor does relapse mean recovery is not going on. Sobriety only means that no mind-altering substance is currently present in a person's system. Relapse is part of the disease of addiction. Relapse is disappointing, but it is expected. It's how an addict learns. The Recovery Outfitters staff, for example, don't "hope" for relapse, but they hope that, if a client is going to relapse, they do it under their care where the client will not be shamed or rejected, but will be guided to understand what led to the relapse and what he might do differently in the future.

Recovery means giving up additional behaviors associated with addiction, such as lying and stealing, and the addict mindset. Honesty with oneself and others is a bedrock of recovery, along with caring about other people, letting go of feelings of entitlement, and becoming people of integrity.

For addicts, real recovery also means finding what motivates them and setting goals that fulfill their Elements of Interest. Once they have achieved a mindset of recovery, they need to create a life to fill the space once occupied by addictive behavior. In recovery, persistent boredom is not only a symptom of ADHD, but also a sign that the addict has not found a sustaining interest or compelling purpose.

Counselors at effective programs like Recovery Outfitters know that relapse begins in the mind before the addictive substance of choice is consumed and before the addictive activity of choice is acted on. Recognizing that thought process is important for counselors, and it is a critical skill to teach the addict himself. That is one reason why working through relapse rather than dismissing a relapsed client is essential. "Do you work through relapse?" is an important question to ask a treatment center before choosing one or referring a client. Learning lessons of relapse is a big step on the path to recovery. Keeping the addict in the proper environment while he explores the thought process that has led to relapse is critical to his recovery. That thought process will revolve largely around boredom, anticipation of boredom, or seeking an escape from boredom.

McWelling Todman, Ph.D., is one person for whom boredom is not the elephant in the room about which nobody speaks, nor a minor condition mentioned only in passing, but a major point in the discussion of addiction and recovery.

Todman, Director of the Mental Health and Substance Abuse Counseling Program at the New School for Social Research, has a special interest in "the functional consequences for individuals who are frequently or chronically bored." In an article on boredom in recovery from substance abuse, Todman suggests that "the experience of being bored 'depletes' the reserves of 'will power' that can be used to bolster restraint in the face of subsequent temptation to use." He says the phenomenon is sometimes called "ego depletion." The boredom management skills "have long ago dropped out of their boredom-coping repertoire, thereby erecting a strong bias toward strategies that invariably lead to drug seeking and drug use."[14]

Another way of stating Todman's first point is to say that boredom is stress; any kind of stress pushes an addict towards relapse for temporary relief. His second point, about loss of "restraint in the face of subsequent temptation," coincides with the impulsiveness of ADHD.

"Anyone who has experienced the cycle of relapse and recovery," Todman says, "quickly becomes aware of the role boredom and idleness plays in triggering their desire to use drugs."[14]

Todman continues, "And because the recovering individual has a limited arsenal when it comes to avoiding anticipated boredom there is a greater likelihood of the individual responding to both boredom and the anticipation of boredom with a sequence of decisions that invariably lead" to relapse. These he calls "unconscious boredom-avoidance strategies."[14]

Todman describes the thought process of the addict approaching relapse as a scenario in which non-addicts—and all of us—engage sometimes; it's also descriptive of ADHD thinking patterns, which set the ADHDer up for addictive relapse because they are already his mode of thinking:

> Consider for a moment an activity that you know will be tedious but which you are obligated to perform (for me this might be things like filling out a tax return or cleaning out the garage). What happens almost immediately after the decision is made to engage in such an activity is that your mind starts to wander to irrelevant but eminently more interesting things that you could be doing. And not infrequently, your actions will follow suit and you will actually begin to engage in an activity different than the one you set out to undertake. A fairly common example of this phenomenon is the bane of all college students: completing the long overdue term paper. You

> are sitting at your desk, finally determined to write that term paper that you have been putting off for several weeks, but then your attention begins to gradually shift to a phone call you didn't make earlier in the day or the television show that you will miss. And of course you rationalize the distraction and the delay by telling yourself that you will only spend a couple of minutes on the phone or an hour watching television. Now imagine the same scenario with a distraction one thousand times more powerful in its perceived attractiveness. Then couple this with an abnormally short list of considerably less potent alternative sources of potential distractions and I think you get the point.[14]

Todman's description of a thought process applies not only to drug addiction but to addictive behaviors such as gambling and problematic compulsive shopping, sex, or internet use.

Recognizing the power of the cues to which addicts are conditioned and which become triggers to relapse, Todman says, "…individuals don't become addicted to substances per se, but rather they become addicted to the experience of taking drugs."[14] Steven E. Hyman and Robert C. Malenka have done an extensive review of research on cue-mediated relapse that supports and explains this description.[15]

Todman continues, "I would like to elaborate on that insight a little by adding that individuals become addicted to the experiences associated with taking drugs only to the extent that they play a role in mitigating and avoiding boredom. If we accept that very simple premise, then the potential tools for managing boredom—current, expected and cued—are fairly easy to discern."[14]

In seven steps Todman gives his recommendations for overcoming boredom. His differ from the ones I present in this book in that he focuses on recognizing, measuring, and tracking boredom, and identifying and avoiding its situational cues, whereas I focus more on recognizing Elements of Interest by examining experiences of joy and bringing these Elements into boring situations.

Todman says, "An important implication of the view that boredom coping is a skilled activity is that one learns to cope more effectively with boredom… Indeed, helping our children form good boredom management skills may be one of the most lasting and beneficial gifts that we can give them, and it may well start with the quality of the early mother–child bond in infancy."[14]

It is because of this opinion, which Dr. Todman and I share, that Part 2 of this book contains age-by-age development of interest-seeking beginning with infancy and suggesting steps to boredom management at home and school, and in career and leisure.

PART 2

Fostering Interest by Age Groups

CHAPTER TEN

Introduction to Part 2: Fostering Interest by Age Groups

A hyperactive, inattentive, or boredom-prone child isn't necessarily a child with ADHD, but these symptoms bear monitoring. Keep in mind, though, that if the child is eventually diagnosed this isn't the opening act of a tragedy; rather, it is the beginning of an opportunity to help that child excel in school and in life.

ADHD is not a disease that can be cured; it's a condition that represents a differentness in the way that left-handedness is different. ADHD is not a childhood phenomenon; it's a lifelong state. As we grow and mature, we learn to adapt to some of the symptoms, but that doesn't mean they go away.

If your child, student, or patient is diagnosed with ADHD, no matter the age, and you have confidence that it's an accurate diagnosis, know that he will most likely face challenges his whole life. The key to success will rest with acceptance of the reality that this child is not like the others. Denial and unwillingness to treat ADHD can lead to escalating discipline issues, loss of self-esteem, and failure. However, there is absolutely no reason that he can't thrive as long as his medical team, parents, and teachers all understand what he needs. When ADHD is recognized, accepted, and treated as an insufficiency of neurochemical stimulation, whose psychological correlate is boredom, ADHD can actually represent an advantage to the child in terms of creativity, motivation, and success. Discovering and using his Elements of Interest is not a substitute for medical treatment but a complementary strategy, the adoption of a mindset that allows him to flourish and his brilliance to shine.

The concepts and language that clinicians, teachers, coaches, and parents use will differ by age, of course, as well as by your professional or personal relationship with the person with ADHD or similar characteristics. Generally at every age, however, it is good to engage in the following attitudes and behaviors when partnering to alleviate boredom:

- *Empathize* with boredom and related difficulties, when expressed. Tell patients, clients, students, and children that you have felt bored sometimes, too. You understand how boredom can sometimes be painful. You regret that expressing it sometimes provokes a negative reaction.

- *Realize* that you are often and typically dealing with boredom avoidance rather than overt expression of boredom. Ask, "How do you feel when you are not allowed or able to… [move around, talk to friends, be challenged, solve a problem, be in charge, have your turn…]?

- *Observe behavior and ask open-ended questions*; listen and accept answers about related behavior: When are you bored? How much does that bother you? What do you do about it? How hard do you expect that to be? How well does that work? What has worked well before? What kinds of things are hard to start? What kinds of things are hard to finish? How do you want to feel about this?

- *Discover Elements of Interest* by observing spontaneous expressions in conversation or casual writing and also by using exercises such as the Top 10 Joys, described in Chapter Four, and the Childhood Pastime questioning described in Chapter Five.

- *Partner* with patients, clients, students, and children of any age to design solutions to potentially boring situations by bringing individual Elements of Interest into those situations as illustrated in Part 2.

Age groups

There is obviously some overlap in the activities suggested for the different age groups. While I recommend you read all the age groups through, if your interest is limited to a certain age group, I suggest reading the chapter on that age plus, where possible, the chapter before it and the chapter after it, in chronological order. Note also that some points will be repeated with age-appropriate variation, but more detail is used for such topics in one chapter than another.

Most but not all of the people used as illustration in this section, as in the rest of the book, have a diagnosis or characteristics of ADHD. The need for interest and for seeking appropriate levels of stimulation is universal. While the techniques for building interest presented in this part of the book may be useful for anyone of any age, for those with ADHD, dealing with boredom is critical.

The age-by-age chapters illustrate a mindset or approach to head off boredom by fostering interest-building. It is designed to guide clinicians to help clients, who may be children, adults, parents, or families. It is designed also to inspire educators to bring Elements of Interest into their classes as well as to teach their students how to be responsible for bringing their own individual Elements into their work. I also directly address parents who are guiding their children with ADHD and its characteristics in concert with clinicians and teachers.

In no way is Part 2 intended to be an exhaustive listing of things you or your clients can do to resolve boredom. Part 2 suggests approaches and offers illustrations that together can promote a mindset of encouraging interest with the knowledge that, without this stimulation, young minds, old minds, and especially ADHD minds are unable to fully engage.

CHAPTER ELEVEN

Infants and Toddlers

Interest begins at birth, if not before! Its Elements soon become apparent. It can be fascinating and fun—and not too early—to be noticing and encouraging the interests of babies.

While it is too early to suspect or determine if an infant has ADHD, parents should be told that the condition is largely inheritable. When one or both of a couple has ADHD there is a significant chance their child will also have it. *ADDitude Magazine* reports that "studies have shown that one-third of all men who had ADHD in their youth have biological children with ADHD," and researchers are currently doing studies of family history and genetic markers.[1] Whether or not there is any reason for parents to consider ADHD, being aware of children's interests and learning to give them enough freedom and resources so they can express their interests is a universally desirable goal.

Elements of Interest

Probably the most apparent and strongest Element of Interest for children of all ages is novelty—something new. Novelty is also a necessity for survival as something new and different can be either a danger to be avoided or something valuable or necessary to explore. A new sound, a new plant, a new person, or a new object has to be identified as well as a new position of an old object or a new time of arrival of a familiar person or phenomenon. Something novel excites the brain by activating the dopamine circuit.

For the newborn, everything is novel. Therefore everything is interesting. From the first flickers of the baby's eyes, you can see that the baby's focus is on his mother's face as he nurses and on his mother's mouth as she speaks. The Element of social interaction is instinctive and develops rapidly with the baby's attention to each new sound, facial expression, or movement of the arms that hold him. Without social interaction, as in an understaffed orphanage, an infant will fail to thrive.

In the slow-motion view of early development, you see a baby focus on the movement of a mobile toy revolving above his head in his crib. You see when he notices his own hand, turning his tiny fist and staring to see how it moves at the same time he feels his muscles pull a certain way, putting visual and kinesthetic sensations together and noticing the beginnings of his own control. What an amazing discovery! He is fascinated with sensory experiences. From pawing at the flower on his printed crib sheet to reaching out for a toy, from making an odd sound with his mouth and voice to doing something that makes his big sister laugh, it's all new, and he is totally engaged. When he is not engaged, he is not bored—he's asleep.

Later, as he grows, he begins to notice possibilities more and more. He becomes curious, and he seeks new sources of sensory stimulation and new Elements of Interest. He fusses when he's bored, and he stops fussing when turned around in his seat to have a new view. He needs to be held and touched and turned and jiggled. He needs to have lots of face time with his parents, siblings, and caregivers. A baby can seem bored and begin to fuss during the period when he can't easily change his position and seek the novelty of new scenes by himself. The drive for seeking novelty is his motivation for learning to crawl. He digs in his toes and pushes with his legs to help him reach a new object. He pulls himself up and stands in order to reach higher objects and experience a new point of view.

Surprise is a special kind of novelty, sudden and unexpected. Surprise in itself can be fun, but anticipation of surprise is even more fun. Dopamine is activated in the brain in times of anticipation of reward even more than for the reward itself. For example, the baby game of peek-a-boo begins as a surprise when an older person hides his face for a few seconds behind his hands or some other object, then pops back into view, saying "Peek-a-boo" or "Peep eye," but soon the game becomes more about anticipation than surprise as the child waits in excitement for what he knows will happen. He doesn't know exactly when his wait will be rewarded. The wait in uncertainty is the heart of suspense. Surprise, anticipation, and suspense are all related Elements of Interest. Best of all, peek-a-boo requires no supplies or toys and can be played anywhere.

As infants grow and experience life, they exhibit more of their innate Elements of Interest. Observation of spontaneous actions tells us about the personalities of our children. Very early on we see which child is the cuddler who hangs out near Mommy's lap and which is the explorer gone from her lap in a flash. We notice which is the physically active one and which is the contemplator, and which one wants his hands on every new object and which one is content to watch and think. We observe the persistence of one child—a problem-solver—who tries repeatedly and with several adjustments in style to pick up a raisin with her inexperienced opposable thumb and forefinger, while another child, after one failed attempt, brushes his raisin off his tray onto the floor and, whimpering pitiably, holds his hand out for a fresh one to be placed directly in it.

Infant toys

Infancy is an age to give a child time to explore, time to get bored with one thing and look around for something new, and time to use all his senses, to manipulate, poke, taste, and chew. He needs only a few resources for this exploration.

Infancy and toddlerhood are the ages for which I favor providing manufactured toys over homemade toys and household objects because toys made by reputable toy companies are tested for safety. Homemade toys or household objects may have loose parts, toxic materials, or unexpected hazards.

I favor toys, basic or elaborate, that meet the little one's Elements of Interest, likely to include novelty, hands-on interaction, color, texture, music, rhythm, and face-to-face social interaction. Experimentation with a wide range of playthings reveals new

Elements. Mobiles over cribs mesmerize babies; musical devices set them bouncing to rhythm. Toys that honk when squeezed or pop open when their button is pushed and soft plush animal toys to nurture, all satisfy their desire for interest.

If, in addition to lots of cuddling and face time, parents give their babies time to be bored enough to seek interest, they will entertain themselves. Parental precautions for their safety may be the only limitation to their baby's freedom.

Toddlers

Toddlers, by definition, toddle, which soon becomes steady walking, climbing, and reaching for new things. As in infancy, their Elements of Interest include multi-sensory experiences such as color, taste, texture, sound, rhythm, hands-on interaction, surprise and suspense, social interaction, and especially challenge. Now that they can walk by themselves, the hunt is on.

Toddlers would never be bored if they had complete freedom. As with all other ages, some degree of freedom is the condition of never being bored, and restrictions on freedom are the only things that stand in the way. Toddlers reach to feel and to hold things that we snatch away in the nick of time because they are too hot, too dirty, too fragile, or too dangerous. Or maybe their little hands are sticky with cereal and, because Mommy is dressed up, she pushes them away. A parent has to supervise and restrict. This is a time-consuming job requiring keen attention from the parent or caregiver.

There is a range of restriction versus freedom that is healthy for a child, and setting boundaries varies by culture and era. Many Native American peoples carried their babies and even toddlers wrapped tightly around the legs and strapped to a cradleboard, especially during frequent travel.[2] By contrast, a television show about children around the world showed toddlers playing with sizeable rocks inside a nomad family's tent and even hitting their siblings with them without causing their parents alarm.

When I was a child, many families kept not only babies but toddlers in playpens except for eating and closely supervised play or rides in a carriage. There were toys in the playpen and the sound of adults and perhaps siblings nearby for company. The toddler was expected to stay there and play for most hours of the day. Some of today's parents ask, "How? My child would scream to get out." Or "My child would just climb out."

The answer seems to be that the parents of yesteryear were so determined that their toddlers stay in the playpen that it never occurred to them to let the child wander around the house investigating things. Investigation time was sometimes limited to the "nursery," that is, the toddler's bedroom where fewer things were off limits. Parents must find a balance they can live with between freedom and safety as well as between freedom and chaos. In making the many related decisions, parents would be wise to consider the Elements of Interest of their toddlers and allow them to express these within healthy limits, not too authoritarian and not without boundaries.

Encourage enjoyment of time alone

The matter of how long to leave your toddler alone to figure out how to interest himself is another important question. Given a variety of toys in his crib or playpen, a child begins to play. First, he may put one toy inside a container and dump it out, push a button to make music, or investigate the face of a toy giraffe. Given time to be bored, toddlers will find ways to entertain themselves for longer and longer time periods.

Elliott is awake one morning and sitting up. The 16-month-old is so quiet his mother only knows he's awake by looking at a video monitor. He is surrounded by toys, blankets, pacifiers, cloth picture books, and stuffed animals.

In this small ten-square-foot world, he plays quietly for a full hour. He pokes his fingers into the painted eyes on a puppy. He turns the pages of the book over. He puts a toy telephone to his ear and turns on his musical mobile with the deftness of one born into the digital age. He talks softly and unintelligibly as he plays. He hears a woodpecker tapping on the outside of his house, and he imitates it, replying "Duh duh duh. Duh duh duh" in rhythmic response. He pushes the buttons on a second musical toy that plays an assortment of melodies and bounces his whole body to their rhythms.

When Elliott's mother hears the music, she knows he's fully awake. She doesn't go to pick him up then, but she knows he'll want to get out of his crib soon. When he picks up his blanket and his favorite toy, stands up, and puts his hands on the sides of the crib, looking outward, she knows he's ready for her company. She doesn't wait for him to cry for her. Her object is to leave him to entertain himself for as long as he can, but not to let him cry lest she reinforce crying as a means of communication.

This early hour of happy play, a few short months before, lasted just a few minutes, but the ready engagement of his interests in the crib and the security of knowing his mother will come when he really wants her has lengthened the span of his self-entertainment. The morning he first calls out "Mama!" for her to come, she is delighted with the pay-off for her patience.

Observing such a waking scene in the crib is one of the most enchanting experiences in the world. From the days of cooing, then babbling, to the age of talking to playthings, the baby is entertaining himself, satisfying his Elements of Interest all by himself. There's the fuzzy texture of the teddy bear, the bright color of the walls, the pattern on the sheets and wallpaper, or just a pattern of light coming in stripes through the window blinds. There's the rhythm of the music and the rhythm he makes banging one toy against another. When he begins to feel the pull of one more Element—social interaction—he's ready to let his parents know their company is required.

Resources: toddler toys

Restrictions increase for toddlers because they can cause so much damage to themselves and others while having no sense of consequences. Toddlers are cuddlers and biters and grabbers just to see what it feels like to cuddle, bite, and grab. As they follow their impulses, they are learning the consequences of their actions.

Toddlers are subject to the conscious or unconscious thought: *"I wonder what would happen if I…? What if I touched it, how would it feel? What if I cuddled it? What if I pushed it off the table? What if I banged it on the floor? What if I banged it on Daddy's face? What if I bit it? What if I hit it with something hard? What if I put it through this hole?"*

Give them something to feel, cuddle, push off the table, bang on the floor, bite, or stick in a hole. There's pretty much a toy available for every one of these "what ifs." There are books like *Pat the Bunny*, where different textures, ranging from sandpaper to fur, can be felt through a hole in the page. There are rubber teething rings to bite, and toys with holes of different shapes to put pegs of matching shapes through—over and over and over. These toys have been around for generations, but the same kinds of toys with updated motifs are being offered anew.

Don't forget what may be the world's best toy: a big cardboard box. A toddler will push it around on the rug, then knock it over and crawl in one end or over the top. He will drop a toy in first, hang over the edge and dive in after it, and then sit up, lie down, and throw the toy out. He will do it without help or attention, but he really likes you to watch him problem-solve as he revels in his skills. When the sides of the box finally break down, he will drag it around. Then he will use the flat cardboard as his special space to sit on. Several Elements of Interest will be satisfied with this one ubiquitous toy.

Encourage a mindset of interesting oneself

If you keep in mind that ultimately a child will need to interest herself, you will develop the mindset—in her and you—that revolves around that responsibility. Watch her find things; don't find things for her.

Instead of handing her one toy and then another, watch her pick up toys and say, "Oh, look. You have a bear." Outdoors you tell her approvingly, "You found a leaf! A pretty leaf." Let her examine the leaf until she decides to eat it. Your approval reinforces the behavior of exploring, finding, and learning and establishes a boundary. She will investigate even without your approval at this age, of course, but even now you can encourage a confidence that allows her to feel comfortable exploring and manipulating new things, while accepting limits.

You cannot know yet if a child has the genetic predisposition for ADHD, but every approach to boredom and interest presented in this book is adaptable to any child or adult and especially valuable for those for whom the stimulation of interest is critical.

Quick points

One-on-one time: Babies and toddlers need lots of face time. Close one-on-one time with parents, siblings, and other adults is how they learn language, socialization, self-worth, and security.

Time alone: They need alone time to learn to entertain themselves. Avoid rushing to them the moment they are awake or fuss because they can't solve a problem immediately.

Boundaries: Give them limitations to keep them safe and to teach them the concept of boundaries by showing and telling them the limits.

Novelty: For babies, everything is new. It's easy to give them novelty just by turning their bouncy chair around or taking them for a stroll. Toddlers take great interest in something new; so give them variety just by putting old things away and bringing them out later when they are "new" again.

Multi-sensory experience: Give toys that provide auditory, visual, and tactile experience. Sing to them, rock them, hug them. Offer them food with different tastes and textures. Let them smell the roses. Use sensory words like *soft*, *scratchy*, *rough*, *smooth*, *bumpy*, *slippery*, *sticky*, *loud*, *quiet*, *warm*, *cold*, and *wet*. Name the colors. Comment on what smells good or looks pretty, and what's interesting.

CHAPTER TWELVE

Preschool, Ages 3–5 Years

In the years before a child begins school, parents and preschool teachers may notice a child who is never still, who rocks in his chair or even jumps up suddenly and knocks his chair over. He also fiddles with things, runs around the room, doesn't seem to listen to directions, interrupts others, and creates disturbance. He doesn't follow instructions and he doesn't wait his turn well. He could be impulsive and hyperactive, meaning "too active," or he could be just especially energetic. A child who is inappropriately active may have ADHD. Children with ADHD, impulsive/hyperactive type, usually attract attention to their symptomatic behavior sooner than those with inattentive-type ADHD alone. Some children can be diagnosed in preschool.

Physical action seems to be his only Element of Interest. As a parent or teacher, avoid complaining, "Can't you ever be still?!" Instead, tell the overactive child, in a matter-of-fact tone, that he seems to need to move around more than many children and you'll try to make that possible. A teacher or evaluating clinician can honestly say to a four- or five-year-old with ADHD characteristics, "Your mother and father tell me that you are very, very active. You run around more than other children. What do you think?" The conversation then can move towards the fact that he truly needs more exercise than most children but there have to be rules about when and where he's active. "Can you help me think of ways you can run and jump and play without bothering the other children? Do you think you can follow a few rules?" The activity level of the hyperactive child is not the whole picture of ADHD, but it is the most recognizable and disruptive symptom and therefore the one you can address most clearly with the child. Excessive action is a child's effort to get more stimulation to his brain. Allowing movement instead of stifling it satisfies a need for stimulation that may help him focus on tasks, listen to instructions, and increase his ability to take his turn.

A child with ADHD without hyperactivity will not likely attract attention until later. For her, as for any quieter child, you may need to observe longer and more carefully to see what Elements interest her.

Partner with a child

Observing what children do to entertain themselves when they are free to choose is key to providing absorbing activities. Someone once said, though only once, "If a child loves to hammer rocks, give him a bigger hammer." This is a metaphor; do not give a preschooler rocks and a hammer. If she is enthusiastic about drawing, give her some crayons and a stack of paper; she won't care if the paper has printing on one side and is being recycled. "Here's a big piece of paper to draw on," you can say. "Let me see if you can keep your crayon marks on the paper." If he likes to rock in his chair and it's not a rocker, consider providing one. David Giwerc, founder of the ADD Coach Academy (ADDCA), often tells of wearing out a series of rocking chairs during his childhood because he was unable even to sit and watch television without being in constant motion. He expresses gratitude toward his parents for providing a means to rock instead of trying to prevent him from rocking. His parents *partnered* with him to relieve his symptoms and meet his needs. As a parent, you can do the same with your child. When you, as a teacher or clinician, show an interest in helping him manage his needs instead of preventing him from seeking solutions, you might open a line of communication previously closed off to you.

Another way to allow a hyperactive child the physical movement he craves is to provide an exercise ball to sit on instead of a noisier rocker. I first saw a ball used as a seat in an Apple Store. It was a small one placed in front of a Macintosh computer, which was sitting on a low table for techno-tots to use. I managed to try out the ball as a seat myself and found it so comfortable that I got an adult-sized one for myself. A child or adult can rock it back and forth or sit still; either way, it's quiet and it doesn't crush anyone's toes. If needed at home, preschool, or a clinical setting, consider marking the do-not-pass line on the floor with masking tape. A parent, teacher, or clinician can say, "If I give you this ball to move around on, do you think that you could stay inside these lines?" Or you can put a bath mat on the floor to show the permissible territory. Alternatively, put a bath mat down and let him sit or lie there. It is good for all children to change position frequently, so sitting or lying should be facilitated.

In preschool, wouldn't the other children want the ball, the mat, or other accommodation the hyperactive child has? Probably. If I had my way, all kids would have exercise balls and mats available as alternative seats. What's a good accommodation for a child with ADHD characteristics is often good for all.

On the first day of school in one kindergarten I saw the teacher put a glob of play dough, a sheet of paper, and two crayons on each desk before the children arrived. They all had something to do with their hands while they waited for everyone to gather. Providing for the Element of Interest I call "hands-on" was a good idea for any child in the class, but a great idea for any child with ADHD. A teacher can expect to have in her class at least one child with this disorder that affects anywhere from 3 percent to 8 percent of children in the United States.[1, 2, 3, 4, 5] Some of the children in this kindergarten class immediately started making shapes with the play dough, others drew on the paper with the crayons, and one stuck the crayons into his play dough and engaged the children next to him in admiring his snail with antennae—and yes, he used the word "antennae." The play dough solution to keeping a child engaged while waiting can be used at the dining table at home or in a restaurant, the doctor's office, or any place where quiet waiting is required.

Preschool teachers are marvelously creative, and in addition have access to books, magazines, and websites full of a year's worth of ideas for hands-on activities with small children. Multi-sensory and hands-on play are examples of a typical child's strongest Elements of Interest, although a few children are squeamish about touching things like fish or getting paint on their hands, and others prefer to watch and listen. It is obviously good to offer activities that address as many Elements as possible to engage a child or group of children so that all may experience the modalities they engage with most strongly. The child with ADHD will benefit from the stimulation of a multi-sensory approach even more than most children.

Imagination creates toys

Imaginative play exists without any resources at all, as demonstrated by the child who sits and daydreams, using only her mind, or the child who rolls down grassy hills or turns somersaults in the living room, using only his body. Throughout time, children (and adults) have had a play life without toys.

Phillip, barely three, entertained himself in the car, in bed, and in lulls in family life with dialogue between his "Two Guys," in reality no more than his two index fingers facing each other. The one speaking at any given time nodded as he spoke, and the other one nodded in reply. Like a puppeteer, Phillip conducted an unlimited array of drama and comedy within about four inches of space and without any props at all. Nobody else could follow what was going on between them, but Phillip did, and that's all that mattered. He always had his Two Guys in his pockets to pull out when he might otherwise be bored.

Creating dialogue with a minimum of props develops before story-telling. Talking to dolls, and dolls talking to other dolls—or indeed dogs or ducks—is very early imaginative play that occupies hours of young children's time.

Phillip also loved Thomas the Tank Engine, the sets of little engines and railroad tracks, and the stories of Sodor Island that help give them character.[6] He has large layouts and many trains, which, though purchased as gifts over several years, represent a sizeable investment. But when he's away from home, his imagination and the simplest of props serve just as well. At the park one day, Phillip lay down on some exposed dirt, took off his Crocs and laid the shoes end to end, and then loaded them with dirt. He moved this two-car freight train around the patch of ground, carrying its cargo, with just as much apparent pleasure as he did with the elaborate train sets at home. He seemed completely oblivious to older children playing close around him on climbing equipment.

Seeing shoes as trains capable of hauling a load of cargo is making a connection between disparate things with some spark between them. Phillip is good at this. Artists, cartoonists, and comedians are good at this. Children with ADHD are good at this.

At this age the power of imagination still applies to the simple box. As mentioned in the previous chapter, the cardboard box heads the list of toys that young children commandeer and remains a favorite for quite a few years. The preschooler's box is sometimes a box and sometimes something else like a boat, a house, a cage, or a car. The other basic "toys" on Geek Dad's list of "The 5 Best Toys of All Time" are a stick, cardboard tube, dirt, and string.[7] The stick, depending on its shape and size, becomes a fishing pole, a sword, a flagpole, or a horse to ride. The cardboard tube is just as versatile, functioning as a telescope, a bullhorn, or a pipeline to convey dirt. Dirt transforms from a battlefield to a mud pie as quick as you can say, "I'm bored with that." The string may be the fishing line on the stick fishing pole, the stick horse's halter or reins, or a snake hanging from a branch. Sometimes a string is just a string.

Elements of Interest as tools

Children are constantly imitating parents, teachers, and older siblings. Anything you do that is aimed at making a task more interesting can serve as a model, even more so if you point out to children what you are doing. When you observe them bringing their own Elements of Interest into a task they might otherwise find boring, acknowledge to them that you notice how they are making it more interesting. In this way children learn from you that making something interesting is a desirable doable skill.

With imagination, the child's and yours, you can teach a very young child to bring Elements of Interest into chores long before he has actual chores to do. When folding laundry and putting it away with a young child nearby, engage him in the chore. If he has seen someone fish or has seen a story where someone catches a fish, a parent can say something like, "Let's pretend we're catching fish." She picks up an undershirt and says, "I caught one! A nice big one. Let's put it in my fish drawer." And she does. Just giving the idea that it's fun to pretend one thing is something else fosters the idea of adding interest to everyday chores. At some point, say, "What can we pretend we're doing that will make this job more interesting?" Consistent engagement of this kind can lead to the day the child will show the parent how to pretend work is child's play.

Time management

Children have trouble with managing time and even with gauging it. "Time flies when you're having fun" is a truism that applies particularly to those with ADHD. The other side of the same coin, "Time drags when we're bored," is equally true. Children riding with their families to a distant vacation spot famously ask, after a 20-minute ride, "Are we almost there?" Their perception of time varies according to the level of stimulation they experience; for children with ADHD their lower-than-normal activation of dopamine makes boring periods of time seem like forever. They can become more realistic about time by experiencing Elements of Interest, such as those offered by music, experienced in particular units of time.

For example, rhythm, melody, humor, and even story can be inserted into a boring task to make it easier to do, as the Seven Dwarfs who hosted Snow White demonstrated and lyricist Larry Morey knew when he wrote "Whistle While You Work" for the 1937 Disney animated film.[8]

A parent or teacher can model and teach several strategies for making toy clean-up more interesting by using the Seven Dwarfs' method. Play or sing the whistling song or another of the Dwarfs' ditties, "Heigh ho! Heigh ho! It's off to work we go," as a timer. The strategy is to pick up toys to the rhythm of the song and deliver them to the toy box for the length of time the song plays, almost three minutes if you use a YouTube version.[9] Changing songs provides the Element of variety, and changing from listening to actually whistling or singing provides additional sensations.

"Let's put your supplies away in one Heigh Ho!" can sometimes be said as, "Let's put all your supplies away in three minutes, that's one Heigh Ho!" After a while, by using music and lyrics, the children will learn how long three minutes feels. "Do you want to do it one more time?" is a good question to ask little helpers when finishing off a job. After a while a teacher might call a six-minute task a "two-Heigh Ho!" job. Just for the fun of it, someone will say, "Let's do a three-Heigh Ho!" job," and putting away supplies will have become fun instead of a boring chore.

Because newness and change are Elements of Interest, a time limit on an activity is a promise of a change approaching, and the anticipation of something new very soon is motivating. I consider the desire for a time limit on a task as an Element of Interest, based on the satisfaction that comes from knowing when the end of a tedious task is near.

Make it new

As much as I favor using props plus imagination as toys, many children have loads of store-bought toys they love, and the arrival of every new one is exciting. Novelty or variety and other Elements of Interest that reflect newness are always good for boosting dopamine. If parents can provide two containers, there can always be "new" toys. In households where toys are plentiful, even too plentiful, parents can engage the child in dividing the toys into two piles. Put one pile in a box called the Old Toy Box. Talk about how much fun the old toys have been and say they are going to rest for a while but they will be back. Then store the "Old Toy Box" away. After a few weeks go by, pack up the remaining toys while the child looks on. Tell her not to worry because you have a surprise for her. Bring out the Old Toy Box again and watch the child welcome each old toy back with as much enthusiasm as if it were new. Then it's time to give the remaining toys a rest.

Avoid packing up toys and switching without the child knowing what you're doing because this routine is not a trick but a lesson about making things new again by giving them a rest. In later years, switching back and forth between boring tasks will make each one more interesting as a "new start." Making something new again can become an important technique for the ADHD child and adult.

Preschool classroom strategies

Children, especially those with ADHD, often need individual instruction, but preschoolers with and without ADHD often lose interest when it's someone else's turn. Here are two ways to give Elements of Interest both to the doer and the observer while they are learning basic academic and life skills.

Children with ADHD don't follow instructions as well as others. Teaching and learning instructions and instructional words can be boring; instructions involve a lot of details that need to be practiced. Prepositional phrases that tell place using words like *under*, *between*, *on top of*, *behind*, *above*, and *near* are harder to learn from listening to conversation than, for example, verbs. Phrases like *more than*, *less than*, *too far*, *too near*, *to the left*, *to the right*, *on your left*, *on your right*, *straight ahead*, *go forward*, and *go around* may have to be taught individually, but groups of these words can be practiced; for example, *to the left*, *to the right*, and *straight ahead* can make a simple game to master those expressions before mixing them with others.

To make practicing them less boring, add Elements of Interest wherever possible. One strategy to use with preschoolers is a variation of the "warmer, colder" game for finding a hidden object. It involves physical activity, mystery or uncertainty, and some amount of competition and applause.

To begin, the teacher hides something out of the children's sight. She picks a child to search for it. Then she gives the child instructions like *go forward*, *stop*, *turn left*, *go under the table*, *reach under the chair*, and *look above the picture*. She doesn't direct the child straight to the object but all around the room, eventually reaching the hidden object. That child hides the object or another object for the next child, and the teacher gives directions to the child. The children who are observing like to say "Under, under" when a child has looked "over." Watching to see if the seeker is correct gives the observers interest and practice in listening to directions. A daily game might give only three or four children a turn, but in a week everyone may have a turn as seeker and many turns as observer.

Prepositions and other words that tell relationships of time and place and size are found in all kinds of directions from instructions on boxes to standardized tests, and many children and adults with ADHD don't have the patience to process these little words. Also these relationships have been found to correlate strongly with math success. Children in environments with impoverished language have been found to fall back in math as well as other areas. Learning these phrases and words and practicing them often in preschool is a critical foundation.

When individual phrases seem mastered, add an additional direction such as, "Go forward two steps and then turn left." The complexity can be adapted to the child's level of mastery, ending in several directions at one time and using more complex phrases like, "Go three steps to the left and pick up the book farthest away." The hidden item is located under that book.

For variety, a student can be chosen to give directions, especially a child for whom the directions game is no longer challenging enough. Variety is an Element of Interest, adding the Element of challenge makes a lesson more interesting, and "putting it in their hands" is a principle that gives children the Element of control.

Another game with Elements of Interest for preschoolers gives practice with numbers and develops a sense of distance. The game requires a child to guess how many jumps it would take to reach a certain chair, table, or other object, preferably one that can be moved different distances away. Or a whole class can guess the number of jumps to cover the distance before one child jumps, and afterwards see who guessed the closest. A variation is to guess how many heel–toe steps it is to a certain spot or object. The child must put her heel against her toe in succession to reach the goal. How many children it takes to reach the door is a question answered by having children lie end to end on the floor. You might finally use a real unit of measurement determined by a yardstick, meter stick, or a one-foot or metric ruler. How many meter sticks is it from Adele to the window? Then Adele gets to flip the stick over, counting how many flips until it reaches the window. Who guessed right?

The "lessons" above will not train a child out of ADHD but will alleviate boredom that contributes to distraction and impulsive behavior in class. The lessons are play. Keep them that way throughout the preschool years as you develop your own array of activities and tools to bring Elements of Interest into the daily lives of the children with ADHD (and without) whom you teach, counsel, love, and live with.

Quick points

Acknowledge hyperactivity: Say, for example, "You need to move around more than some children. Let me see you take a walk all around the room without touching anything, and then come back to me."

Teach interest: Point out what seems interesting to you or to the child. Avoid the word "boring."

Partner with the child: Say, for example, "Let's work together to make this task more interesting. Let's try this new way."

Use your story-telling voice: Use lots of expression of feelings of surprise, delight, or sadness. Quiet, even-toned, adult voices don't interest small children so much. Let your inner actor come on stage.

Give children hands-on experience: Let him touch, hold, feel, and manipulate things. Choose things that are safe to handle. All talk without doing is boring.

Give children challenge: Children often say, "Let *me* try." Let them try.

Present the same thing with a new wrinkle: An object or activity doesn't have to be entirely new to pique interest. In fact, doing the same thing with one noticeable change is often enough to excite children. Change locations, colors, sizes, positions, or order. Think how you can change a routine that is becoming stale.

Promote imagination: Silly is just fine. "Let's imagine we are birds and we are picking up sticks to build a nest" can mean let's pick up the crayons and put them in the crayon box.

Make it grown up: Make an object more interesting by using it yourself first while the child observes. For example, if you want to use a chance to play with play dough or a toy truck to reward a child for a desired behavior, play with the play dough yourself first, making snakes and balls as he watches, or run the toy truck along the table and up your arm. Then offer him the object when he does something you want to reinforce. The commonplace toy is more interesting to him as a reinforcing token now that you, a grown up, have shown an interest in it.

CHAPTER THIRTEEN

Elementary School, Ages 6–10 Years

Ages six to ten, elementary or primary school age, is a time when more children begin to be evaluated by clinicians—perhaps referred by teachers. Symptoms teachers and parents report are hyperactivity, inattention, and forgetfulness. If ADHD is diagnosed, you as the evaluating psychiatrist, other clinician, teacher, or parent may use the name ADHD when talking with the child but, in my opinion, you should not use it before some ground work is laid.

With young children, professionals and parents can refer to the reason for the evaluation as "talking about your special way of thinking." The concept of boredom as key to ADHD is a nonthreatening way of introducing the condition. "That special way of thinking turns on and off a lot. It turns on very strong and quick when activities are interesting; it turns off when things are boring. Have you ever noticed anything like that?" Whether or not the child is diagnosed with ADHD, the emphasis on Elements of Interest and ways to escape boredom or shape boring situations is valid and beneficial for any child.

At the point when you see the need to give the special way of thinking a label, I recommend *All Dogs Have ADHD*, a charming picture book by Kathy Hoopmann, an informative and positive introduction to ADHD for children and adults, in spite of its appearance as a book for young children.[1]

I also recommend *7 Habits of Happy Kids* by Sean Covey. The chapter introducing the very first habit is titled "Bored! Bored! Bored!" and the desired habit to learn for dealing with boredom is "Be proactive."[2] That chapter in the children's book, like the book you are now reading, shows a child that boredom is a valid emotion, that it is his responsibility to deal with his own boredom in positive ways. Notice that the animal character in the book has an appropriate degree of freedom, resources, and time to make that doable. Clinicians, teachers, and parents can read and discuss the boredom chapter with children, making an additional point that some children are bored more easily and often than others. These are said to be "boredom prone." Teach this concept to children who fit the description, especially those with ADHD. Tell them that their special way of thinking is so active when they are interested and so much slower when they are bored that learning special ways to seek interest will help them reach their goals.

This is a good age to begin to formally explore children's individual Elements of Interest, using methods described in Part 1, Chapters Three through Five, especially the Top 10 Joys exercise presented in Chapter Four. As a teacher you will find it useful to know more about your students and to develop a mindset for using their strongest and most common Elements. Teachers who are recognized for being great teachers have a personal relationship with their students. The more you know about them the more easily this happens. Both teachers and parents have told me they find the Top 10 Joys exercise reveals important things about their children that they didn't know before. The exercises in those chapters can also facilitate establishing a partnership with a client or patient in counseling.

Children avoid boredom naturally

Sadie was on a weeklong visit to her grandfather's home. He didn't have a swing set or bicycle or neighborhood children to play with or even very many toys. While he had certain activities planned, they by no means filled the week, and he had some of his own interests to pursue part of each day. Was Sadie bored? No. Sadie was eight. Any eight-year-old can entertain herself (and others) if given sufficient freedom and a minimum of resources.

Sadie wasted little time before exploring her grandfather's garage out of simple curiosity. First, she asked his permission. There on a shelf she found a box about a foot long and fashioned like a treasure chest, a novelty and a catalyst for her creative expression. Without any prompting, she was off and running. First, she decorated the chest, a hands-on project that engaged her for a rather long time. As her imagination took hold, she tore a sheet of paper into small pieces and began to write clues on them in sequence from "Start Here" to the end where she would hide the treasure chest outside. The clues were not too explicit, but gave enough information to keep a search party going; this task required problem-solving. She spent quite a happy time devising the path from one clue to the other, visibly reveling in her skill, which means a surge of dopamine was activated each time she paused to admire her handiwork. When the clues were done and hidden, she looked for something intriguing that would fit in the box to serve as treasure. She gathered small objects from around the house and secretly put them in the treasure chest. The "treasure" would be returned to its place when the game was over. Following the clues was the point of this endeavor; nobody was going to keep anything.

Creating the game engaged her by providing multiple Elements of Interest: curiosity, imagination, problem-solving, reveling in skill, and hands-on activity, but there was more excitement to come. Granddad, drafted as the treasure hunter, was happy to supply the pay-off. Sadie enjoyed suspense, curiosity, and surprise, as she watched her grandfather work his way from clue to clue. She is well equipped with Elements of Interest to apply to a lifetime of potentially boring situations in work and play.

While watching children enjoy their Elements of Interest, it's good for parents to go one step further and remark on the Elements involved in this play (theirs and hers) so that the child learns to recognize and value them herself: "I had to work hard to figure out those clues. You thought of really good clues that were just the right challenge for me. Not too hard and not too easy. Challenge is one of my Elements of Interest." Or, "And I was so surprised when I opened the chest! I love surprise!"

"Play is the work of the child," said Maria Montessori,[3] who developed the Montessori system of education that features educational, hands-on play. Knowing how to play creatively hones the tools for keeping happily engaged in work or play at any age.

While allowing children to initiate their own play is the most rewarding approach, six to ten-year-olds will often accept ideas from teachers and parents like Betsy's mother. Betsy and her friend Trisha were both their parents' only children and without each other they would have been loners all summer. Betsy's mother picked up Trisha every day of their school vacation to take her and Betsy to the beach, to the dock to fish, or to a good place to pick blueberries. One day, for something new to do, she told them about a contest the small town was holding in order to rid the area of ragweed, which caused hay fever for a lot of people. The person who pulled up the most ragweed and delivered it, roots and all, to the town hall by a certain date, well before these weeds would flower, would be the winner. Betsy's mother asked, "What do you think of that?" Betsy and Trisha, nine and ten, didn't have to be asked twice.

It was a challenge they thought they could handle well, a competition they thought they could win. It was novel, physically active, and involved other Elements of Interest, notably a sense of purpose. Because Tricia's grandmother was allergic to ragweed pollen, Tricia understood the purpose especially well. The Elements of purpose, achievement, and possible acclaim became more important than the $25 prize, which they'd split. Betsy's mother had to drive the girls around looking for ragweed and haul the piles of weeds in the trunk of her car, but she had signed on for that at the outset and, in fact, nurturing her child's interests was one of her own strongest Elements of Interest. On dreary days the girls pulled up weeds instead of going to the beach; on good beach days they stopped on their way home to gather a few armloads.

If a parent said to a child, "I'll give you $12.50 to pull weeds every day for several weeks," what response would he likely get? On the other hand, suppose the parent said, "You and your friend can do something outdoors that will be a big help to your grandmother and other people with allergies," and he might get a different answer. Kids hear the call of their individual Elements of Interest.

Interest promotes harmony

Engagement in interesting activities is good for families, classes, and other groups as well as individuals. When we're not bored, we get along better together. Clinicians often see families that complain their children fight with each other, especially when one or more has ADHD. While children being separately occupied results in a period of peace, if one of them, often the one with ADHD, is not engaged in something interesting, he will, you can count on it, go to the other one, who is doing something interesting, and cause a disruption to provide himself with the stimulation of drama his brain craves.

However, children don't fight when they are focused on a mutual interest. Children voluntarily engaging in an activity together requires that both be drawn into the activity by at least one of their Elements of Interest; an Element that appeals to one may be different from the one that attracts the other. Different Elements account for the different roles children take in their play. This is just one reason that promoting interest is as valuable an emphasis to teach families as conflict-resolution skills.

My daughter, visiting me with her children, was complaining about the state of one of my closets. "Do you really need all these things?" she asked. No, I admitted. "Well, why do you keep them? You're never going to use them." Maybe I wouldn't use them, but somebody might. Shortly after that exchange, her two children, then six and nine, went into the closet where they found a cuddly, stuffed green alligator that I had used as a table decoration for a party on behalf of the author of a book entitled *Alligator Creek*. The children also found bandannas in the closet and tied them around their heads (apparently alligator hunters wear bandannas). Without a word of discussion, one child picked up the tongs from the fireplace and used them to seize the alligator by the neck while the other one ran to grab a pillowcase from his bed to keep the reptile captive. He held the pillowcase open while she worked the flailing alligator into the sack. They jubilantly repeated this daring act several times before their play morphed into a different adventure. The way I look at it, it's always good to have a stuffed alligator in your closet.

Several points to notice are these:

1. Children between six and ten can jolly well entertain themselves using their imagination and the props at hand. It's good to have appropriate materials to inspire them and to give them freedom to use these or they may find more troublesome ways to entertain themselves.

2. Kids of this creative age, especially those with ADHD, who tend to be unusually creative, see connections between things that aren't packaged together (literally and figuratively) better than other kids—that's the bright side of thinking of more than one irrelevant thing at a time, as ADHDers do.

3. I repeat, kids don't fight while their Elements of Interest are most engaged. These two children who played together very well during their youngest years had a tendency to irritate each other once their age difference came between them. But on this occasion, curiosity drew them to the contents of the closet, and then the whirring machinery of their brains said, "What can we do with this?" Then the Elements of hands-on action, challenge, and reveling in skill—it's not so easy to put a stuffed alligator into a pillowcase with fireplace tongs—all came together in a play activity, and the siblings became best friends again for a while. This sounds a bit like "keep them busy so they won't fight," but it is not busyness they seek. If you gave them a boring chore to do together like clean up the den, they would soon be bickering about whose mess this was and whose job it was to do what and saying, "You're not doing it right." Boredom brings discord; interest brings children (and adults) together in cooperation.

4. Keeping resources, that is, props and materials, around for children's use motivates them to entertain themselves. While they can do something even with nothing, they can do more with something.

Games people play

Kids enjoy card games from simple ones like Go Fish to collectible ones like Pokemon and commercial board games like Shoots and Ladders and derivative games with other popular motifs. The game of Monopoly, that old classic based on the theme of buying real estate in Manhattan, has been "thoughtfully adapted" into a board game for elementary school kids called Monopoly Junior. A grandparent reviewer of the game said, "I've always hated Monopoly. My grandkids love Monopoly, though, and this faster-paced Monopoly is bearable to me."[4] It features amusement park images kids can relate to, giving it greater relevance—an important Element of Interest—to today's kids' lives. Faster-paced, it takes only a half hour to play. Speed is also an Element of Interest for many kids and granddads.

Like commercial game marketers, children themselves make up new games and adapt them on the fly to suit their Elements of Interest. Most games kids play, especially outdoors, from hopscotch to king on the mountain, were invented by kids and passed down from kids to younger kids. They jumped rope and made up songs to accompany the rhythm. These are not adult inventions. The names and rules change over time and in different localities, with each new adaptation involving their Elements of Interest—competition, reveling in skill, rhythm, speed, and physical action, to name just a few revealed in these games.

Encouraging games and the Elements of playing and inventing them is good for children of all ages, and the creativity involved translates to making adult tasks more interesting. "Make a game of it" is one of the ways people get through boring tasks they can't escape.

To keep from being bored themselves, adults sometimes make up a game that meets their own Elements of Interest to play with their children. Cindie and her father, waiting in the car while her mother was shopping, shared this routine: As they watched people walk by their car, carrying groceries or pushing strollers, scowling or smiling or talking to companions, Cindie's father began to make up thoughts these people might be thinking or the comments they might be making to each other. He imitated the passers-by saying the lines he imagined. "He would, of course, come up with all kinds of funny things," Cindie recalls. "I used to beg him to play that game all the time. Of course, then I did it with my kids. We'd be out somewhere, and they'd request, 'Say what people are saying!' I think we've even done that fairly recently!"

The game provides the Element of humor, regardless of the quality of wit employed, and it can be useful when played by children together even without a witty adult to do the comic lines. Children can be great comedians when they have an audience—applause is an Element of Interest—and other children make an appreciative audience.

The Treasure Chest

There are those who understandably want very neat homes and storage space. If you haven't used something in a year, get rid of it, their advice goes. There are also adults, often grandparents, survivors of the Great Depression of the 1930s, who say, "When I was a child, we didn't have to be entertained; we found something to do." Like Sadie and the alligator hunters, the old timers probably "found something" and asked themselves, "What can we do with this?" Where they often found things was in sheds out back, attics, basements, barrels in storerooms of all kinds, in the tack room or barn, and there weren't many restrictions on their use, since the objects weren't always reserved for a known purpose. I wish for the same resources for the newest generation.

Parents and teachers may designate a similar place to put odds and ends of no further use to adults so that kids may find new uses. While preschoolers have an Old Toy Box and a New Toy Box, school-aged children need what I'll call a Treasure Chest, taking a cue from Sadie, a feature at home and at school to which they have access as their imagination requires. Suggest the kids decorate the inside walls of the closet or the outside of a big box or trunk. Applying their artistic whims to the Treasure Chest increases their sense of ownership and increases the likelihood that they will try to honor the maxim, "A place for everything and everything in its place."

Parents, teachers, and the children themselves can put toys and gadgets and materials like toothpicks and paper clips into the chest, along with leftovers like beads from a broken necklace, a metal object that belongs to something but they don't know what, a small toy an unknown visitor left behind, used greeting cards, some pieces of a game for which the rest of the pieces are lost, some sea shells picked up at the beach, and a bag of large acorns with caps like French berets gathered under an oak tree. Artists make works of "found art" of such things; kids will do the same. I have a figure of an old lady a child made from mussel shells; one large one serves as a long black skirt, and a small double shell opened forms a vest on top of the skirt. The head is a periwinkle with a face painted on it and whose spiral point is her topknot of hair. Her feet are two tiny snail shells. She's stuffed with cotton from a first aid kit, which is then glued to a backing of cardboard. For what purpose was this made? None. Its creation was an exercise in Elements of Interest for a child whose problem-solving Element led her to figure out how to do each step and who enjoyed hands-on tasks. Working alone, in this case, was a stronger Element than social interaction.

With novelty being a chief Element of Interest, especially for those with ADHD, the arrival of a new trinket or material to arrive in the Treasure Chest every now and then is likely to become the center of just such a creative scenario as Sadie invented. It's like handing an object to a performer in an improv show and letting them turn it into an interactive skit on the spot.

Free rein inside the Treasure Chest gives options essential for experimentation. Teach children to ask for other materials they may need, with the understanding that a parent may say "No."

In addition to the Treasure Chest, families of school-aged children need an additional shelf, drawer, or cabinet designated to contain basics that I call "raw materials" kids are allowed to use, for example paper, poster board, crayons, colored pens with washable ink, blunt-tipped scissors, paste, and tape. The figure of a woman made of shells, for example, required glue or paste, cardboard for a backing, and colored pens to draw the face and color her hair. A tool box with pliers, screwdriver, and a roll of duct tape is often a good gift for a child whose Elements of Interest include hands-on use of a variety of materials.

Clinicians can emphasize to families that basic materials allow more interest to be expressed in more sensory modalities, and they often cost less than many complicated toys. The point of all this is not just to keep children from being bored now, but to establish habits of exploration and creativity to last a lifetime in work and play.

Use basics, do it from scratch

What about *real* toys? I'm not at all opposed to them in reasonably limited numbers. But remember the noted preference children often have for the box a toy came in over the toy itself? The box, mentioned in an earlier chapter, made "Geek Dad" Jonathan Liu's "The 5 Best Toys of All Time" list. Liu's other items were: stick, string, cardboard tube, and dirt.[5] The stay-at-home dad described at length how kids use these, and he mentions also some dangers. I also asked friends, clients, and assorted kids to add their own items to it. These consultants agreed the top 10 toys surely might include: a container (pool, watering can, or puddle) or source (sprinkler, spigot, or hose) of water; popsicle sticks; pipe cleaners; drinking straws; a shirt cardboard; or the wire hangers that come from the cleaners with freshly laundered shirts. Parents and teachers can show kids how to cut the hanger with a pair of pliers by bending or twisting the wire back and forth till it breaks and in the process learn why the wire gets hot as you twist it. Don't know the answer? Look it up together on wiki.answers.com. Ask the kids to add to the list of top 10 toys, with the limitation that their choices all be basic materials not intended as toys. This challenge will spark their interest in itself.

Going even more basic, school paste, wallpaper paste, or even flour and water applied to strips of torn newspaper makes paper mache to drape over discarded plastic bottles to make angels or bears. Also, while commercial Play-Doh is a basic material, making play dough from scratch from recipes found on the Internet is a step in the direction of interest.

Speaking of dough, for most children, making bread and kneading the dough by hand is a treat that satisfies their interest with hands-on experience. A child from six to ten can also learn to make biscuits from scratch. The farther we get from the origins of familiar objects, the more interesting the idea of making them ourselves becomes. I recommend the classic tale of "The Little Red

Hen and the Grain of Wheat," in several early-grade reading levels, to accompany this activity.

Making butter from cream, by shaking it in a closed container, engages multiple Elements of Interest, from the curiosity and surprise to the physical exercise and even social interaction because it takes a long time to make butter this way and a child will need helpers. As a longer-term project, growing a small patch of potatoes or peanuts or Brussels sprouts will yield the Elements of surprise and purpose. Many children don't know a peanut grows underground on the plant's roots or Brussels sprouts grow directly on the plant stem; they learn by planting, tending, and harvesting some. Digging potatoes is guaranteed fun for this age group. It takes them back to basics, the best point for them to start experimenting with cooking or gardening. The value is not just the knowledge of where things come from, but empowerment comes from knowing that they can begin at the very beginning and create something from scratch.

Freedom: Put it in their hands

David, a single father, asked his eight- and ten-year-old daughters what they wanted to do during their summer vacation. He didn't want them to spend these precious hours in front of the television. The younger girl said, "Watch movies." The older girl said, "How about if we *make* a movie?" David smiled, knowing it was not as far-fetched as it might sound. He and some friends had attended an "unconference" the previous year, a get-together-and-do-something workshop for adults, and they had decided to organize a similar experience for their children. The parents pooled their technical skills and decided a movie was feasible, and they could even teach the kids some of their skills. When the families got together for the first time, the children brainstormed the film's subject matter, plots, and characters. Later they figured out how to do props, locations, and costumes. The story was in the children's hands, the problems were (mostly) for them to solve, and the parents went along for the ride, offering filming equipment, logistics, and other resources. The company of other children and self-directed experience were the chief goals. The parents advised sparingly. They were fully responsible, giving or withholding permission, but the kids were leading the charge. The parents filmed the final product, a silent movie titled "Fish and Chips: Zombies vs. Ninjas,"[6] and then it was time for popcorn. The movie, the end result, was not as important as the process. The process constantly met the Elements of Interest of David's girls—hands-on interaction, humor, challenge, social interaction, problem-solving, purpose, physical action, and reveling in their skills. Their summer was anything but boring.

Putting choice into young children's own hands, encouraging them to experiment rather than to perfect, and avoiding criticism or overpraising the results frees children to seek interest. The encouragement to seek is empowering for all children, as it was for these young film-makers; it is the essential tool for a child with ADHD who must constantly create stimulation for himself through multiple Elements of Interest.

- *Freedom can be messy.* A woman from Minnesota had a solution for boredom when it was too cold to play outside. What did her boys play outside when it was warm? They played for hours with toy cars in the dirt. When temperatures dropped, this mother allowed them to cover the table with a plastic cloth, dump 25 pounds of flour on the table and make roads through it for their cars. Give that woman a medal! The flour could be lifted off for Sunday dinner by gathering the corners of the plastic cloth and making the terrain into a bundle for the next day. Yes, it took some vacuuming but think of what freedom! I personally would have opted for corn meal or kitty litter as a little easier to handle, but use what you have, what you can buy cheap, and what you can live with.

- *Freedom can be dangerous.* One mother's kids broke down a box and used the larger pieces for sleds to slide down on the bare wood of a flight of stairs over and over again. Many children have done this without incident. However, a child could hit his head on a banister or tip over at the bottom. You don't have to stop the fun, but be aware of the risks and take precautions.

- *Freedom means there will be some undesirable outcomes.* Meredith and Kenny, six, and seven-year-old siblings contemplating a free winter afternoon, decided they wanted to paint. Fine, except they didn't have any paint. So they gathered up their wax crayons and put them in a container on the radiator to melt them into paint. Melted crayons didn't work very well as paint, but tending to the melting pot made for an interesting afternoon in their room. The children's parents punished them when they discovered this activity.

You and the parents you counsel will do better to say, "How did that work?" and "What did you learn?" This does not mean that kids don't have to clean up any messes they make. They do. That's part of what they learn. "How will you get these drips of wax off the floor?" is certainly an appropriate question that says something about responsibility. Avoid sighing at small disasters. In that long or staccato sigh a parent emits when displeased, the well-intentioned child hears unspoken words of criticism that inhibit not only further experimentation but their willingness to ask you for permission first.

Reading and writing

While many children prefer physically active, hands-on activities to thinking activities, many children with ADHD love to read. Some hyperfocus on what they are reading just as others do on computer games; you can't tear them away. Children don't want to read boring books, and they often avoid assigned books, but they pursue their own Elements of Interest via the written word just as they do in their imaginations. Whether they are reading e-books on portable devices in a car or in their private hideout behind the hedge, they are constructively occupied. Whether they are reading old books like *Little House on the Prairie* or newer books about Harry Potter, silly books, or even comic books, reading for interest is building skill for reading "better" books later, which is the ticket to an education. In the early years of school, just the act of reading—reading anything—allows them to encounter new vocabulary, develop fluency, and build the habit of reading to avoid boredom. The skills of reading and writing will be the main avenues for academic success, which is now their job.

The makers of Thomas the Tank Engine enhance the interest in that line of toy trains by accompanying each train with a story of its adventure on Sodor Island,[7] and the trains likewise increase children's interest in reading or hearing adults read, which is equally valuable for a beginning reader.

To bring several Elements into reading, bring a dog! Some schools and libraries offer children's programs where a certified therapy dog[8, 9] and its owner volunteer as a team. The dog listens attentively and responds appreciatively to a child reading a book aloud to him. A Library Dogs' spokesman says, "…every day we're learning there's more than just cuteness when this happens. The smiles on a child's face, the wagging tail of the dog, the excitement of doing something different (even forbidden in some public places) proves there's anticipation when it comes to reading in this particular setting. And that's what it's all about. Youngsters of all ages are not only learning to read, they're looking forward to it. They're learning to love to read."[10] This quotation from LibraryDogs.com describes ADHD kids' favorite Elements of Interest: novelty ("something different"), rule-breaking ("forbidden"), suspense ("anticipation"), and social interaction ("smiles" and "wagging tail"). The child also enjoys practicing his reading aloud before his visit in order to do a good job for the dog, though a key feature of this approach is that the dog is not judgmental. If there's not a reading dog in your area for readers who need encouragement, consider starting one at your school or library.[11]

Story can truly be an Element of Interest in itself, whether truth or fiction. When teaching children of low reading and writing levels, I have sometimes asked the children to write true anecdotes from their own lives. After they have written the stories, I ask them to write five questions at the end of the story for readers to answer, showing that they comprehended the story. One question might be easy, another harder. Some questions might be subjective such as "What was funny about the dog house?" Or "Who was nice in this story and why do you think so?" I check the stories and questions for correct language and spelling as well as clarity and coach the child to make it entirely correct. Then they exchange stories. They read their classmates' stories and answer the questions at the end. The exchange offers the Element of social interaction, as the young authors check to see who got their questions right and discuss the stories.

Bringing Elements of Interest into school

By the age of "real" school, when children are aged six years old and up, there are usually too many children in a classroom to tailor every learning experience to the individual Elements of Interest of each child. However, you will find knowing what motivates your students very useful and can be learned with remarkable efficiency by using the Top 10 Joys exercise described in Chapter Four. The exercise can take the place of the infamous "what did you do last summer?" essay and reward you with more information than you can get from that assignment. Even though you are not able to adapt lessons to every child's needs, keeping the most common Elements of Interest in mind leads to surprising ideas like the following:

A fifth-grade teacher in Louisiana dubbed her classroom the Great Hall of Hogwarts School, drawn from the enormously popular series of Harry Potter books. As in the books by J.K. Rowling, the teacher provided a Sorting Hat[12] to group the students into four "houses." She awarded or withdrew points from the houses rather than individuals so a criticism or praise wouldn't single someone out. The ones in the same house helped each other, and houses competed in achievement. This arrangement offered several Elements of Interest, initially the Elements of surprise and novelty as they first encountered the familiar motif with all its accompanying pleasure. Like Harry Potter and company, the students soon experienced the Element of affiliation with others in their houses, enjoyed special group interaction with them, and finally were motivated by competition among the houses.

One of the advantages of affiliation is that it increases the motivating power of competition. When teams compete at school in academics, sports, and other activities like fundraising or social projects, it's more effective if the groupings are long term. In more than one school I know well, the grouping began in elementary school, where the announcement of the random assignments to teams is very exciting and lasts throughout the school years.

If a teacher chooses to group students by, for example, reading ability, any competition arranged between the groups obviously must not be in reading. Use whatever criteria for competition is useful and motivating or none at all. If competition is desired, consider competing based on the most interesting way to do whatever is to be done: making the most interesting picture, using the most interesting word, finding the most interesting plant. Seeking interest is a goal worthy of modeling, intentionally teaching, and reinforcing.

Remember also that competition is not an Element of Interest for all children, and generally less so for girls. Note also that social interaction in doing tasks is not always an Element of Interest. Every child needs to learn to interact socially and with increasing comfort. However, children for whom one-on-one interaction is preferred to group activity, that is, "individual contributors" who want to work alone, need to be recognized and given outlets or respites from group activity. A group of children may work these things out by themselves naturally, perhaps by letting one child execute a part of a given plan by herself.

Teachers can use variations on the Hogwarts School model to make classes interesting. There are endless options, and you may find that choosing a theme brings details to mind more easily. Adding the Element of relevance, for example, a teacher can create a theme related to a current field of study such as a unit on water in science, with houses designated as lake house dwellers, river boat crew, ocean liner passengers, and oasis tent nomads, where the groups learn everything about the water of their dwelling—water sources, use, creatures, pollution, conservation, regulation, etc.—and make presentations to the other houses.

In planning any classroom activity, consider the Elements of Interest that are most common—novelty, multi-sensory aspects, social interaction, hands-on activity—and ask yourself, for example, "How can we add a hands-on Element to our theme?" Like any Element, hands-on aspects can be applied to all kinds of learning to make it more interesting to students.

Second graders in one school, in their second year of using Cuisenaire rods to learn about manipulating numbers, enjoyed this variation: They watched a teacher cut carrots into halves, thirds, and quarters. The teacher then gave them bananas and plastic knives to cut the banana into halves and quarters or thirds as instructed. This hands-on, multi-sensory exercise was planned in place of snack time so that the children could eat the segments while the teacher said, "How many pieces is this banana cut into?... Three... So if Juan eats one of the pieces, what part is he eating? Yes, a third. How many thirds are left? Two thirds, that's right. There are three thirds in the whole banana and one third of this banana is gone." Texture and taste were Elements added to the hands-on, multi-sensory activity.

A fifth-grade class learning the scientific method started with accurately recording observations. The teacher provided students with their own plastic tubs with holes in the tops into which they put *Armadillidium vulgare*, commonly called pill bugs or roly polies, which they found in parks or their own yards. One child told me she found her specimens under a cinderblock in the backyard. There's nothing more hands-on than collecting roly polies. The children recorded their little crustaceans' reproduction, growth, change in color, and shedding of shells, as well as features of the environment such as moisture, light, temperature, and food, which they varied systematically. They learned about hypotheses and variables and how to use their data in drawing conclusions. The Element of nurturing was added to the learning experience when some of the children kept their specimens as pets for more than a year after their formal study.

In one primary school, the Element of purpose was added to an exercise in learning number sequences: Children on the playground who wanted a particular swing or other piece of play equipment that was currently being used by another were required to "count for" their turns. First graders had to count, one, two, three, all the way to 50 or (later in the year) to 100, at which point the user of the item had to relinquish it to the counter. Second graders had to count by twos to 200 to get a turn, which took between two and four minutes. Third graders counted by threes to 300, fourth graders by fours to 400, and fifth graders did multiplication tables.

The children were willing to do this task, which held interest for them because of its Element of purpose—getting their turns with a desired piece of equipment.

The children counting for a turn added another Element, rhythm, as their counting became a singsong chant. Any learning task that requires repetition may be done in rhythm; for example, reciting the names of the monarchs of England set to the tune of "Good King Wenceslas," as English children have sometimes done. Older children can make up rhymes to help take the boredom out of learning lists.

The Elements of urgency and challenge were added to the task of learning multiplication tables in a third-grade class. Every week, the children drew slips of paper with a different "times table" written on it and then performed a Minute Multiplication Test on the selected table, their recitations timed digitally. "When I drew the 12s tables," one student said, "it got harder. When the minute was almost up, it got exciting and a little bit stressful." With the right amount of challenge, kids with ADHD may thrive on urgency, which creates a dopamine surge and which they often create at home by waiting till the last minute to do their homework. Urgency creates interest, but too much challenge for the time allowed also creates anxiety.

Interaction is an important Element of Interest for most people. Many children like to go to school just for that; they make temporary and lifelong friends in school. The interaction between the teacher and student is also paramount. Most of a class period is used in group interaction. Many children crave one-on-one interaction as a more important Element. Most successful people can name teachers as mentors and even remember certain moments of interaction that made a significant difference in their future success. As a college freshman, Ryan remembers a fifth-grade teacher who took him aside when his behavior was particularly "off the wall" and told him how she too had a lot of trouble in school because she had ADHD. She told him she understood what was hard for him, and she reassured him that he would find his way. Through understanding his needs and tendencies and exercising a great deal of diligence, which he says was particularly motivated by a special middle school teacher, he is now succeeding academically and socially in his first year of college.

I once read a study in which matched classes were compared on various measures according to whether the teacher gave students individual greetings as they entered or left the room. In one class the teacher spoke to each child by name, adding as often as possible an appropriate personal detail like "I like your sweater," "I hope your leg feels better," or "Did you remember to take your math book home?" and sometimes just saying "Have a nice weekend" or "I hope the rest of your day goes well." The classes where the teacher addressed each child individually were more engaged and did better academically than the classes addressed only as a group. There are lots of hard-to-control variables in such a study, such as the warmth of the teachers, but I am not surprised by the findings. One-on-one interaction is an Element that makes any activity more interesting. I highly recommend that teachers stand by the door, dismissing children one-by-one and speaking to each child as they leave; missing some will be inevitable, but catching each one at least some of the time shows interest and attracts interest in a class.

Similarly, calling on individuals often for ideas, answers, and actions creates interest. That teacher technique entails thoughtful execution. There is the child who wants to answer every question, even waves her hand frantically while panting to be chosen; she may be someone with ADHD controlling herself as best she can. And there may be a child with ADHD who impulsively blurts out answers because he can't control himself. Instead of being rewarded for his interest, he has often been criticized for not waiting to be called on. There may be another child who doesn't say anything and is reluctant to be called on; perhaps she hasn't been paying attention. Whether a child has ADHD or not, offering the Element of social interaction in your lessons can be amazingly beneficial.

The goal is not for a teacher to replicate these examples, but to develop a mindset of bringing Elements of Interest into lessons so that the skill comes naturally and easily. When a teacher plans a lesson for its learning value, deliberately and regularly insert Elements into it. Experiment. Anything new automatically has the Element of novelty. Develop this mindset in students by asking them, "How can we bring an Element of Interest into this task?" Or "What Elements made this lesson more interesting?" When they become aware that seeking interest is one of the objects of learning, they will more readily begin to find, supply, and invent ways to make learning more interesting. The child with ADHD will benefit the most of all.

One of my most memorable uses of Elements of Interest as a tool in the classroom came before I'd formally started to explore individual Elements as outlined in this book, but I knew a good bit about children because I had my own. That year, I was trying to interest and motivate children for whom one sensory modality was missing—they were all profoundly deaf—so a lot had to be going on visually or kinesthetically to sustain interest. They were reading lips, a difficult visual task, so when I turned my back for a few seconds to write on the board, for example, I lost their attention as they could no longer understand what I might otherwise say. I frequently reclaimed their attention with difficulty as they had begun to play or interact with each other while my back was turned. In this class, one boy cried out in protest frequently and then caused an uproar complaining that the others caused him grief by their behavior, which at first I could not actually catch them doing. I mistakenly focused on calming the protester down, trying to get him to ignore whatever the others were doing that bothered him. Things did not go well.

As I began to understand the dynamics of the class, I realized that the one who disrupted my class, causing me to lose the attention of all my students, was being teased or even bullied by silently mouthed words and vulgar gestures by the others. When this happens, I've found, there are several or many who enjoy the disturbance and serve as an audience and there are one or more leaders. I considered what motivated them. First, they liked drama. For many that is an Element of Interest and a reason to stir up trouble. When they get bored, they figure out who they can get to fight, cry for help, or get in trouble. They also like an audience for the scene they incite. The Element of Interest that requires an audience can be used positively or negatively.

To solve the problem, I had to provide some drama of my own. So I created a reward system for their quiet attention to me that had some drama involved. I devised a mystery that was far more important than the reward. Elements of Interest are almost always more important than reward, especially for those with ADHD. On a Monday, I put an empty can on each student's desk, and when they asked what it was for, I said I wouldn't tell them. Curiosity, which in itself is an Element of Interest and the enemy of boredom, kicked in big time. The first time I noticed someone paying solid attention to the lesson, whether it was what I was saying or some math or reading he was doing, I put a popsicle stick in his can. Nobody knew what that meant. I wouldn't tell them. I did the lessons as always, but every now and then put a stick in several cans belonging to the most attentive students. By now everyone was looking at me. It took no more than five minutes to achieve this initial rapt attention.

Three days passed before the novelty wore off and one of the students was doing something other than attending to the lesson. I took a stick out of his can without a word. The others instinctively, it seemed, put their hands over their cans as if to prevent a similar loss. By this time they knew what the stick was about and behaved accordingly. At the end of the week, I asked them to count their sticks and everyone who had ten turned it in to me in exchange for a pack of gum wrapped with a collectable card.

What would happen next week? Would I do the same? I wouldn't tell them. This went on for weeks, during which I had their full attention and almost no disruption. I changed the reward occasionally, but not always. Novelty, unpredictability, mystery, drama.

One Monday, I took ten sticks out of one child's can and replaced it with a stick I'd painted red. The child protested that he'd lost nine sticks. I said, "But you have a red stick." The children chattered about what that new stick meant. Without explaining what I was doing or when I'd do it again, I kept the mystery going. The next day, I replaced ten sticks in other cans with a red stick. It took the rest of the week for them to discover that the red stick had the same reward power that the ten regular sticks had, and I had near-perfect attention the entire week.

Several of the children hoarded their sticks. When one day some time later I took ten red sticks from the can of a very attentive student, and replaced them with a blue stick, the class certainly figured out what was happening, although they were behind regular students in math. They became extremely eager to get a blue stick, and some declined to turn in their red sticks on Friday for a reward. They were aiming for the blue. The small reward expected was simply not as interesting as the suspense, an Element that stimulates many of us. This practical use of base-10 sticks also helped these children in math class when we began to study borrowing.

Keep in mind that the reward of gum with collector cards and other equally small tokens was never the main point. These kids had all the gum they wanted at home. It was about the common Elements of Interest of novelty, uncertainty, mystery, drama, and, for some, my personal recognition of their good behavior, a quiet equivalent of applause.

Have you forgotten about the boy who was disruptive in class? So did the other students. Peace reigned. Attention and motivation soared.

I don't recount this decades-old story so that you might replicate it, but to give you an example of keeping Elements of Interest in mind as you design methods of reaching educational goals.

Marcelo Suarez-Orozco, a distinguished professor of education at UCLA, in his article aptly titled "The Elephant in the (Class) room,"[13] not only points out that the elephant is boredom, but emphasizes that a great failing in education in the United States is the insufficient teaching of foreign languages. Elementary school, if not preschool, is the time when children best learn language and the ideal time not only to expose them to multiple languages but to teach them to the point of mastery. He says that immigrants who flock to the U.S., especially urban areas, come speaking many foreign languages, but their grandchildren no longer know them. He paraphrases sociologist Stanley Lieberson in calling this nation "the world's largest cemetery for languages," even during an era when being bilingual or multilingual is hugely valued in the marketplace. "Foreign languages are boring to us," Suarez-Orozco says.[13] I believe that for many years the separation of most Americans from large numbers of people speaking a language other than English made the study of a foreign language somewhat irrelevant. Modern transportation and technology have bridged the situational gap. Knowing many languages has now become relevant, and relevance is certainly a powerful Element of Interest.

Learning a foreign language can be just as interesting as using one's mother tongue as long as it's presented in interesting ways. *Dora the Explorer*, for example, the television series featuring a seven-year-old Latina and her friends,[14] introduces a sprinkling of Spanish words to preschool children. Dora and Dora products have become hugely popular, and children find their use of Spanish in the shows not boring but enriching through their novelty. The producers of these shows seem to have studied the Elements of Interest well; problem-solving is one of Dora's chief Elements of Interest. The Dora shows are available in Spanish with a sprinkling of English,[14] and it seems children raised on Dora in English with sprinkles of Spanish might move right on to learning from the Spanish version by connecting it to what they already know about Dora. Moreover, by exploring with Dora, they could learn any of the more than two dozen languages from Swedish to Hindi for which there are Dora adaptations. There are other comparable educational programs designed to teach children a second or third language; I single out *Dora the Explorer* for its proven success in engaging children's interest. The idea and practice of using educational media, of course, is hardly new but widespread; many schools use media well for teaching foreign language. The same high-interest design has been and can be applied to any language and become a staple of every classroom. Also, among our many immigrants are grandparents of current students, who could be valuable resources as volunteer or paid "visitors" conversant in their native languages. These would not so much teach in the formal sense, but tell stories of their childhoods in other countries or their journeys to their new country, or ask the children about their lives. The telling of their stories would bring social interaction, novelty, and many more Elements of Interest into the learning experience that not only children with ADHD require but all children.

Challenge: Too hard, too easy

As Csikszentmihalyi wrote, too little challenge equaled boredom, and too much challenge caused anxiety. The perfect amount of challenge allowed a person to be in a state of "flow."[15] For a person with ADHD, challenge may be a critical Element of Interest; he will seek it. When he finds the right degree of challenge, he may slip into flow so intensely that he can hardly be pulled away. He doesn't hear you say, "Put up your books now, and get out your maps." He won't refuse to disengage—he can't disengage. The stimulation of the activity will be too precious. You will have to touch him on the shoulder or even close his book for him. His kind of hyperfocus is flow, the ideal state of engagement; he needs plenty of opportunities to find it in positive, productive experiences.

A classroom is also likely to include children, with or without ADHD, who have tuned out because the work is too easy, and those who have given up because it is too hard. Either way they are bored. They may daydream or sleep or draw pictures. They are not disruptive, just inattentive. A child with the inattentive type of ADHD will be among them. The child with the hyperactive/impulsive type of ADHD will be forced by his need for stimulation to take matters into his own hands. He may disturb those who are working in an effort to enjoy social interaction or provoke drama or he may simply be moving around, even running around, exercising his Elements of Interest. The teacher must tailor the solution to the child, a nearly impossible task with so many to attend to.

One fifth-grade teacher put two gifted math students out in the hall with sheets of more challenging work to do so they wouldn't have to hear the repetition of explanations they didn't need or wait for average students to catch up. The two in the hall were happy to be occupied with work hard enough to be challenging. When they chose to consult each other or collaborate, adding social interaction to the task, so much the better. This solution obviously depended on them being willing and able to interact quietly without supervision. Being given appropriately challenging work tends to improve behavior.

Students for whom the work is too hard need a different placement for that subject, or time with a resource teacher who can give one-on-one attention.

Accommodations and advocacy in school

The task of a teacher is to help each child reach her potential; that often requires accommodations for the child with ADHD. Kirk Martin, behavioral consultant and founder of Celebrate Calm, teaches research-based interventions to educators and parents.[16] He has suggested, for example, that a teacher let a child with ADHD lie down on the floor and look up at the ceiling while she talks because it helps him concentrate in a way that looking a teacher in the eye prevents. Martin advised another teacher to give a hyperactive child a very specific job to do approximately every 15 minutes or when she saw him looking bored or fidgety. The job Martin mentioned on a recent *ADDitude Magazine* webinar was to come forward to the teacher's desk when she gave a prearranged signal, take her water bottle from her desk, fill it, and return it to her. This little bit of exercise eased his restlessness. She explained to the child why she was doing this; it was their little secret. She also encouraged him to stay focused for increasingly longer periods.[17] Any little job that requires moving around may help a fidgety child.

That accommodation was designed for an individual child and could obviously not be done for the whole class. However, when helping a child reach her potential means involving more of her Elements of Interest in the delivery of lessons, the specific adjustment is probably better for all the children in the class. Moreover, adopting it for everyone reduces the stigma of special treatment for the child with ADHD.

The task of educational consultants and clinicians is to advise parents to advocate for their children in school and to advise educators on how they can better serve their students with special needs. As a parent or a professional, you will almost certainly need to advocate for the child with ADHD. It takes imagination and experimentation to find strategies that allow a child with ADHD to fully engage his interest.

Ideally a school has the services of a highly trained team of teachers, educational psychologist, and principal, along with teaching assistants, interns, teachers in training, and volunteers. Making this ideal a reality requires a strong commitment of resources and leadership in the community.

Quick points

Notice children's spontaneous expression of interest: Comment to them, "You seem to be interested in all the different colors," "I notice you like to build things," or "You often bounce to the music. That feels good, doesn't it?" This gives them one-on-one attention as well as making them conscious of their choices.

Learn children's Elements of Interest by their Top 10 Joys: Ask a child or a primary class to write and/or draw pictures and tell about their happiest times.

Talk about ADHD: Whether you label the condition or not yet, tell children with ADHD or similar behavior that they need more stimulation than some children and that they can find ways to find interest by being curious, learning more, being active, and participating in class. Tell them you will help them find a good time and way to do this.

Make it new: Change themes, topics, and routines when interest begins to wane. Learn how long they can focus well, and adjust lengths of lessons or activities accordingly.

Encourage harmony through interest: When children get testy with each other, bump the stimulation level up enough to distract them from their differences and get them engaged in something together.

Be subtle: Bring out a new game or toy or activity and begin to use it in front of them. Attract them to it before you invite them to share it with you or take it over. The subtle presentation increases curiosity and gives them a sense of choice.

Put it in their hands: Ask children, "How can we do this?" or "What can we add to this?" or "What would be more interesting?" or "What do we need now?" Try to incorporate their ideas in activities.

Encourage reading: Read aloud to children from high-interest material a little more advanced than they could read themselves.

This can be an end-of-the-day activity at school or home, and it passes the time on family trips. Give them purpose by asking them to read recipes to you when you (and they) are cooking or simple instructions for other tasks. "What does it say first?" you ask. "What next?" Read in front of them for pleasure.

Encourage social writing: Ask children to write letters to people not in their household, like thank-you notes, birthday messages, and newsy letters. Writing serves the Element of social interaction. A child will be thrilled when he gets a letter back.

Encourage purposeful writing: Ask them to write lists for themselves or for you. "Let's think what we need for the party. Write them down while we think of them. We need ice cream. Write that down." Give writing a purpose, which is an Element of Interest. Writing, of course, is an essential academic skill; moreover, written record-keeping is required throughout life. Children with ADHD benefit from record-keeping as soon as possible to keep them on track.

Encourage writing for interest: Encourage creative writing such as poems and stories. Encourage children to keep a journal on trips and special activities or outings. Say, "Write down the interesting things you are doing. You'll enjoy reading about it later."

Encourage art: All kinds of art forms make children's lives interesting. Some may develop into adult hobbies or careers.

CHAPTER FOURTEEN

Middle Schoolers, Ages 11–13 Years

Middle schoolers are cool. No more kids' games or cute songs for them, then suddenly they revert to child's play. We have to treat them more like a grown-up now, but expect them to be kids. They will say, "Dad, I'm not a baby." Then they act like two-year-olds. Next they surprise us with some very mature behavior or sophisticated observation. Kids this age are not boring. Kids with ADHD are even less so. Their off-the-wall humor makes us laugh, and their antics make us cringe. Their difficulties in school become more difficult as the need for up to six hours of chair-sitting each day is now typical.

Talk about ADHD, boredom, interest, and substance abuse

More diagnoses of ADHD are made at this age, and among them educational specialists are now seeing the inattentive-type ADHD more frequently than earlier when hyperactivity was the most noticeable marker of the disorder.

Clinicians, coaches, teachers, and parents can talk to 11 to 13-year-olds about ADHD, the neurotransmitters, and the brain. You might show them a three-dimensional model of the brain. Whereas a younger child might think, *you mean I'm crazy*, middle schoolers can understand brain differences in more accurate terms. Don't talk down to them. They are ready to hear this information. They may even be relieved to hear it and to give the source of their frequent difficulties a vocabulary and adult explanation.

Show them diagrams of synapses[1] as you explain how dopamine and other neurotransmitters help electric impulses cross small gaps between synapses in the brain, taking "messages" to all parts of the brain. Tell them that sufficient or normal dopamine aids the flow of impulses through the reward circuitry and can make children feel more satisfied, while too little dopamine seems to make them restless or bored.

Let them know there is medication that "increases the activity of chemicals called dopamine and noradrenaline in areas of the brain that play a part in controlling attention and behavior. These areas seem to be underactive in children with ADHD. It is thought increasing the activity of these chemicals improves the function of these underactive parts of the brain."[2]

Be sure they know that exercise, especially aerobic exercise, also increases the activation of the neurotransmitters involved in attention and motivation.

Guide them especially to pursue stimulating interests. The experience we call "interest" activates dopamine, just as boredom slows dopamine down. I encourage you to try the techniques in Chapters Three through Five to help middle school children discover their individual Elements of Interest and Chapter Six to learn how to choose interests and to use them to make activities more interesting.

Also tell them about people who have had ADHD and successfully pursued great sources of interest. Suggest they research successful ADHDers for a school project or just for fun.

Middle school is an age when kids' curiosity and interest-seeking behavior will lead them to experiment. They will treat boredom, whether current or anticipated, by trying something new—whether alcohol, pot, pills, or breaking rules. Many children try mind-altering substances without becoming dependent or addicted, but the neurochemistry of ADHD brains makes dependence on such chemicals more likely as they crave relief from boredom, the racing mind, or the hyperactivity that has been their chief response to lack of stimulation. They may also want to dull the feelings of failure they may have experienced when they forget to do tasks or do poorly in school.

Health writer Carl Sherman, Ph.D., says:

> Experts urge parents to start talking to their kids about the matter at an early age. If you wait until fifth or sixth grade, it may be too late. Let your child know that having ADHD raises his risk for trouble, that he is more vulnerable to addiction than are his non-ADHD peers. Make sure your child understands that the best way to avoid trouble is to avoid illicit drugs altogether, and to wait until adulthood to use alcohol (if at all).[3]

Families that model abstinence or moderate use of alcohol may reduce the risks further. Consider the attitude you convey about the use of alcohol and cigarettes before your child has a problem.

It falls to parents and teachers to make home life and school as interesting as possible, so that cravings for something novel to do, activities with a purpose, and pursuits that offer other strong sources of the Elements of Interest are fulfilled.

Sports and activities

Options for sports and extra-curricular activities expand for middle schoolers. Many have been playing on sports teams since preschool where skills, discipline, and strategy are in the beginning stages for all kids. When an outfielder is caught looking everywhere but the game and misses an easy catch, the repercussions of her inattention are rather slight in the early grades, but sports become more competitive in middle school. While skills, teamwork, and social interaction of sports are important to develop, some sports are definitively better than others for ADHDers. Even more than other kids, they need the exercise to get neurotransmitters activated, but their inattention, impulsivity, and difficulty following directions make team sports more difficult for kids with ADHD. Baseball, for example, requires attentiveness even when there's no immediate action; an outfielder may never get a chance to field a ball in a whole inning, but must be ready to make the game-winning catch any second. Paying attention while waiting is not an ADHD strength.

The consensus of experts quoted in *ADDitude Magazine* is that sports involving individual performance are far better for the child with ADHD than team sports.[4] Swimming, diving, and gymnastics are all excellent because ADHDers can concentrate fully—hyperfocus, in fact—on their own performance when they are "on," and then let their attention wander when they are not performing. One-on-one sports such as wrestling and tennis are also good games for constant action and focused attention. Most sports involving individual performance or one-on-one focus still involve teams for camaraderie off the court or field. The most highly recommended sport for an ADHDer is a martial art, particularly taekwondo. "Martial arts are all about control," says Patricia Quinn, M.D.—control of the body and the internal control of meditation. Instructors teach step-by-step rather than coach, so there is little time for distraction.[4] Martial arts are competitive, and there are teams for social interaction and team affiliation, to name three Elements of Interest, without the complicated strategies of sports like football and basketball, which are low on the list of ADHD-friendly sports.

Playing in a band and singing in a choir or chorus provide the Element of music and rhythm, obviously, but also social interaction, reveling in skills, applause, and maybe competition. Professor of Neurology and author Oliver Sacks, M.D., says, "Nothing activates the brain so extensively as music."[5] Dopamine levels rise as people listen to music, and playing it or singing to it adds to the stimulation. Music has structure, and listening to it develops a sense of structure, rhythm, and time. As in sports, solo performing or performing throughout a piece offers an opportunity for intensity without waiting for your turn as is necessary if playing in a symphony. Art classes help children develop visual focus and give the brain sensory stimulation; color, texture, and design provide interest. Cooking classes cultivate responsiveness to the sensory qualities of taste, texture, and design of presentation.

Electronics or computer clubs are ways to be involved with a group and also learn individual skills. Electronics kits for different levels can engage a middle school child's Elements of Interest. Forget reading directions, he will jump in and start making things. Expect blown circuits; every one that goes up in smoke is a lesson.

Computers involve individual performance and learning by doing. Middle schoolers will benefit from trying many avenues of interest outside of academics; a few will develop full-blown passions. All of these mentioned fulfill the need for a variety of Elements of Interest; they are mentally or physically active and involve hands-on activities and many senses. They all build skills and serve a purpose.

Freedom: Put it in their hands

The responsible child is allowed choices, tries to make them wisely, and learns from positive outcomes and from mistakes. Freedom with supervision allows middle school-age kids to pursue their Elements of Interest. Preteens want more freedom—and are looking for ways to get it one way or another. Let them know that freedom is earned when they are willing to accept reasonable limits and take responsibility.

Given an opportunity, an ADHD child will surprise you with originality. One evening Jason asked his father if he and a friend who was visiting could cook some chicken for dinner. Mike agreed, but before turning them loose, the single father showed the boys a few things about cooking, especially about using the stove safely. He also showed them his supply of seasonings in the cabinet, advising them to use sparingly and season by taste. Then he left the room. In due time, Mike was called to dinner and served a plate most notable for a sizeable portion of deep purple chicken. The boys had added food coloring to taste. "It was good to let them experiment," Mike said, who, like his son Jason, has ADHD. "If we had to throw the whole batch of chicken away, it wouldn't have been the end of the world." As it was, food coloring is flavorless and Mike ate the purple chicken along with the boys, without revealing his lack of enthusiasm for its color. Jason's friends have always enjoyed coming to his house; Jason's dad hit the right balance of supervision and freedom, and his laid-back attitude about experimentation made them feel comfortable. Their interest-seeking that evening ran the gamut of Elements of Interest, including novelty, social interaction, hands-on interaction, taste, smell, and especially color.

Resources: The junkyard

Middle school-age children need equipment or supplies for the activities mentioned above: sports require such things as balls, nets, and uniforms; arts require musical instruments or art supplies; and cooking requires the raw ingredients. These are the resources that you can list, plan, and put on a budget. But ADHD ingenuity comes out best when youngsters pull together things in unexpected ways, satisfying their Elements of Interest such as novelty, surprise, risk, uncertainty, humor, and so forth. They find interest in a variety of unexpected materials. Like the toddler, but on a grander scale, they think, *I wonder what would happen if...*

Once I took my grandsons on an outing to a llama farm for something interesting to do. They enjoyed watching and petting the llamas well enough, but the success came from an unexpected detour on the way home. (Unexpected/surprise/unpredictable is a common Element of Interest.) I was driving down a country road when I passed a sign for a junkyard. I turned around and went back. Sure enough, we found an old-fashioned junkyard with wide paths running between high walls of junk piled up on either side: old tricycles and wagons, building materials, and unidentified objects. The yard was complete with a fire barrel to warm the hands and provide a hot lunch for the old man attending the business. A true junkyard dog was on duty for security. The place offered novelty by the pound. There was a big scale marked by a sign that stated the price for one pound of junk, any junk. The boys were excited as they went down the aisles singling out items as "cool" and "weird." (Weirdness is a middle school Element of Interest!) I gave them a limit of $5 each to buy what they wanted. Think how much they learned about size and weight and materials trying various desirable items on the scale! They both were pleased with their purchases. The older boy had selected a sign for the end of their driveway reading: "This space is reserved for the Employee of the Month." Their parents weren't pleased with the idea, but it looked good on his bedroom wall for a year. The success of this venture really became clear when, as a teenager with a driver's license, he called me up and asked me where that junkyard was because he wanted to take his girlfriend to see it! Any time you do something a teenager wants to reenact for his girlfriend, you can count it a success.

The notion of a Treasure Chest is just kid stuff now; preteens need a Junkyard to collect materials to experiment with. The Junkyard is often their bedrooms, but space in a garage or basement can be set aside for their tools and materials. As parents you will see items of junk pulled out frequently and may wonder what's going on. Let kids know this Junkyard is open for your inspection at any time, then check in and supervise. Freedom for middle schoolers does not mean "Private. No admittance." Oversight and freedom promote safe but unique expressions of children's Elements of Interest.

School

Middle schoolers are creative, funny, and enthusiastic about any novelty that will break their infamous tedium. Many of the American comic strips in my collection begin with a kid saying, "I'm bored," especially about school. One such cartoon depicts the monumental boredom of its middle school character Holly, but from time to time shows us the "good guy" teacher. In one comic strip, the good teacher announces to the class that they will do the whole day's work using an English accent. They not only exuberantly use their stereotyped version of an English accent throughout the day's lessons, we are led to believe, but in the next day's comic strip, Holly demonstrates her accent to her mother and grandmother and the whole family takes it up. The novelty lasted for hours.[6] True to life? Where else do cartoonists get their ideas?

A teacher once told me that teaching middle schoolers was great because they were curious, fun, and funny, and could have a grown-up conversation, but were "still a little bit scared of you." That is changing. The age when they are still a little bit scared of you is younger and younger, and bad behavior in some schools is problematic. This is not a book about discipline, but making a class truly interesting, strongly engaging students' interest, is the best way to make them behave well. It's when they are most bored that they start making their own entertainment, pursuing their Elements of Interest of drama, comedy, rule-breaking, physical action, and social interaction in disruptive ways. You are lucky if you can be more entertaining than they are, but not everyone can leap onto desks to get their attention like educator Ron Clark famously has.[7]

Teachers must purposefully include Elements of Interest every step of the way. When the students come into Lisa's sixth-grade classroom for the first time, the technology education teacher gives them graph paper to staple together to make a Technology Journal. "They love graph paper," she says. Why? "Because it's different from the lined paper they've been used to." Novelty. It's also a symbol to them of more advanced work; it carries prestige, which is also an Element of Interest for many people. The sign of more advanced work may appeal to some because they expect it to be more challenging. Challenge is a very strong Element of Interest for some students. The first thing these sixth graders get to do on their new graph paper is draw a device that they use much of the time and that they don't want to live without. Making the task about something they are already very interested in is smart, and making it about each individual student is even more interesting because everyone's chief Element of Interest is himself!

Lisa says, "I used to think that if students were busy they weren't bored. But later I realized that they can be busy but bored; they're attending to their work just because I've told them to do it." She has learned to take great care in making lessons interesting by adding Elements such as surprise, novelty, multiple senses, challenge, and interaction. She cares about their attitude toward the work.

Lisa also tells me her plans for her upcoming seventh-grade Technology class called "Invention and Innovation." She's going to start with the definitions and distinctions between the two concepts because the curriculum she's been given begins that way. Beginning with definitions is logical. It's also boring. So Lisa has picked a YouTube video of a product of technology "because that will be unexpected." She has just named an Element of Interest that motivates most kids, those with ADHD all the more so: the unexpected. You could also call it surprise. The video shows a remote control skateboard that can go uphill, go slowly downhill, and do what an ordinary skateboard can do but with a touch of the remote control the rider carries. Nobody in the class has seen such a device. It is "weird." The novelty of the device attracts the students, as does the animation, the multi-sensory aspect that adds vision and sound to the words of the definitions. The example is more specific and less abstract than the definitions. Being specific or concrete, if not an Element of Interest, is a characteristic that allows people to visualize a picture or hear a sound in their minds, providing sensory imagery. In short, the video of the remote control skateboard is more interesting than the technology lesson would have otherwise been. Beginning with this video also sets the students' attitude: This class is going to be cool instead of "Boooooring."

"Is it an invention?" Lisa asks about the remote control skateboard, when class begins. "Is it an innovation?" The definitions develop from the characteristics the students themselves provide, and Lisa sorts them into two columns to create two definitions. Interaction instead of just listening to lecture—or definitions—is an Element of Interest. Check off step one of today's lesson. Later the students will be guided to think of inventions and innovations on their own.

Lisa may not have been thinking of those students with ADHD who are *unable* to attend to things that are not interesting. They are the ones chewing their pencils and daydreaming while definitions are discussed or sharpening their pencils too often just for a chance to get out of their seats. While her intention to inject interest in every step of her curriculum is fortunate for her whole class, it is critical for those with ADHD. Chances are she has at least one student with ADHD in each of her classes.

Put into their hands: School version

Lisa follows TechTalk.com during the summer to gather ideas for making her classes more interesting, and she finds videos on YouTube to illustrate concepts. I give her preparation a thumbs up!

Teachers can go even farther to promote interest-seeking. "Put it into their hands" means give the job of making subjects interesting to the students themselves. For example, give them a term or concept or one manageable part of a topic in their book or curriculum to investigate before a class lesson comes up in class. You could give them instructions to "find one interesting thing about this topic" or find one really cool video or image that illustrates a principle or fact. The main requirement is that it must be interesting. That, you can tell them, is a criterion for their grade for the assignment as long as it is on the assigned topic.

The assignment of finding something interesting about a topic is better done in advance of the class lesson on the topic. Searching for illustrations of topics they've already studied is far less interesting than searching for things they don't yet know about.

The teacher can collect the copies of facts or pictures and review them. On the day that a particular fact or picture becomes relevant, he can pull it out and ask that the student who brought it read it to the class, pass the picture around, and tell how it illustrates a point on the lesson's topic. The teacher asks for the best ones to be shown; the rest are put on display. Some kids will take up the challenge to make their fact chosen, some will not. Challenge and competition are not Elements of Interest for all the children.

You could have the class vote on whether a student's offering was actually interesting. You could make the judgment yourself. You could announce different criteria before each new assignment: the shortest, the most useful, the weirdest. Or you could name a particular Element of Interest they must satisfy.

There must be a process for finding assigned facts or images, which you may have to teach. You can give students the resources for adding Elements of Interest to their lessons by directing them to science sites or sites especially for science teachers. To avoid consuming too much time Googling or disappearing down Internet rabbit holes or unreliable sources, you can give them a list of sites you will allow them to draw from; offer them points for picking items that no one else has found on those sites. If they want novelty, let them produce it. On top of a Google list for search words "jr. high science" is The Science Spot (www.sciencespot.net), where there are lesson plans and "starters," a treasure trove of activities with worksheets collected from creative teachers. Another site is www.aboutschool.com/8science.htm, which directs us to other sites on particular subjects eighth-grade science students study. Be open to a student saying, "I didn't see anything I wanted there but I went to…and found…" Curiosity is the interest motivator. Encourage it.

Kids already care about interest; they hate to be bored, but they may have been requiring you to bring it to them. Putting it into their hands empowers them to seek interest on their own.

Some people may complain that you are making the kids do your work. Reply "Thanks!" because they have complimented you. Then add, "That's the best way for them to learn!"

Relevance

Once I taught French to seventh graders in the same year that I taught tenth and eleventh graders. I was given traditional language books for the older students who had been taught French for several years the same way I had been taught—boring. Each chapter of the book had a vocabulary list to memorize followed by a piece of an ongoing story in French about a 19th century woman who, as I recall, was struggling to find the right fabric for a dress she was to wear to the opera to look elegant enough for the man her parents expected her to marry. It was probably a famous story made simpler for us, but not more relevant or funny or surprising or reminiscent of any other Element of Interest we desired. After wading through the story in French day after day, we turned the page to find a new point of grammar and a chart of pronouns or verbs to memorize and some exercises to write out using the vocabulary, the pronouns, or the verbs. As a first-year teacher, just as I had done as a first-year French student, I dutifully went through the book, unaware that I might have had the freedom to redesign the whole approach if I only had the time and materials. I didn't ask. It was embarrassing for me, even painful, to drag these youngsters through a process that bored us all.

I describe what was then the traditional teaching method, only so you will appreciate the glee with which I discovered what I was given to teach the seventh graders that same year. The program included recordings of simple and natural conversations between actual French school kids about doing things contemporary French kids do. There was a lunchroom scene at school where the kids complained about the food, a flat tire in the car when the family was on the way to the beach, and a party being planned for after a game in which the school football team might win a regional championship. Hello, relevance! I don't have to tell you that relevance is a big Element of Interest for most people but especially kids. "What is this for?" they want to know. The seventh-grade students were assigned to memorize the lines of the dialogues by listening to them over and over, and then to present this dialogue in class as a sort of skit. In this curriculum, there were also fast-paced, game-like exercises done loudly while standing up. Action! Grammar was introduced in small doses when the need arose in the dialogue—relevance again—not in a rote format or order. I do not recall having a boring moment in that class. The summer after their second year of this approach, some of these students went to France and actually spoke and understood the language passably. Purpose!

Fortunately, an audio-lingual approach with materials relevant to young students is often, but not always, used today. When teaching language or any subject, ask, as the kids do, "What is this for?" Bring the teaching closer to its real use to keep it relevant and purposeful.

Flipping allows more interaction in school

Forging relationships between students and their teachers is known to be motivating as social interaction is an important Element of Interest. However, teachers don't have time for much interaction with individuals in large middle school classes. How do teachers find time to interact with individual students when there is so much knowledge to pour into their heads so they can meet educational criteria?

One solution is popularly called "flipping." Some teachers in Georgia have begun to experiment with flipping in middle schools. Here's how it was reported on television news in August 2012.

> "What you traditionally have always done as homework will now be done at school. And what you've traditionally done in the classroom will now be done at home," teacher Ashley Miller explained to her students at Dodgen Middle School in Marietta.

> The idea is to have students watch the lectures at home so they can use class to focus on interactive exercises that make the lesson stick, or simply to get hands-on help with their homework. Students already seem sold on the idea.
>
> "Sometimes in class I have trouble focusing or I just don't get it at all and I can't really rewind a teacher. But at home I can rewind it as many times as I need to," said Maddie Sell.[8]

Students with ADHD in particular know all about "trouble focusing." With the flipping method, they can listen to lectures lying down, sitting up, or walking around, giving them more opportunity to ease restlessness. The lectures can be played as many times as necessary and on computers, smart phones, or tablets almost anywhere, and such repetition is the equivalent of studying, only better.

The teachers in the Cobb County, Georgia, schools mentioned above are not putting the lectures on the Internet but burning them onto DVDs for television or Flash drives to transfer to computers. The new technology, often thought to take away from personal interaction, in the case of flipping, allows more time for interaction between teachers and students.[8]

The very thought of "flipping" gives a rush of dopamine to the brain. Any method that facilitates interaction and other common Elements of Interest is going to mean better education and more engaged students.

Quick points

Use humor: Don't "try" to use humor. Adults remember as their best teachers and mentors the ones who used humor naturally; and what those people said and did has stayed with them. Whether you are a clinician, teacher, or parent, and you think of a funny story that illustrates a point, tell it. Say what you would say to an adult. Middle schoolers "get it." Of course, you will keep your topics and language appropriate.

Use surprise: Do the unexpected. Sometimes that's humor. Sometimes it's doing things in a different way. Sometimes it's not doing something they expect. Sometimes it's wearing an attention-getting outfit that's relevant to a school topic. Ask them to do something interesting that they don't expect to be asked to do.

Be an actor: Teachers may tell relevant history stories in a funny or dramatic way, playing the role of the prime minister in a history event, the inventor in a science project, the farmer in a geography lesson, or the character in a piece of literature that the class is studying. Let willing middle schoolers act out roles based on their study.

Teach interest: Discover middle schoolers' Elements of Interest by the exercises of the Top 10 Joys and Childhood Pastimes. Interpret their Elements from these exercises and ask them if your interpretations seem right to them. Accept their interpretations. Tell them why interest matters. Teach them to seek it. Tell the ones with ADHD that this is critical for their success and satisfaction.

Put it in their hands: Set limits but give middle schoolers choices. Ask them for solutions and negotiate the best ones they suggest. Ask them how they would best learn this topic or accomplish that task. Let them know they are not running the show but that you are listening; you care about their preferences because they will learn very little if they have no interest.

Make it relevant: Whatever task you want youngsters to perform or lesson you want them to learn, ask yourself why it matters to them. Ask them. Your sense of importance or future importance is not enough. It's hard to make any child share your sense of importance, but children with ADHD are unable to be motivated by importance, only by interest. Relevance, like purpose, and other Elements, can begin to interest them. Find a hook.

When they say they are bored, listen: When preteens mention boredom, tell them it's their responsibility to "Escape It or Shape It". Explore with them. Ask them what bores them and when. Listen for "too hard," "too easy," "the same old thing," or "what good does it do?" These are the opposite of their Elements of Interest. Instead of asking what would be less boring, ask how it could be made easier, or more challenging or different. Ask them to explore "what good does it do?" Writing the question "What purpose is…?" into a search engine can provide a usefulness for almost anything, and amazingly, "What good does…do?" or "Why do we need…?" work almost as well. Somehow, if the Internet says it's good for something, it carries weight. Ask them to tell you what they learned.

CHAPTER FIFTEEN

Boredom and ADHD in High School

The teen years are mostly about high school—its academics, activities, and social life. By the time children reach high school, they begin to more clearly recognize on their own when boredom creeps into their lives. If they start high school knowledgeable about their ADHD diagnosis, they're also better able to influence what the high school experience will be like for them. Recognizing how boredom interacts with the learning experience gives them countless opportunities to intervene on their own behalf. Educators also can do much to include Elements of Interest into classwork and assignments for the benefit of all students including those with ADHD.

Teens are generally sophisticated enough to understand the basic roles of neurotransmitters active in ADHD. Clinicians and teachers can guide them to sites like mybrainnotes.com and textbooks on the workings of the brain. Language teachers could accept ADHD as the topic of an essay or term paper for a student with ADHD. A science teacher could assign the topic for the student with ADHD or to another interested student who might give a presentation to the class. Encourage the student with ADHD to speak about how the condition affects her. Such a project or presentation will inform the student, classmates, and, most of all, her teachers on the biology behind ADHD and the psychological effects on her academic life.

Along with coaching high school students in techniques to arouse motivational chemistry, clinicians and teachers can coach parents to partner with students to overcome this chemical deficit by giving them the freedom to experiment with different time frames and different coping techniques.

Clinicians often talk about seeking accommodation for ADHD students to help them adapt to a difficult situation. If the student has a good understanding of ADHD, it can sometimes be more effective if she herself discusses the accommodation with her teachers. Doing so takes it out of the realm of adversarial confrontation and can often result in a more positive relationship.

In a history class, a teacher assigned each student a major project that included a research paper and a final presentation to the class. Rick was struggling in this class, but the teacher recognized that he was trying hard, so she assigned him, as his project, the job of producing maps and other graphics in support of the other students' presentations. She knew this task was a better fit for Rick's hands-on, artistic Element of Interest. He would also learn more from viewing history through these graphic representations than from listening to the lecture-style presentations. The fact that the teacher made this adjustment without the need to negotiate with Rick's parents helped to strengthen the relationship between them.

Dialogue between the student and his parents, between the parents and the teachers, and, more importantly, between the student and his teachers will reap bountiful rewards. Acceptance of ADHD by all the links in the chain will ensure understanding and increase the likelihood of a successful educational experience.

Boredom in high school

Kids with ADHD aren't the only ones who are bored in school. Half of the high school students in the United States are bored every day, and 17 percent of them are bored in every class, concluded the 2009 High School Survey of Student Engagement (HSSSE), based on 42,000 high school students in 103 schools in 27 U.S. states.[1] These figures are about the same as previous years for the annual survey conducted by the Indiana University Center for Evaluation and Education Policy (CEEP).[1]

"Just 41 percent of the students in the 2009 survey responded that they went to school because of what they learn in classes. Only 23 percent said they went because of their teachers. Around a third said they went because they enjoy being in school." Of students who have thought about dropping out, 42 percent said they didn't see the value in the work they were asked to do.[1]

If half the students are bored every day and many don't value the teachers or what they learn, think of the plight of the student with ADHD who is easily bored and has difficulty finding sufficient interest to keep him attentive.

What do students want in order to feel engaged? Responses on the HSSSE included a clear desire for more opportunities to be creative, and 65 percent agreed or strongly agreed with the statement, "I like discussions in which there are no clear answers." They wanted intellectual challenge, discussion, and debate; they wanted hands-on projects in art, drama, and technology projects, especially group projects.[1]

Like students with ADHD, the surveyed students preferred teaching methods that offer a large number of the Elements of Interest described in earlier chapters, especially experiences that are interactive, challenging, and hands-on. They want to learn and demonstrate learning through its use or purpose, a powerful Element. They can tolerate an Element of uncertainty, which favors curiosity and experimentation.

Various responses to the findings by schools involved in the study indicate that educators are trying to learn from the HSSSE data.

Yazzie-Mintz, director of the survey, reported on some of these responses. What they learned revolved around creating stronger relationships between school staff and students.

Kealakehe High School in Kailua-Kona, Hawaii, has focused on building relationships between school staff and students. "They say they used to focus on relationships a lot, but 'No Child Left Behind' has made them focus on tests and outputs," Yazzie-Mintz said.[2]

The prevalence of disaffected students revealed by the HSSSE has prompted the Chesterfield County district in central Virginia to concentrate on that issue. "They've tried to focus on listening to those kids, having people work with them more closely and bring them back. Not just to force them to be in class and do the work, but to attend to their needs."[2]

The principal of Yorkville High School in Yorkville, IL, said, "There was an assumption that 'if we teach it, you will learn it'... What we're learning from the engagement data is 'personalization.' Engagement will drive structures."[2]

At the tiny Explorations Academy in Bellingham, Washington, "Their whole idea is really engagement," Yazzie-Mintz said. "They do active learning, hands-on projects, and they've used HSSSE really to see if they're walking the walk."[3]

Homestead High School of Fort Wayne, IN., has been adjusting its structure with help from a federal "Small Learning Communities" (SLCs) grant. SLCs are often referred to as "schools within schools," establishing more concise groups of student coursework within the structure of a large school. Smaller grouping promotes closer relationships.[2]

Yazzie-Mintz said, "These schools are starting to see that when you engage the students, get them interested and keep them in it, student outcomes—including achievement—will increase."[2] These selected efforts to increase engagement, which is almost synonymous with interest, should ease the difficulties of students with ADHD as well.

The need for people who will listen to their concerns is especially important for children with ADHD. Krystal, now a young mother, remembers the pain of boredom in high school classes and how she could not bear to read long passages, let alone whole books, for assignments even though her reading comprehension was excellent. Especially, she remembers being discouraged from expressing these difficulties to her family. "We all do things we don't like to do" was a frequent response. She was not diagnosed with ADHD until adulthood and still feels the lingering effects of shame for disliking school and anger for not being understood.

Physicians, clinicians, and others in the helping professions can guide children with a diagnosis of ADHD to understand their own needs for stimulation in the form of interest, and they can work with teachers, families, and others to provide common Elements of Interest in schools and other settings.

The "flipping" model of education described in the last chapter was initiated deliberately for the purpose of increasing face-to-face, individual, and personal interaction between students and teachers. By turning class lectures into take-home videos and using class time as "time with the teachers," the connection between students and teacher is significantly increased. One Georgia high school teacher says he did not begin to record his lectures and save class time for interaction so deliberately.

"It was really by accident. Students initiated it," said Willis. "They were asking me, 'Hey, Mr. Willis, can you record some of the lectures that you're doing in class?'" Readers will recognize the value of letting students initiate strategies.[3]

"…I can say for sure student engagement has gone through the roof. And I think student engagement is correlated with student achievement," said Willis.[3]

What does the class do with the class time that has been freed up by sending videos of lectures home?

"On the day we visited Willis' 9th grade Physics and Engineering class, students were reinforcing the concepts they had learned in a recent video, by creating a PowerPoint presentation on it," the reporter said. On other days there may be quizzes on the material.[3]

The use of technology for communication is often thought to have a negative impact on relationships but, in the case of flipping, it frees up time "to build up the kind of relationships that will help them learn. "It's about bringing that human relationship back into the classroom where you're not distancing yourself from the student. You're right there with them," said Willis.[3]

Organizational skills

Disorganization is one of the biggest problems caused by ADHD in school and everyday life. It too is related to boredom. Up till now, parents have largely enforced or provided organization. Mom has said, "I found one of your shoes on the back porch. I put it on your bed. Do you know where the other one is?" Teachers have said, "Bring a big spiral notebook with three sections. The first section is for…"

For teenagers, the shift to taking responsibility for organizing their own life is often difficult. Jeremy, perhaps the most ADHD teenager in the comic strips, was reluctantly listening to his mother explain the new family organization board where everyone could find "reminders, appointments, lists, and general information." Jeremy said, "I thought that was what *you* were for?"[4] The creators of "Zits" know what they are talking about. Parents and teachers try to shift responsibilities for keeping track of things to their teenagers. They tend to resist. Teens with ADHD truly *can't* keep track as well but they can learn strategies.

Order, meaning orderliness, is an Element of Interest. Some have it, some don't. Even in preschool, at clean-up time, some children automatically put the toy cars in the car box, or the crayons with the other crayons. They hold up scissors and ask, "Where does this go?" Order interests them. Other children have no interest in sorting; they sweep everything on the table into one jumble and put it into any empty space.

When a child with ADHD and little interest in order becomes a teen, he still doesn't care about order. Order is boring to him, and he is even less interested in the process of putting things in order. More than other teens, if the ADHDer is not interested in putting things in order, he *cannot* bring himself to do so on a regular basis or for a long period of time, and neither reward nor punishment will make much difference.

Anika is a teenager whose bedroom is a mass of confusion. She says with astounding sincerity, "I don't know why Dad says my room is a pig pen. I think it's *interesting*." Interest is what counts. She does want to be able to find things, and she does like—but doesn't love—a neat room, but she isn't much interested in keeping it that way.

Having a place for everything and putting it there when he's finished with it is a great principle to teach, coach, and counsel an ADHD teen to do. Parents say, "It's just as easy to put it in the proper place as it is to drop it in a chair." For the ADHD teen, it's not. The following is the way it might go.

Jake picks up the list of the names and phone numbers of his basketball team from a kitchen drawer where the family's directories are kept, so he can call someone for a ride to practice. He walks toward his bedroom to find his cell phone. The short, uneventful amble through the familiar dining room, living room, and dimly lit hall offers little stimulation. He allows thoughts to drift through his mind, seeking an object of interest, but none take hold. In the den, he sees his kid brother happily absorbed in watching television. Jake sees him as a potential source of stimulation, but not while he is lying still. Jake picks up a pillow on the sofa and lobs it at his brother's face. "Hey!" his brother yells, and throws the pillow back at him. Jake ducks and the pillow knocks the sheet music off the piano behind him. "See what you did," Jake chuckles, feeling a bit perkier.

That little bit of conflict, an Element of Interest, gets his dopamine going. He remembers he had something he wanted to do. But what? Oh, yes. Get his cell phone. But what's his teammate's number? He had a list. Where is it? It's gone. Disappeared into thin air. His mother's usual query "Where did you last have it?" is incredibly annoying. If he knew where he last had it, he'd know where it was.

His mother is annoyed that her sheet music is scattered on the floor. "Who did this?" she asks. The younger boy doesn't answer but scoops it up and replaces it on the piano. Mother sighs. The next day when she sits down to play the piano, she picks through her sheet music and finds Jake's list of basketball team names and numbers between Brahms' "Lullabye" and "When the Saints Go Marching In."

Jake didn't "forget" that he had laid his team list on the piano when he became distracted by the sight of his brother; he was never aware of laying it down. As his mind leaped to the more stimulating prospect of starting something with his brother, laying the list down was an involuntary, unconscious act of which he had no memory.

Replay this pattern through preparation for school, breakfast, social studies, language arts, lunch, math, culinary skills, and detention, and you will have Jake's day. He learns some stuff, sits next to his girlfriend at lunch, gets a few short pieces of schoolwork done, and enjoys some camaraderie, especially at detention. It's not all bad, but it's not as good as it could be—if he could only manage his ADHD and the necessity for escaping moment-to-moment boredom.

There are skills he can learn and situations to which he can adapt. There is also medication.

ADHD and medication

If your child, student, or patient is diagnosed with ADHD, no matter the age, and you have confidence that it's an accurate diagnosis, consider the benefits of properly dosed medication that is recommended for the child by a physician who specializes in ADHD. ADHD is not just a childhood phenomenon, it's a lifelong state. As we grow and mature, we learn to adapt to some of the symptoms, but that doesn't mean they go away.

Every fall, when a new school year began, Luis's father withheld his son's ADHD medication, to see if the teenager still had ADHD or if he could now manage without medication. After Luis was served with his third detention in the month of September, his father relented and started up the medication again. Had this parent understood that his son would not outgrow the condition at adolescence, he could have saved them both a great deal of grief by letting the boy begin the school year with the help he needed to stay focused. The learning time Luis lost in successive years of this pattern by his father could have a lifelong impact on his education. Those first few weeks of classes are critical to learning new material.

The medication helps Luis focus, but it doesn't tell him what to focus on. He has to establish organizational habits consciously. Keeping a calendar, whether digital or on paper, writing on it as soon as a new appointment is made, and checking the calendar each morning are habits worth developing. Writing down a list of things to do the next day and putting his homework in his backpack the night before a school day are things that can help make the next day more successful. He can't learn these habits all at one time, though. Clinicians, counselors, and teachers can help. ADHD coaching is especially helpful for choosing and developing better habits. For example, a coach might ask a client, what is one thing you do every day without fail? He likely brushes his teeth every day. She asks which organizational habit he wants to establish first, then suggests he write a reminder on a sticky-note and put it on his toothpaste so that he is reminded of the desired action to do it right then before he brushes his teeth. He continues placing reminders until that habit is established, then picks another habit to train. Similarly, putting his backpack on his bed pillow could serve as a reminder to put his homework and other essential materials into the backpack the night before school. At the beginning of each period of work, writing down a list of what must be accomplished during that period should be helpful. Referring to this checklist gets a student on track again when his mind wanders. The coach and student monitor the success of such strategies and adjust accordingly.

Time management

Dr. William Dodson, an expert in adult ADHD, says that in the early years before cell phones were ubiquitous, he used the presence or absence of a watch as part of his assessment for ADHD. Those with ADHD rarely wore watches! They didn't care about time.[5] They focused on something as long as it was interesting and discontinued or put off something that was boring.

Neither is time highly motivating for the teenager with ADHD, and his experience with the passing of time is inconsistent. A boring class seems like forever; an exciting game on the computer that he plans to play for just five minutes may become an hour—it just seems like five minutes.

As a coach, I sometimes help a client with ADHD find her optimum focus time to spend on a certain type of task. Laura, for example, finds writing papers hard to organize and hard to concentrate on, and therefore she gets bored and becomes distracted by more interesting thoughts. She can do math problems rather easily; problem-solving is one of her Elements of Interest. She loves designing and crafting ceramic pieces; hands-on work deeply engages her. She observes that the longest she can focus on writing the paper is 12 minutes. She can do math problems for about 30 minutes without her mind drifting, which is about long enough to finish half of one evening's homework. She can focus—or hyperfocus—on ceramics for an hour and a half or even two hours. Knowing her optimum focus time helps Laura plan. She can schedule her day using focus time as her planning unit. Because writing her paper requires longer than her 12-minute focus time, she may use the "make it new" strategy. Just as preschoolers can put half their toys away for "a rest," and then bring them back later as "new," Laura can put away the writing task after 12 minutes and start something new. The next free period, she returns to the first task, alternating types of work to make each of them new again. Sticking to a task after its focus time has run out is unpleasant and usually unproductive.

I encourage students with time management difficulties to use a digital timer for *everything*. As soon as the alarm for one appointment goes off, set an alarm for the next one. Make it a habit. Or preset all appointments for the day on a cell phone the night before. New applications on cell phones allow amazing flexibility to suit the focus time of any ADHDer, and one app will even count down the time for them in a pleasant voice.[6]

Timing strategies help with procrastination, a major force that holds teens with ADHD back. I asked a high school student what in the past had ever motivated him to start his schoolwork. He said, "Being close to a deadline." Urgency is his Element of Interest. A deadline close at hand was a sort of emergency involving fear that he wouldn't meet the deadline. For some people, especially those with ADHD, fear is experienced as excitement; both trigger arousal chemicals in the brain that are necessary to focus. The sensation is not unpleasant but motivating. This student met most deadlines by a marathon work session right before an assignment was due. Sometimes he couldn't finish and missed some deadlines. He agreed that starting early was a good idea; he just couldn't do it. Not understanding his need for urgency, his parents nagged him earlier and earlier to start on an assignment, making the very thought of doing it harder for him to bear. Moreover, the nagging didn't work.

He and I worked on creating a sense of urgency sooner, using imagination, one of his strong Elements of Interest. He enjoyed acting in school plays; getting into a role was easy for him. Like a director, I asked him to imagine himself in an emergency situation involving the project and to create a dialogue with himself or with an imagined person about what had to be done immediately and to speak this dialogue out loud with dramatic flair. "Hurry, hurry, you have to have an outline by noon. Here's the paper! Here's the pen! Do it before the enemy comes!" Or "The fuse is getting shorter. Write the opening paragraph before the bomb explodes!" Or just, "The curtain is opening, write your opening line before the audience sees you." The monologue didn't have to be clever, just passionate. This high school student also wrote down the real deadline in small letters on his calendar, and he wrote the earlier, imagined deadline in big red letters. He learned to create a surge of excitement for himself whenever he looked at those red letters. He had to do this for each step of a project. He still finished the whole assignment at the last possible minute, but at least timely completion was possible because he'd done some of the work earlier, and he was energized by the final push. Ask students to experiment with techniques to bring Elements of Interest into work that soon becomes boring and report their effectiveness. This is an important way for professionals to learn new techniques to pass on to other students.

Risk-taking and safety

Risk-taking is an Element of Interest for many with ADHD that, like urgency, involves the Element of uncertainty and some degree of fear, enough to be exciting and therefore stimulate the activation of dopamine. Some risk-takers are drawn to physical risk, others to social risks or to both. The challenge is for ADHDers to choose experiences that provide their desired amount of risk-taking without too much actual danger.

In competitive sports, there is obvious physical risk. In contact sports, there's the risk of pain and injury that some teens avoid. Such risk does not deter the kid with ADHD. There's also the social risk of losing or performing badly. Players have to risk losing in order to seek a win; the very thought increases dopamine activation. Experts recommend, however, that children with ADHD participate in sports involving individual performance such as gymnastics, singles tennis, or martial arts, as discussed in Chapter Fourteen, rather than team sports because of attention issues. Individual sports also offer competitive events and coaches, trainers, and officials to provide supervision and increase safety.

Some other kinds of physical activities can give teens with ADHD the feeling of risk without undue danger. Riding on zip lines, for example, provides the speed and experience of being high in the air that excites a person in the same way that danger does, but a strong cable and harness provide safety. Whitewater rafting with an experienced guide and the sport of rock climbing with safety equipment provide the same kind of thrill with managed risk.

Performing on stage, either in live theatre, stand-up comedy or especially improvisation, appeals to ADHDers because, among other reasons, these activities involve social risk. To bomb on stage in front of an audience is embarrassing and a deterrent to many people, but those with ADHD often experience nervousness before performances as a form of excitement that allows them to focus and therefore perform at their best. Performing in improv theatre involves a great deal of additional uncertainty; players can't rehearse their performance but rely on quick, zany response to unexpected stimuli. An interesting description of an improv class with young students illustrates the Element of social risk:

> About midway through the hour, the students played a game called "Museum." In the game there is one museum security guard. The rest of the students play seemingly inanimate "exhibits" in the museum. As the security guard walks through and around the still "exhibits," the students wait for a moment when the security guard is not looking and change positions. If the security guard catches someone moving, then that person is out. Throughout the game, the teacher was encouraging students to take "big risks," to make the most of the moments when they were out of the guard's line of sight by significantly changing their poses. When a student would take a big risk, she would reward them with acknowledgement and praise. The students adopted her attitude. They, too, admired big risks taken by their peers. Positive peer pressure came into effect and the game became increasingly interesting as students got over their fear of being out, hoping to instead be congratulated for taking a big risk.[7]

The "museum game," in which some of the students have to learn to accept more risk in spite of anxiety, comes more easily to those with ADHD because the risk of being caught is often exciting to them, putting them in their comfort zone of stimulation somewhere between boredom and anxiety.

Kids whose Elements of Interest do not include risk or competition usually don't want to engage in a sport but prefer an activity that involves skilled artistry, such as dance, music, photography, or other art forms. Clubs and performances that revolve around these activities provide the Elements of social interaction, reveling in skills, physical activity, and applause.

Organized sports and activities offer many Elements of Interest to teens while managing danger. Finding ones that suit a teen with ADHD is a good way to keep him stimulated but safe. What we don't want for our teens is serious risk-taking and rule-breaking. Dangers accompany unorganized social interaction like large impromptu parties and out-of-town trips without parents or other adults.

Nonconformity and freedom

In one high school robotics course, after studying each set of physical principles and associated calculations, student teams programmed their robots to perform tasks in competition with the other teams' robots. In the first competition, each robotic vehicle had to complete an obstacle course made of a series of two-by-four boards lying in its path. The team that arrived at the end of the course the fastest would be the winner. One such event illustrates the clash between limits and innovation. The programming of robots was done by calculations involving the size of the wheels and the number of rotations necessary to cover the distances between and around the boards. Owen's team modified the wheels, making them giant sized, and then simply drove their robot over the obstacles, arriving at the end in the shortest time. There was no rule saying they couldn't drive over the obstacles, but the teachers did not award Owen's team the win. The students, appreciative of the novel approach, protested that its victory should have stood. The teachers were also appreciative of the clever solution and did not scold Owen's team, but they had to make a judgment call about how much to reward or reinforce out-of-the-box strategies versus how much to discourage "tricks" that might get out of hand.

"We didn't like to do the expected thing," says Owen, a 17-year-old diagnosed with ADHD. Nonconforming thought processes are a hallmark of ADHD, and "thinking outside the box" is a highly valued trait for the entrepreneur, inventor, promoter, and others who seek new products and new ways, but there are always limits. Owen hastened to add, "We were bright and we understood the physics and math. We did the final competition seriously [which was the final exam] to show we could do the work." It seemed a good balance of creativity and limits.

Walking the line between rules and originality, and between regulation and interest, is an art that teachers and parents must practice daily with teens in general and those with ADHD in particular. In many diverse issues like orderliness, noise level, meeting curfews and deadlines, following rules, or dressing appropriately, parents and teachers have to decide how much to bind and how much to bend. Remembering that nonconformity is an Element of Interest that stimulates the ADHD mind may help ease the impatience you may feel when the teen doesn't toe the line. The line was most likely drawn for the purpose of order. The ADHD teen more likely seeks interest on the wilder side of the line.

Reading Shakespeare, a case in point

Students with ADHD, like many without ADHD, often say that reading Shakespeare is high on their list of boring things they have to do in school. What might seem just the right amount of challenge to a drama student seems like drudgery to others because translating it from Elizabethan English is too slow and too hard. Reading Shakespeare is devoid of other Elements of Interest necessary for engaging the ADHD mind. Relevance to their lives and purpose is not readily apparent.

In commiserating with students who find Shakespeare tedious, I suggest a solution: Allow the students to read the selected play all the way through in modern English first. Entire Shakespearean plays translated into modern English, side by side with the original, are available on nfs.sparknotes.com, among other sources. The quicker run-through facilitated by the modern reading allows students to do a detailed study of the original play after they've grasped the whole. If they don't understand the whole, they are going to hate, hate, hate the details of the reading in the Bard's own eloquent words. This goes double for students with ADHD.

Alternatively or in addition, show a film that represents the original story accurately. It may take a week to show all the acts in class, but if it's worth studying, it's worth the time required. Better still, if a play is currently being produced at a local theatre, college, or high school, arrange for the students to go to a free dress rehearsal or low-cost preview. Finally, allow time for the students to act out the most exciting or famous scenes in class. Going through the scenes in character, physically acting, not only brings additional Elements of Interest into the study of the Bard, but the performance of these plays harks back to the original form and purpose of theatre. Shakespeare was never meant to be read but to be performed, seen, and heard on stage. When modern students are allowed to take the same steps that Shakespearean actors, like modern actors, probably took at the Globe Theatre—from quick run-through, to close study, to performing—they are being truer to the process of Elizabethan theatre than the snail-paced readings that often pass for studying Shakespeare today.

Planning for life after high school

Some students are planning on following in particular career paths or getting jobs where people they know have gone before; others are counting on waiting till they graduate to look around at what is available for the next step. Some students are drawn early to think of going to a college or university where their friends are going, where the sports teams are their favorites, or where their parents went and hope they will go in turn. However, a student with ADHD would do well to consider a range of options well in advance of graduation.

In their next-to-last year of high school, students with ADHD need to think about choosing appropriate fields in the job market or post-high school education. The junior year is a good time for them to be working with school counselors or educational consultants to explore colleges, vocational studies, and other options to see which is the best fit.

The college option

Typical university-level teaching practices vary from country to country. In some, university classes are "teacher oriented," consisting of long lectures with little interaction between teachers and students. Also large quantities of reading are assigned from which test questions will be drawn with little instruction about what might be expected on the exam. Few instructors in these countries are expected to acknowledge the individual needs of students. In other countries, interaction with students is common and considered a hallmark of good teaching. Study guides and practice sheets may be distributed to students, and instructions for papers are specific. Professors may be knowledgeable about ADHD and willing to adapt their teaching to accommodate different learning styles.

Colleges and universities in some countries are required by law to offer accommodations and provide resources for students with ADHD and learning disabilities. For example, in the United States all colleges and universities that receive any federal funding must provide "reasonable accommodations" for students with ADHD.[8] Interpretation and implementation of this law varies, and information about accommodations and resources are best gleaned program by program. One source of information on U.S. colleges is *The K&W Guide to College Programs & Services for Students with Learning Disabilities or Attention Deficit/Hyperactivity Disorder*, which is in its eleventh edition.[9] Under the Equality Act 2010,[10] universities in the United Kingdom provide resources and accommodations for students with disabilities including ADHD.[11]

Even in countries where accommodations and resources are required for the learning disabled, these may not be widely available in practice, and ADHD in particular may not be considered a disability. "There's been a great deal of resistance to even believing there is a disease," said Mary Baker, president of the European Brain Council, a Brussels-based non-profit organization representing doctors, patients, and companies that work on neurology and psychiatry issues.[12] Conversely, those who do consider it a disability may conclude that any student with ADHD, though gifted, is simply not university material. Acknowledgement of ADHD as a disability deserving treatment and accommodation may become more widespread in 2015, when the World Health Organization's International Classification of Diseases is revised.[12]

In addition to providing available information about university services for students with ADHD, high school counselors and educational consultants can advise students to visit prospective colleges and talk, by appointment, to the admissions office as well as the student support center, learning center, or student disability support center. It is also helpful to talk to instructors in specific fields of study. Students with ADHD who have recently attended colleges are an excellent source of information about which schools, professors, or major programs are most receptive to working with students with special needs. Gathering information about resources, accommodations, and application processes for these services at a variety of colleges and programs can be a part of the school counselor's or educational consultant's guidance for students.

A comprehensive article from help4adhd.org on choosing a college and obtaining help includes a list of 14 questions counselors, parents, or students themselves may ask student disability support staff. For example:

> "Is there a ADHD–LD specialist on the staff of student disability services?"
>
> "Do members of your staff actively advocate for students with ADHD when they encounter resistance to accommodations from a faculty member?"
>
> "Has there been an organized program to educate faculty members about supporting students with ADHD and LD?"[13]

High school advisors on college entrance and medical and educational consultants should be informed and willing to guide high school students through the process of gathering supportive documents including a recent psycho-educational assessment, a medical history, and a list of previously provided accommodations that may be required to receive accommodations and services in college. This guidance will include help in applying for accommodations for college entrance examinations.

In general, encourage a student with ADHD to consider small colleges with small classes and professors whose job is teaching, not doing research. The small college greatly improves the chances a student with ADHD will forge a relationship with professors and will experience some hands-on, interactive teaching, discussions that add meaning and purpose to the learning, and more of his Elements of Interest. Large lecture halls with PowerPoint presentations likely hold the attention of an ADHDer for about ten minutes, and in a large freshman course, no one will notice that he sleeps through the rest.

Also the huge university with hundreds of students in core courses often gives tests with multiple choice, matching, and other little puzzles whose answers are easy to grade by the hundreds. If a student with ADHD happens to be good at converting material learned through reading and lecture into this kind of test, he will be at an advantage there. If he can explain what's important about an issue or process but gets distracted while coming up with answers to questions in that format, he will be at a disadvantage.

On a big campus a student may find some classes so boring that she just doesn't go. Not attending classes is a big cause of failure in college. In a small school, the professor will more likely know the student and, when they meet in the hallway on the way to lunch, the professor may say, "We missed you in class today." The personal attention encourages attendance and performance.

Where colleges with programs to support ADHD are not available, it's especially wise to recommend smaller colleges where there is an emphasis on teaching rather than research and where class size is smaller. While a mentor, advocate, or very accommodating professor may be found anywhere, these are more likely to be found in undergraduate colleges without graduate schools. Professors whose teaching satisfies an ADHDer's Elements of Interest are known by reputation as great teachers or interesting teachers the world over. Educational advisors in high schools can try to identify the teaching colleges that seek this kind of instructor.

When possible, hiring outside coaches and tutors is also beneficial, especially those trained specifically in ADHD. Coaches often work by phone or Skype with clients all over the world. While the ADHD Coaches Organization (ACO) promotes ADHD coaching worldwide,[14] and ADD is listed as a specialty under Personal Coaching in the International Coach Federation (ICF) directories by country and language,[15] most countries do not have an ADHD coach listed. However, with modern technology, coaching can be done between countries when language skills allow. Consider also the Edge Foundation, which connects high school and college students with Edge-trained ADHD coaches.[16]

Parents, coaches, teachers, and other professionals should also prepare students for self-advocacy. Help them develop the same kind of professional documentation they would need to attend a university with an accommodations program for ADHD. As part of a "self-advocacy kit," provide handouts about ADHD and special needs and special recommendations for students that they can offer admissions staff and judge their prospects by the responsiveness they receive.

Even when universities have special services for students with ADHD, students will often have to be their own advocates. One student attended a large university which offered ADHD accommodations and was given extra time for taking tests. In his first year of study, he had trouble taking accurate notes from lectures accompanied by PowerPoint displays. He failed the first test in one class because there were mistakes in the notes he'd taken and studied diligently. He then asked the professor to give him a copy of the PowerPoint file as a guide to organizing his notes. Before he had a chance to ask the support center for note taking services, the professor gave him not only the PowerPoint file, but also a complete set of his accompanying class notes. All it took was asking, but he had to ask. In some universities, class outlines and other guides are posted on-line for all students.

Two American students with ADHD, whose international exchange experiences were shared with Mobility International USA (MIUSA), reported finding their stay in other countries—one in Eastern Europe and one in Asia—to be valuable experiences. However, the classes in the countries they visited were difficult, and professors were not familiar with ADHD or accommodations for the condition. One student said, "I talked with professors and told them, 'I'm struggling with this…' I kept them informed and they were more willing to work with me and give me tips on how to deal with studying differently."[17] Meeting individually with professors during their scheduled office hours often works best in any country.

Institutions of post-secondary learning that specialize in certain areas best suited for ADHDers include schools for culinary arts, music and art institutes, or computer skills programs; studies in these areas are hands-on and multi-sensory, satisfying these common ADHD Elements of Interest, and some involve performance, applause, and other Elements. Students with ADHD may also seek colleges and universities that have successful experience with "bundling" academic and non-academic courses along with resources that prepare them for success in the workforce.

When college isn't a goal

Not every high school student is interested in traditional college. His Elements of Interest suggest a different kind of stimulation. If a student is in that group, help him explore other options. Many community colleges and vocational schools can help a high school graduate develop specific, job-related skills needed in industries like healthcare, the computer industry, and many other areas of employment. Young people who receive this kind of training are critical to our economic system. Apprenticeships can prepare aspiring plumbers, electricians, and carpenters for pursuing valuable hands-on skilled work at good wages. Moreover, Elements of Interest offered by vocations requiring training different from a college education can be critical to the activation of an ADHDer's dopamine. Mechanics get the stimulation of problem-solving and working hands-on. Chefs doing hands-on food preparation enjoy the rapid pace of making meals on demand and the artistry of creating sensory appeal with food. Firefighters and other first responders are excited by the rush of an emergency; physical action and urgency are a firefighter's Elements of Interest. There are a whole host of technical jobs where students who don't have the interest or focus to pursue a traditional degree can find satisfaction and full employment. Freelance work is good for skilled ADHDers, who can do one time-limited project after another, each one new and different and often with different people. Sales jobs provide challenge, uncertainty, risk, skill, and social interaction where the ADHDer can display his winning personality. Selecting the right path to employable skills will have a tremendous impact on a young person's ability to cope with and take charge of his ADHD.

Quick points

Be flexible: One high school allowed a student with ADHD to take Art History to fulfill her history requirement; Art History was normally considered as an art course. In the class, the teacher showed slides of paintings and architecture and related these to historical issues and events.

Add Elements of Interest to assignments: One high school teacher, instead of just requiring students to learn the elements of the periodic table, required pairs of students to compose a jingle or rhymed list containing all the information and recite it to the class. The students became extremely familiar with the elements doing this more creative task, which included rhythm, novelty, social interaction, and more Elements of Interest.

Do it from scratch: Students have calculators to do any kind of math now, but understanding underlying principles can be enhanced by going back to the old-fashioned way. For example, teach students how to make a slide rule out of paper, using a ruler and a table of logarithms. This task fixes the mathematical basis in their minds by adding hands-on and multi-sensory Elements.

Start early planning for college, vocational training, or job search: The year before the final year of high school is ideal for those with ADHD and their advisors to find appropriate placement compatible with students' special needs.

Help students put together an "advocacy kit": Consider including a one-page explanation of ADHD, professional recommendations for accommodations, references to laws relevant to disabilities in school and job opportunities, and a personal essay about the student's difficulties, accommodations, and success.

CHAPTER SIXTEEN

Adulthood

In the years after high school, many people with ADHD will find jobs or do military service; many will go on to further training or seek university degrees—either with career goals or with little idea where they are headed. Many will not know they have ADHD, and their lack of that knowledge will keep them from seeking treatment and from understanding what Elements they need to keep in their lives. They will often end up bored in their jobs.

Learn more

Younger workers without specialized training may be working in low-paying jobs, hoping to work up to better jobs. They may be capable of a great deal more challenge and skill than they are using in such jobs, but they may not yet have that skill or proven that they can accept more challenge. They are learning.

While some people would prefer to stick with what they know well already, for many learning is an important Element of Interest. They perk up when they hear they are about to learn something new. Learning means encountering and integrating new knowledge, new skills, and new experience into the old and familiar. Novelty is a basic Element of Interest for someone with ADHD; novelty or newness is the basis for Elements like variety, the unexpected, surprise, and learning. Learning also involves challenge. If a person in a low-paying job takes learning challenges to heart, learns quickly, uses his new skills, and gives a little extra effort, he often comes to the attention of a supervisor and wins an early promotion to a higher-paying job, where he can again repeat the cycle of newness and challenge that learning a new job offers.

Collier works for a grocery store where he bags groceries, probably the lowest-paying customer service duty in the store. The 18-year-old may not think bagging groceries is a particularly interesting job, but he says, "I enjoy it better than most of the jobs in the store."[1] He is not bored because he has found ways to put Elements of Interest into his bagging duty. First, he took his training seriously. Bagging is a hands-on job involving learning new things to which he has added speed, problem-solving, competition, mastery, reveling in his skills, and even applause. Despite the job's repetitiousness, "It takes a lot of finesse to know what goes in the right place at the right time," he says. "It starts with technique. Then there's weight distribution. Then speed." He details principles like not putting glass next to glass, separating cold items from not-cold items, cushioning crushable things, and balancing the weight evenly among bags. "It's better to be slow and have great technique," Collier says, although speed is his forte.[1]

Perhaps he enjoyed a little friendly competition with other baggers in his store. The grocery store chain promoted that Element of Interest by sponsoring a statewide grocery-bagging contest. Competition was stiff: The top finishers got the job done within seconds of each other, Collier says, while satisfying bagging requirements such as the weight of the bags that had "to be within a half ounce of each other." Collier won third prize and a small amount of money he's saving for college,[1] where he will no doubt go on to use that same diligence in learning challenging subjects. If he wants a summer job at the grocery store, I doubt the store manager will offer him the bagging job again just because he's the best bagger; I'm betting he will be offered a higher-level job because he has proven he learns new skills well and strives to perfect them. Having the mindset of making tasks interesting by learning more and doing more than the minimum necessary is stimulating; it makes the dopamine get up with us in the morning.

Whether president of a company or floor scrubber, what makes a task or job interesting is often the right amount of challenge, a common Element of Interest. Evelyn's job was unchallenging and therefore boring. But she couldn't get a more interesting job unless she could read better, and learning to read had never been interesting; it was too hard for her and too slow-going for a story to catch her interest.

Evelyn's steady job at a hospital cleaning operating rooms after surgeries included one of her Elements of Interest—it was hands-on work—but few others. She longed to increase her challenge and skill level and to interact with people by taking their vital signs and drawing blood. She was confident she could do the desired job well; she had watched others do the procedures and had handled the instruments. The job required reading and writing down names and numbers, the kind of reading she could do. What she couldn't do was read the questions on the written test necessary to qualify for the job. So she set out to learn to read better at a literacy program where I volunteered.

After working with Evelyn on phonics for a few weeks, it was clear to me that she had a specific learning disability. Learning disabilities frequently accompany ADHD. Hers was not a disability in reading comprehension but in a specific word-processing area. She had zero ability to sound out a word from its spelling, even to know what letter a word might begin with from its sound.

Evelyn could not overcome the specific learning disability from which she suffered, but she could increase her recognition of words, which was her strength. She had an excellent memory for sight words that were useful for her, like street signs and labels. But she did not recognize enough words to spend much time reading. The way to best learn more words is to read more words, but Evelyn read so poorly and so slowly that she and I were both bored.

As a volunteer tutor, I was instructed to use several different materials, exercises, and avenues of reading instruction in each session, but I soon gave up on the avenue where she was completely blocked and the booklets written for her beginning reading level. Instead I offered her more of the experience she lacked—reading for interest. I brought her adult books I chose for interest and a personal and conversational style, memoirs primarily, often bestsellers. I read these aloud to her at a normal speed while she followed along word by word and line by line. Just as I'd done with children and you probably have, too, I began to stop midsentence and let her fill in the next word or phrase, using her word recognition and the context. I was entirely amazed at how she could follow and enjoy this kind of reading.

I started bringing Evelyn newspaper articles on topics that might interest her because of their relevance to her life. Relevance is a common Element of Interest. One day I brought her a news item about the death of our zoo's most beloved primate, a gorilla named Willie B., whom she had visited several times as a child. The aging gorilla had died of pneumonia. I didn't bother asking her to sound the word "pneumonia" out because she had no ability in phonics and because of that pesky initial *p*; I simply told her the word; she was already familiar with the disease. Several weeks later she was reading aloud to the literacy program supervisor from a book he had brought when she came to the word "pneumonia." I could see it coming and held my breath. She read the word as if child's play. The fact that it begins with a *p* but has the sound of an *n* was irrelevant to her as a pure sight reader. The supervisor asked Evelyn how she had been able to read that difficult word. She said, "I saw it in a newspaper article about Willie B.'s death." At that moment I knew that Evelyn was ready to read the kinds of words and questions on the test for the job she wanted at the hospital. I knew, not because pneumonia is a health-related word, but because she remembered it and could read it in a different context. Learning to read for the test involved a strong Element of purpose, and for that purpose Evelyn had been able to learn the question words like *who, what, where, when, and which one* and the names of the instruments and procedures to pass the written test for the higher-level job she wanted.

I recommend that anyone bored with a chore do more, not less, by exploring a new technique, a new aspect, or new facts about that activity to renew interest. Becoming an expert in something, whether it's bagging groceries, reading, or watching grass grow, brings in many Elements of Interest.

Yes, watching grass grow.

Know more: Watching grass grow

"More boring than watching grass grow" is a phrase people sometimes use to describe the most tedious passage of time. But a woman in Lincolnshire, England, is paid to do just that and she finds it fascinating. At the beginning of a typical day, Helen Southall counts out 400 grass seeds and checks their growth every week. She inspects blades of grass on lawns and fields to see that they are growing to the right height. Her days are filled with grass and more grass. Most of us would tire of grass in less than an hour and a half—nine minutes if we have ADHD. That's because most of us don't know a lot about how many kinds of grass there are, which grass is best for what purpose, how fast grass is supposed to grow (five centimeters in 14 days is good, Mrs. Southall says), and why it doesn't sometimes do what it's supposed to do.[2] The more we know about a subject, the more interesting it becomes. The grass seed analyst for British Seed Houses can tell you why she loves her job, and in doing so, she names her Elements of Interest, which are much the same as most people with ADHD. There are many different species of grass grown for many different purposes. Weather varies, from season to season and year to year, creating different problems, and she's a problem-solver. "It's always fascinating when you find a new seed type." She loves the "challenges involved in creating golfing greens and well-seeded sports pitches." Reveling in her skill, she says, "It's so rewarding seeing a stretch of perfect green grass and knowing that it has grown right because of my work."[2] There's change, variety, something new, purpose, problem-solving, challenge, and pride in her skill. Besides all that, she likes to spend her days outdoors.

The message for ADHDers, of course, is not that they should become grass analysts, but that they might consider learning all they can about the work they do in order to find it more interesting. They can pick an aspect of their job that they are not necessarily required to learn and become an expert in it. The interest generated by increasing knowledge is what makes people spend an hour on the Internet that they didn't intend to spend—ADHDers know this pattern well. They have searched for a single fact and found it, but, seeing there was more to learn, they followed a trail of links learning more and more beyond what they originally wanted to know. The more you know about a subject, the more interesting it can be.

Notice the difference in the interest levels of people watching a football game. The ones who know a lot about the game are exclaiming about a move well done or complaining about an opportunity missed, while the ones who don't know the game lose interest or, expecting to be bored, come only to see the fourth quarter and eat the peanuts.

How serious is boredom anyway?

"You Really *Can* Be Bored to Death" began a headline reporting a study of more than 7500 government workers in the United Kingdom who were monitored for 25 years. At the end of the study it was found that those who had earlier reported being the most bored were 40 percent more likely to have died.[3]

In 2009 Annie Britton and Martin J. Shipley, researchers at the Department of Epidemiology and Public Health at University College London, wrote, "In a rare moment of idleness one day, we pondered whether the expression 'bored to death' has any basis. Are people who are bored more likely to die earlier than those who are not?"[4]

Participants aged 35–55 who self-reported boredom during the previous four weeks as "not at all," "a little," "quite a lot," or "all the time" were given the same test three years later, and then after 25 years their death rates were compared.[4]

"We also found that those with a great deal of boredom were more likely to die during follow-up than those not bored at all." In particular they died of cardiovascular disease (CVD), even though those known to have CVD at the outset were excluded from the study. "However, the state of boredom is almost certainly a proxy for other risk factors."[4]

Part of the reason for the earlier death of those who were bored may have been that they turned to unhealthy habits like smoking, drinking alcohol, and snacking on unhealthy foods, in which case it was not boredom that killed, but the harmful attempts to escape boredom.

Proxy or not, boredom is stress and, one way or another, stress kills.

Government work, by its very nature, may lack some Elements of Interest that are characteristic of people with ADHD and that are more abundantly available in the private sector, notably entrepreneurship. The profit motive itself may involve, for example, more risk-taking and competition than government jobs usually offer. Were the bored workers in the British study in the wrong environment? Were they not able to seek their Elements of Interest? Or do they not know what these Elements are?

The stress of boredom, however, is hardly limited to British government workers. In an article from the United Kingdom titled "Poll: Bored at Work? Don't Worry, So is Half of America," some findings taken from a 2013 Gallup poll showed that 52 per cent of US employees were "not engaged" by their work and were just "going through the motions."[5] An additional 18 percent were "actively disengaged"—so unhappy in their jobs that they went out of their way to undermine morale. Only 30 percent of employees said they were regularly engaged or inspired by their jobs. These employees had fewer accidents and incurred less healthcare costs than the least engaged while turning out more problem-free products.[6]

The authors of the book *Boreout!* describe the progression of boredom on the job and the compounding of boredom by the unproductive strategies workers use to avoid it—mostly, they do less and less of the boring work and their increasing idleness basically makes them even more bored; sometimes they instigate drama or engage in other behaviors harmful to the company to give themselves some stimulation. "When employees are understretched, unmotivated and immeasurably bored, and then actively try—paradoxically—to maintain this condition, they are clearly suffering from boreout," Rothlin and Werder say.[7] They conclude, "We maintain that most employees want to develop and to put their abilities to the test. And they want challenging work that gives them meaning. To get that, they are also willing to put in more effort."[8] That goes double for workers with ADHD for whom boredom on the job is especially intolerable.

Freedom on the job

This brings up the issue of freedom, which is always a factor in resolving boredom. If employees are not given freedom to make things less boring, they will more likely express their boredom in the quality of their work. Boredom-prone workers would do well to factor company culture into their job selection.

Some jobs have by their very nature more freedom to incorporate Elements of Interest. Sales jobs are often good choices for ADHDers because salesmen often have a lot of freedom to express their style as long as they make sales. Also, one "No" response sends an ADHDer to a new situation, a new potential client, a new challenge, a new problem to solve for a client, a more creative approach, and the freedom to go at a speed and with a flair that is satisfying.

A lot of people with ADHD opt to become entrepreneurs because it involves risk, challenge, and freedom. One entrepreneur I coached had started a successful wholesale business in novelties. What product could be more appropriate for his ADHD! He traveled the world looking for appealing new goods to sell. He had brought other Elements of Interest into the business as well. He had his office in a long warehouse, which he managed by walking up and down the length of it many times a day, talking to people, and checking on things. This management style has been called "management by walking around," a perfect style for an ADHDer, involving the Elements of Interest of physical action, social interaction, and variety. This entrepreneur was in constant motion, which gave an outlet for his hyperactivity. This business was not his first enterprise nor his last; like most entrepreneurs, he started a series of businesses. Some succeeded and some failed, but the important thing was that he wasn't stuck in an unchanging situation. He turned over the boring parts of one business to someone who found it more rewarding and went on to design something new. The freedom to design work around the entrepreneur's own Elements is a key facet of entrepreneurship.

Freelance work similarly affords a person with ADHD a lot of freedom to design her life. She can take short projects with the Element of time limit and the knowledge she can soon start on something new. "Making it new" is a chief strategy for avoiding the boredom inherent in ADHD.

Personal life

The workplace is not the only environment in which people with ADHD must fight boredom. People with ADHD must be proactive in bringing Elements of Interest into their home and social lives on a regular, even daily, basis. A heartwarming account of a family doing just that is told in a *Parade Magazine* article titled "Dinner with the Smileys."[9] This family does not, to my knowledge, have members with ADHD but was experiencing a loss they needed to face by seeking new sources of interest.

Sarah Smiley and her three boys were seeing the boys' father off for a year-long deployment overseas with sadness. When one boy said to his father, "It will be weird not to have you at the table," Sarah said, "Then let's fill Dad's seat. We'll invite people over for dinner. Shoot, we can invite someone every week if you want." She remembers that she said it reflexively, not thinking it through. "I'm not a cook. I hate small talk," she says. The boys, however, took her idea and ran with it. One wanted to invite his teachers, and the youngest, not yet in school, asked, "Can we invite the President? Or the Mayor?" The result was a dinner guest every week ranging as far as the boys' imagination could go, from a U.S. Senator from their state of Maine to the local weatherman. Their guest list included a zookeeper, a symphony conductor, and a baseball historian, and a principal who had lost her son in an army helicopter crash. The days went by, and "we filled them with interesting people and role models," Sarah says. When Dad came home, 60 of the guests from their 52 dinners came to the airport with the family to welcome him home.[9] The year of interesting people took boldness and imagination, and resulted in enrichment of the lives of the Smileys and, I feel confident, of their guests. What it took was willingness to issue invitations and be prepared for turndowns. It took curiosity; it provided Elements of Interest, including uncertainty, surprise, learning, a bit of nonconformity, some altruism, and, of course, social interaction, with an Element of applause along the way.

As with all examples of interest-seeking in this book, I'm not suggesting people in the helping professions should urge clients to replicate this feat of hospitality, but that they should encourage them to be imaginative and proactive in engaging their Elements of Interest. When a patient or client is hampered by boredom, encourage them to "Escape It or Shape It." You might begin a brainstorming session with the question, "What could you do to shape the feeling of emptiness or boredom into a satisfying experience?"

Midlife: Do what your Elements of Interest crave

Whatever course young people with ADHD may pursue, there is a good chance they will change course—change schools, jobs, and activities—from time to time throughout the years just as many of those without ADHD do. Resetting a course is a product of learning.

"Typically, you tolerate a mismatch for a short period of time in your early jobs while you are learning the ropes," says human resources professional Emory Mulling, author of *The Mulling Factor*. "A consciously chosen, temporary mismatch for a good reason is altogether different from misemployment that you haven't identified, can't control, and have no hope of leaving."[10]

As an illustration of someone who almost stayed in such a mismatch, here is the story of a man named Mike whose ADHD was not diagnosed until midlife. He took a series of different hands-on jobs from working in the engine room of a Great Lakes tanker to laying bricks. He attended college, but without diagnosis and treatment was not able to earn a degree, in spite of intellectual brilliance and willingness to work. He learned a lot on his own and from the many business courses he took. He worked at jobs where he continued to learn while providing value to his employer.

Mike's Elements of Interest, like those of many with ADHD, included newness, that is, starting something new, problem solving, speed, challenge, and—as the nuns who had been his school teachers could attest—rule-breaking and an aversion to authority. He also needed a relatively short time limit on projects, and a promise of a change when a project was done, so that he could begin something new.

After a series of very different jobs, Mike became a corporate accountant and was soon excruciatingly bored by the repetitiveness of the work, which he had long ago mastered. Every month, his tasks were the same, only the numbers were different. There was no variety, no challenge, no creativity, no risk-taking, no rule-breaking, no novelty, and no problem-solving, none of Mike's Elements of Interest. Then one day his company was threatened with closure by the State of California because his branch office employed safety methods for its workers that differed from the safety standards followed by competitors and other branches of the same company. The issue had to be tackled immediately or hundreds of people would lose their jobs. Nobody in the branch wanted to take on the fight. Nobody but Mike.

Mike says he was "uniquely unqualified" to tackle this job, but, in fact, his ADHD made him uniquely qualified for the job, and he lobbied for it. "I had to take it," he says, meaning he desperately needed the freedom, the challenge, the problem to solve, the new ground to plow, and the sole responsibility for the project so he wouldn't have to negotiate every decision with anyone. Mike had neither the resume nor the experience for the job, but nobody else in the company did either and Mike was convincing. He was given the project, which everyone expected would fail, and he began working on it 20 hours a week, in addition to his regular full-time job, for the six weeks until the case went to court. He was energized by the challenge, the risk, the freedom to do the project on his own, and the urgency of a deadline.

"Sure, I was worried about it," Mike says, "but I had confidence because I had done a series of jobs for which I was unqualified and inexperienced and I succeeded at them. That's how I got where I was. I was eager for this one."

The lawyer who would draw up the brief was not experienced in the content of this case. Mike told him, "You don't have to worry. I know the law and I believe that the innovative safety measures we use are actually better than the ones the rest of the world uses. I can demonstrate that." While the lawyer was expected to put the content into the proper legal format, Mike had taken several college courses in business law so he followed a format he'd learned to organize the material. The attorney declared the brief perfect and signed off on it without change. Mike pled the case himself and won. He named this victory as one of his Top 10 Joys. He got no monetary bonus for this grand effort, and the lawyer—the attorney of record—while warmly acknowledging Mike's work, got the credit. Mike never regretted the slight. His effort was never about the money or the credit; it was about fulfilling his Elements of Interest. For six weeks, he had freedom from boredom. He recognized it as his great escape.

Learning from that experience, Mike began to shape his career to one where he could analyze problems and design solutions. He became a software developer where every project was challenging, each presented a different problem and often a new client, and each had to be completed in a limited time, which meant he could soon begin work on a new problem, perhaps for a new client. By knowing what he needed, Mike recognized the opportunities when they arose and went after them. Knowing that each project had a specific plan and a well-defined end-point relieved him of the frustration he'd faced as a corporate accountant. He escaped boredom and satisfied his individual Elements of Interest. Had he recognized these Elements earlier in his life, he says, he would have been able to take a more efficient course to satisfaction.

Some people, unlike Mike, find their calling early and then allow themselves to be promoted out of it. Educators whose main Element of Interest is the teaching process often do such a great job that they are promoted to principal, a job where they are involved in the profession of education, but they are no longer teaching! They are managing! A highly motivated teacher may not only be a terrible manager but be bored stiff with the administrative duties. She may not only miss the teaching process but the social interaction with students and the intense engagement or "performance" that keeps a teacher "on" all day. Similarly, the people well suited for making commercial loans thrive on making the deal. The manager of the commercial loan department doesn't necessarily make deals but manages the overall finances and loan management of the department. These jobs in the same industry offer different Elements of Interest. It is more important for a promotion to promise a way to satisfy these Elements than to offer more money.

In later years

Planning ahead for retirement involves financial issues and lifestyle decisions. Professionals can help clients in their later years to factor their Elements of Interest into their lives as finances, activities, and lifestyles change. Now is a good time to revisit with them their sources of Elements of Interest. New experiences may now find a place on the list of their Top 10 Joys described in Chapter Four; make it a Top 20 Joys to reflect the longer and more recent span of years. Restrictions such as poor health and financial need may determine whether these joyful experiences can be recreated, but in any case the Elements of Interest in those experiences remain. The new question is: How can we bring those Elements into life today at this age?

Freedom is the great benefit of retirement. What is it about a career path that has prevented ADHDers from shaping their lives to suit their special needs for novelty, action, risk, problem-solving, and all the other Elements especially desired by those with ADHD? These restrictions will be gone. What changes in lifestyle will we make to suit our lifelong need for stimulation? Those who needed physical action and hands-on activities to get their dopamine going but were stuck in a desk job for 50 years can now putter around their homes to their heart's content, fixing things, planting new plants, or starting new hands-on and active projects. If they don't need to fix, plant, or start new projects, they can do these things as volunteers for those who do need things fixed or planted. If we don't finish our projects in retirement, there's no one to fire us or dock our pay. We can pursue our Element of accomplishment at our own rate and only for as long as we want. Those who have longed to get away to explore new things for weeks at a time but couldn't now have the leisure to do so. Changing locations brings novelty and the new beginnings ADHD continually seeks. Now is the time to make a "bucket list" of things to do in our years of freedom from formal employment.

Those facing more stringent budgets in retirement can try adding to the exercise of Childhood Pastimes (described in Chapter Five) a new exercise in which retirees remember what they did for interest and pleasure when they were very young on starting salaries and relatively unencumbered. The subsequent quest for their own homes, financial security, and perhaps the arrival of children and the pleasures that come with these pursuits may obliterate the pleasant memories of free or low-cost pursuits in their youth. Some can recall the walks in the park, the free public concerts, or the picnics anywhere the scenery is different from home. Remember the days we started a fire in the grill and spontaneously (impulsively!) called up young friends to come over and bring their own meat to cook beside ours because nobody we knew could afford to provide extra for guests? A potluck dinner with a circle of friends—planned weekly or on the spur of the moment—can bring that camaraderie back when money may be shorter but the need for social life is equally important. Senior travel groups like Elderhostel International now offer travel on a budget just as backpacking and hostel stays used to do for kids in their footloose youth. We can't be young again, but we can be freer to be ourselves and less critical of our ADHD ways.

Health concerns like loss of mobility, vision, or hearing may increasingly restrict the pursuit of Elements of Interest, but recalling these Elements helps plan new or modified interests. I remember a woman who always wanted to write. She'd written poetry in her youth, but later when she was working and raising a family she didn't have time to write. In her later years she had plenty of time. She wrote longer pieces then, a memoir, stories about funny things that had happened to her, and reflections on lessons learned. She shared the memoir and funny stories with her children and grandchildren. A few she told to her grandchild's class as history! She shared her lessons learned at programs at her church. When in the hospital, she recited her poems to the staff and volunteers, and some of her poems were published in the hospital newsletter. When her arthritic hands and vision made writing too difficult, she recorded thoughts on a digital recorder her children provided.

Technology makes a lot of activities possible for those with disabilities. Professionals in fields such as occupational therapy can help the pre-digital generation accept and use new technology. Besides advancements in vision correction and hearing aids, captioning on television allows the hearing impaired to watch movies they didn't have time to see before, and increasingly common captioning devices in movie theaters makes watching new movies enjoyable. Technology facilitates reconnecting with family and friends who might have been allowed to drift out of our lives; we can use a phone or keyboard to get in touch. Many a friendship and sometimes a romance has been rekindled by taking the initiative to seek out a voice from the past.

In our later years, many aspects of life become different from earlier years, but the Elements of Interest remain the same. New or modified expressions of the Elements remain to be discovered at any age.

Quick points

Boredom is stress: Escape It or Shape It. It's not healthy. Don't try to endure it.

Learn more, do more: Learning less and doing less because something is boring makes it more boring. Add an Element of Interest. Become an expert.

Seek ADHD-friendly jobs: Sales, first responders, emergency work, physically active work, freelance jobs, work where people come to you face to face, work where you go to different people in different places, and work that offers you your Elements of Interest.

Become an entrepreneur: Start small and risk, but not too much. Hire out the impossibly boring jobs. This is not an uncommon story: a college student opens a sandwich or ice cream stand in a rented stall; he enlarges the menu; he sets out a table and a few chairs; he rents a restaurant space; he moves to a larger place; and then he turns that business over to someone else before it gets boring and starts another restaurant or business.

Seek interest in your personal life: Interest is not just for work or education. Intentionally bring Elements of Interest into your free time.

Don't accept a promotion out of an interesting job: Taking a boring job for more money is not worth it. If you must have more money, seek one that offers your Elements of Interest.

Change something: Changing jobs often used to be a negative sign, but not any more. Don't be afraid to change a job for more interest. If that's not practical, put your desk on the other side of the room. Get a new hairstyle. Move. Surprise yourself.

Imagine: Pretend what you are doing is something else more interesting or imagine that you are doing it for a different, more desirable reason.

Solve a problem: Pick something that's been bothering you and schedule a time to solve it. Make a plan with a time limit and a sense of urgency. List the benefits. Ask for help from a friend or hire a coach. Find someone to be accountable to. Make it an event to begin and end instead of a long-term nagging condition. Repeat whenever life gets boring.

Redo the Top 10 Joys exercise every few years: Especially at retirement age, renew your pursuit of your Elements of Interest in new ways.

CHAPTER SEVENTEEN

Conclusion

ADHD appears to be largely a condition of lower-than-normal activation of dopamine in the brain, and boredom is its psychological correlate. That is why stimulants are often prescribed to increase the ability to focus on a chosen task, topic, or activity. The word *chosen* is important. With no other obligation, people with ADHD will choose what is most interesting at the moment; indeed, the same may be said for all of us. The ability to *choose* what is of immediate or long-term necessity or benefit *instead of* what is most interesting has to be learned. It is not provided in the medication. The skill of knowing what to choose as an object of focus will be learned only when focusing on that choice is actually possible.

An infant focuses on what is interesting; satisfying basic drives for survival are its only interests at birth, but almost immediately after those are satisfied, we see interest-seeking beyond the survival instincts. No obligations apply. See an object of interest, reach for it, creep to it, pick it up, taste it, chew it, throw it, and ignore all "no, no" commands. Moreover, in a world full of interesting things and with a brain more and more filled with interesting thoughts, jumping from one to another point of attention is natural and fun. As life goes on, obligation increasingly shapes behavior. Choosing to focus on less interesting things in order to fulfill obligations requires structure often in the form of rules, marching orders, calendars, digital timers, parents, drill sergeants, and to-do lists. Individuals with ADHD need such enforcers of structure more than most because boredom is leading them more persuasively astray in search of interest than those without ADHD, who have normal levels of dopamine coursing through their brains and, importantly, the brain's reward circuitry.

The salient ways to resolve the dilemma of ADHD are to match one's obligation with the most interesting means of engagement and to make obligatory behavior more interesting. Knowing these are the desired objectives is the first step. Achieving them is the second. I offer the concept of the individual Elements of Interest as a tool and recommend the mindset of satisfying these Elements as a practice.

Perfect satisfaction is illusory, but deep satisfaction in stimulating moments is possible. Multiplying, extending, and stringing together such moments can follow.

Mihaly Csikszentmihalyi, who defined flow, describes an ideal state in a less-than-ideal world that we all experience, and that people with ADHD experience with more difficulty:

> A person who has reached the point of being able to resonate his abilities with the surroundings, whatever they are, is in harmony with the world. He can be in solitary confinement or in a boring job; but as long as he knows how to respond to the few stimuli around—through fantasy, scientific analysis, or intervention—he will still be enjoying himself… Extrinsic rewards will be less needed to motivate him to put up with the hardships of existence. A constant ability to "design or discover something new," "to explore a strange place"—the rewards that people experience in deep flow—will be enough to motivate action.[1]

Many of those with ADHD have achieved that state of flow; they have proved it exists, even, or especially, for them. In such states, their executive function works just fine, confirming that the stimulation of interest is chiefly what their brains desire.

We cannot be in flow all of the time, but gaining the ability to recognize which of our behaviors are boredom evasion and learning to consciously seek Elements of Interest will provide mile markers along the road to satisfying engagement.

ENDNOTES

Chapter One

1. Hallowell, E.M. and Ratey, J. (2006) *Delivered from Distraction.* New York: Ballantine Books, p.109.
2. Carroll, R. (n.d.) "Panic, Seeking, and Play in Psychotherapy." *Thinking Through the Body.* Available at www.thinkbody.co.uk/papers/panic-seeking%20-play.htm, accessed on 30 January 2014.
3. Waugh, L.D. with Sweitser, L. (1999) *Tired of Yelling: Teaching Our Children to Resolve Conflict.* Atlanta, GA: Longstreet.
4. From a conversation with Lyndon D. Waugh, M.D., 5 June 2013.
5. Spacks, P.M. (1995) *Boredom: The Literary History of a State of Mind.* Chicago: University of Chicago Press, p.2.
6. Dodson, W.W. (2002) "ADHD: The basics and the controversies." *Understanding Our Gifted. Open Space Communications* 14, 4. Davidson Institute for Talent Development. Available at www.davidsongifted.org/db/Articles_id_10262.aspx, accessed on 17 April 2014.

Chapter Two

1. Dobbs, D. (2013) "Restless genes." *National Geographic Magazine,* January 2013, p.45.
2. Dobbs, D. (2013), p.50.
3. Dobbs, D. (2013), p.1.
4. Walters, P. (2013) "Exploration: Risk takers." *National Geographic Magazine* January 2013, pp.58–67.
5. Chandler, C. (2010) *The Science of ADHD: A Guide for Parents and Professionals.* Chichester: Wiley-Blackwell, p.121.
6. Young, J.L. (2010) "ADHD and crime: Considering the connections." *Medscape Education & Mental Health* at Medscape.org, article 719862. Available at www.medscape.org/viewarticle/719862, accessed on 30 January 2014, citing Young, S. (2007) "Forensic Aspects of ADHD." In: M. Fitzgerald, M. Bellgove and M. Gill (eds) *Handbook of Attention Deficit Hyperactivity Disorder.* New York: John Wiley & Sons, pp.91–108.
7. Young, J.L. (2010), citing Retz, W. and Rosler, M. (2009) "The relation of ADHD and violent aggression: What can we learn from epidemiological and genetic studies?" *International Journal of Law and Psychiatry* 32, 235–243.
8. Baldwin, N. (2001) *Edison: Inventing the Century.* Chicago and London: University of Chicago Press, p.65.
9. Goodin, K. (n.d.) "Famous People with ADHD." Available at Parenting.com, www.parenting.com/gallery/famous-people-with-add-or-adhd?pnid=111949, accessed on 30 January 2014.
10. Perrault, S. (2009) "Entrepreneurs with ADHD." *Psychology Today.* Available at www.psychologytoday.com/blog/entrepreneurs-adhd/200909/7-habits-highly-successful-entrepreneurs-adhd, accessed on 30 January 2014.

11. Branson, R. (2013) "Richard Branson Biography." Available at www.biography.com, www.biography.com/people/richard-branson-9224520?page=2, accessed on 30 January 2014.
12. Bateman, C. (2009) "Why You Play Games." *International Hobo*. Blog article. 4 February 2009. Available at http://blog.ihobo.com/2009/02/why-you-play-games.html, accessed on 30 January 2014.
13. The Myers & Briggs Foundation, www.myersbriggs.org/my-mbti-personality-type/mbti-basics, accessed on 17 April 2014.
14. Indiana University Center for Evaluation and Education Policy (CEEP). (2009) "Charting the Path from Engagement to Achievement: A Report on the 2009 High School Survey of Student Engagement." Available at http://ceep.indiana.edu/hssse/images/HSSSE_2010_Report.pdf, accessed on 30 January 2014.
15. "Latest HSSSE Results Show Familiar Theme: Bored, Disconnected Students Want More from Schools." *IU News Room*. 8 June 2010. Press release. Available at http://newsinfo.iu.edu/web/page/normal/14593.html, accessed on 30 January 2014.

Chapter Three

1. Brantingham, E. (2012) *Two Under Two*. Blog. Available at http://mrandmrsbrantingham.blogspot.com, accessed on 30 January 2014.
2. Parvin, P. (2013) "The Secret Lives of Faculty." *Emory Magazine*, pp.34–41.

Chapter Four

1. Csikszentmihalyi, M. (1975) *Beyond Boredom and Anxiety: Experiencing Flow in Work and Play.* San Francisco: Jossey-Bass; (1990) *Flow: The Psychology of Optimal Experience*. New York: Harper and Row.

Chapter Five

1. The Myers & Briggs Foundation, www.myersbriggs.org/my-mbti-personality-typr/mbti-basics, accessed on 17 April 2014.

Chapter Six

1. Smith, R.P. (2010) *How to Do Nothing with Nobody All Alone by Yourself.* Portland, OR: Tin House Books. (Originally published in 1958.)
2. James, L. (2013) "Movercise™ Cooking—Ginger Chicken." Video. Available at www.theladywiththemoves.com, accessed on 30 January 2014.
3. Dodson, W. (2013) "Secrets of the ADHD Brain: What You Absolutely Need to Know about the Condition." *ADDitude Magazine ADHD Expert Webinar*, 30 July 2013.
4. Briggs, H. (2012) *Absolutely! The Memoirs of Harry Briggs, Ph.D.*, p.106. Available at Lulu.com, accessed on 31 January 2014.

Chapter Seven

1. Martin, K. (2013) *ADDitude Magazine ADHD Expert Webinar*, September 2013.
2. Briggs, H. (2012) *Absolutely! The Memoirs of Harry Briggs, Ph.D.* Available at Lulu.com, accessed on 31 January 2014.
3. Sweitzer, L. (2011) "Second chance: Twenty-ninth in a series of success stories of alumni." *The Outfitters Post 11*, Summer 2011. Newsletter of Recovery Outfitters, Inc., pp.8–15.

4. "Service Dogs for Veterans Returning from Iraq and Afghanistan." Available at www.puppiesbehindbars.com/service-dog-program/service-dogs-for-veterans-returning-from-iraq-and-afghanistan, accessed on 30 January 2014.
5. King, M.L. (1963) "Letter from a Birmingham Jail." Letter, 16 April, 1963. African Studies Center, University of Pennsylvania. Available at www.africa.upenn.edu/Articles_Gen/Letter_Birmingham.html, accessed on 30 January 2014.
6. Lovelace, R. (1919) "To Althea, from Prison." *The Oxford Book of English Verse: 1250–1900.* A. Quiller-Couch, 1919 edn, No. 348.

Chapter Eight

1. Dodson, W. (2013) "Secrets of the ADHD Brain: What You Absolutely Need to Know about the Condition." *ADDitude Magazine ADHD Expert Webinar*, 30 July 2013.
2. American Psychological Association. (2006) "Multitasking: Switching Costs." Available at http://apa.org/research/action/multitask.aspx, accessed on 31 January 2014.
3. Gallagher, W. (2009) *Rapt: Attention and the Focused Life.* New York: The Penguin Press, p.9.
4. *New Oxford American Dictionary*. Available at www.oxforddictionaries.com/us/definition/american_english/deliberate?q=deliberate, accessed on 30 January 2014.
5. Csikszentmihalyi, M. (2000) *Beyond Boredom and Anxiety*, 25th Anniversary Edition. First published in 1975. San Francisco: Jossey-Bass Publishers, pp.35–36.
6. Csikszentmihalyi, M. (2000), p.36.

Chapter Nine

1. "Edward: Success Stories." (n.d.) COPAC. Available at www.copacms.com/success-stories, accessed on 30 January 2014.
2. Sherman, C. (2007) "Addiction and ADHD Adults." *ADDitude Magazine*, February/March 2007. Available at www.additudemag.com/adhd/article/print/1868.html, accessed on 30 January 2014.
3. "Substance Use and Dependence Following Initiation of Alcohol or Illicit Drug Use." (2008) The NSDUH Report, 27 March, 2008. Available at www.samhsa.gov/data/2k8/newUseDepend/newUseDepend.htm, accessed on 30 January 2014.
4. "ADHD and Substance Abuse." (n.d.) WebMD. Available at www.webmd.com/add-adhd/guide/adhd-and-substance-abuse-is-there-a-link, accessed on 30 January 2014.
5. Cloninger, C.R., Sigvardsson, S. and Bohman, M. (1988) "Childhood personality predicts alcohol abuse in young adults." *Alcoholism: Clinical and Experimental Research 12*, 4, 494–505. p.431. Abstract. Available at www.ncbi.nlm.nih.gov/pubmed/3056070, accessed on 30 January 2014.
6. Bishop, F.M. (2001) *Managing Addictions: Cognitive, Emotive, and Behavioral Techniques.* Northvale, NJ and London: Jason Aronson.
7. *New Yorker Magazine*, 22 June 2009.
8. Bishop, F.M. (2001), pp.182–183.
9. Bishop, F.M. (2001), p.230.
10. Chandler, C. (2010) "Addiction, Reward, and ADHD." *The Science of ADHD: A Guide for Parents and Professionals.* Chichester, West Sussex: Wiley-Blackwell, p.211.
11. Chandler, C. (2010), pp.211–212.
12. Chandler, C. (2010), p.233.
13. Chandler, C. (2010), pp.211–213.
14. Todman, McW. (2012) "Recovery from Boredom (Part 2): Boredom Maps and Conditioned Cues." *Seeking Equilibrium: Social Dysregulation, Psychopathology and Self-Medication*, 23 July 2012. Available at www.psychologytoday.com/blog/seeking-equilibrium/201207/recovery-boredom-part-2, accessed on 30 January 2014.

15. Hyman, S.E. and Malenka, R.C. (2001) "Addiction and the brain: The neurobiology of compulsion and its persistence." *Macmillan Magazines 2*, 695–703. Available at www.sacklerinstitute.org/cornell/summer_institute/archive/2005/papers/hyman2001.pdf, accessed on 30 January 2014.

Chapter Eleven

1. Muenke, M. and Berg, K. (n.d.) "Is ADD/ADHD Genetic? Genes as a Cause of ADD/ADHD." *ADDitude Magazine.* Available at www.additudemag.com/adhd/article/653.html, accessed on 30 January 2014.
2. "Native American Cradleboards." (n.a.) Available at www.native-languages.org/cradleboard.htm, accessed on 30 January 2014.

Chapter Twelve

1. "Attention-Deficit/Hyperactivity Disorder (ADHD): Data & Statistics." (2013) Centers for Disease Control and Prevention (CDC). Available at www.cdc.gov/ncbddd/adhd/data.html, accessed on 31 January 2014.
2. "How Many People Have ADHD?" (n.d.) Available at ADDitudemag.com www.additudemag.com/adhd/article/688.html, accessed on 31 January 2014.
3. Schwarz, A. and Cohen, S. (2013) "A.D.H.D. Seen in 11% of U.S. Children as Diagnoses Rise." Available at www.nytimes.com/2013/04/01/health/more-diagnoses-of-hyperactivity-causing-concern.html?adxnnl=1&adxnnlx=1387296209-0V3Jq5Met1x0X1mRQ1jXAw, accessed on 31 January 2014.
4. "Attention Deficit Hyperactivity Disorder." (2011) FastStats. Centers for Disease Control and Prevention. Summary Health Statistics for U.S. Children: National Health Interview Survey, Appendix III, Table VI [PDF—711 KB]. Available at www.cdc.gov/nchs/fastats/adhd.htm, accessed on 30 January 2014.
5. Castellanos, F.X. and Tannock, R. (2002) "Neuroscience of attention-deficit hyperactivity disorder: the search for endophenotypes." *Nature Reviews: Neuroscience 3*, 617–628. Available at www.nature.com/nrn/journal/v3/n8/abs/nrn896.html, accessed 30 January 2014.
6. Thomas & Friends: Games, Videos & Activities for Kids (2013) Available at www.thomasandfriends.com, accessed on 31 January 2014.
7. Liu, J.H. (2001) "The 5 Best Toys of All Time." Available at http://archive.wired.com/geekdad/2011/01/the-5-best-toys-of-all-time, accessed on 31 January 2014.
8. Morey, L. (Lyrics) and Churchill, F. (Music) (1937) "Whistle While You Work." Song. Walt Disney Productions animated movie *Snow White and the Seven Dwarfs*. Available at http://kids.niehs.nih.gov/games/songs/movies/whistlemp3.htm, accessed on 31 January 2014.
9. Morey, L. (Lyrics) and Churchill, F. (Music) (1937) "Heigh Ho." Song. Walt Disney Productions animated movie *Snow White and the Seven Dwarfs*. Available at www.disneyclips.com/lyrics/lyrics29.html, accessed on 31 January 2014.

Chapter Thirteen

1. Hoopmann, K. (2009) *All Dogs Have ADHD.* London and Philadelphia: Jessica Kingsley Publishers.
2. Covey, S. (2008) *7 Habits of Happy Kids.* Simon and Schuster Books for Young Readers. New York: Simon and Schuster.

3. "'Play is the Work of the Child,' Maria Montessori." *Child Development: How Parents Can Promote Healthy Development in Children and Teens*. Available at http://childdevelopmentinfo.com/child-development/play-work-of-children, accessed on 31 January 2014.
4. Adcox, S. (2014) "Monopoly Junior: A Kids' Version of the Classic Family Game." Available at Grandparents.about.com, http://grandparents.about.com/od/reviewslists/gr/MonopolyJunior.htm, accessed on 31 January 2014.
5. Liu, J.H. (2001) "The 5 Best Toys of All Time." Available at http://archive.wired.com/geekdad/2011/01/the-5-best-toys-of-all-time, accessed on 31 January 2014.
6. "Fish and Chips: Zombies vs. Ninjas." (2011) YouTube.com. Video. Available [with Adobe] at www.youtube.com/watch?v=60C1OhVthLM, accessed on 31 January 2014.
7. Thomas & Friends: Games, Videos & Activities for Kids (2013) Available at www.thomasandfriends.com, accessed on 31 January 2014.
8. "Tail Waggin' Tutors, TDI's Reading Program, Children Reading to Dogs." (2013) Available at www.tdi-dog.org/OurPrograms.aspx?Page=Children+Reading+to+Dogs, accessed on 31 January 2014.
9. "Reading with Rover." (2013) Available at www.readingwithrover.org, accessed on 31 January 2014.
10. "A Dog in the Library?" (2014) Available at www.librarydogs.com, accessed on 31 January 2014.
11. "R.E.A.D.—Intermountain Therapy Animals." (2014) Available at www.therapyanimals.org/R.E.A.D.html, accessed on 31 January 2014.
12. Rowling, J.K. with illustrations by GrandPré, M. (1998) *Harry Potter and the Sorcerer's Stone (Book 1)*. New York: Arthur A. Levine Books, an imprint of Scholastic Press, hardcover edition.
13. Suarez-Orozco, M. (2013) "The Elephant in the (Class)room." *US News and World Report*, 19 September 2013. Available at www.usnews.com/opinion/articles/2013/09/19/3-ways-to-combat-boredom-and-close-the-global-education-gap, accessed on 31 January 2014.
14. Available at http://en.wikipedia.org/wiki/Dora_the_Explorer, accessed on 31 January 2014.
15. Csikszentmihalyi, M. (2000; first published in 1975) *Beyond Boredom and Anxiety. 25th Anniversary Edition*. San Francisco: Jossey-Bass Publishers, pp.35–36.
16. Celebrate Calm. (2014) Available at www.celebratecalm.com, accessed on 31 January 2014.
17. Martin, K. (2013) "Stop School Stress: 10 Ways to Improve Focus, Social Skills, Daily Routines." *ADDitude Magazine ADHD Expert Webinar*, 17 September 2013.

Chapter Fourteen

1. "The Synapse." (2012) *Neuroscience for Kids*. Available at http://faculty.washington.edu/chudler/synapse.html, accessed on 31 January 2014.
2. "Ritalin (Methylphenidate): How Does It Work?" (2013) NetDoctor. Available at www.netdoctor.co.uk/adhd/medicines/ritalin.html, accessed on 31 January 2014.
3. Sherman, C. (2013) "Addiction and ADHD Adults: Part Two." Available at www.additudemag.com/adhd/article/1868-2.html, accessed on 31 January 2014.
4. "Game On: Picking Sports for ADHD Children." (2013) ADDitudeMag.com Available at www.additudemag.com/adhd/article/5708.html, accessed on 31 January 2014.
5. Rodgers, A.L. (2013) "Music: Sound Medicine for ADHD." *ADDitude Magazine*, Summer 2012. Print. Online, ADDitudeMag.com. Available at www.additudemag.com/adhd/article/9558.html, accessed on 31 January 2014.
6. Eliot, J. (2013) "Stone Soup." Comic, print. *Atlanta Journal and Constitution 12*.
7. Wilson, K. (2011) "Why Every Educator Needs to Hear Ron Clark." *Pure Joy 4*, November 2012. Available at http://teachandinspiretheblog.blogspot.com/2012/11/why-every-educator-needs-to-hear-ron.html, accessed on 31 January 2014.

8. Lindstrom, R. (2012) "Teaching Model Gains in Popularity." 11Alive.com, 17 August 2012. Available at www.11alive.com/news/article/252504/40/Will-flip-classrooms-flip-test-scores, accessed on 31 January 2014.

Chapter Fifteen

1. Indiana University Center for Evaluation and Education Policy (CEEP). (2009) "Charting the Path from Engagement to Achievement: A Report on the 2009 High School Survey of Student Engagement." Available at http://ceep.indiana.edu/hssse/images/HSSSE_2010_Report.pdf, accessed on 31 January 2014.
2. "Latest HSSSE Results Show Familiar Theme: Bored, Disconnected Students Want More from Schools." *IU News Room*, 8 June, 2010. Press release. Available at http://newsinfo.iu.edu/web/page/normal/14593.html, accessed on 31 January 2014.
3. Lindstrom, R. (2012) "Teaching Model Gains in Popularity." 11Alive.com, 17 August, 2012. Available at www.11alive.com/news/article/252504/40/Will-flip-classrooms-flip-test-scores, accessed on 31 January 2014.
4. Scott, J. and Borgman, J. (2009) "Zits." *Atlanta Journal Constitution.* Comic strip.
5. Dodson, W. (2013) "Do You Have Adult ADHD? Signs and Symptoms You Should Know About." *ADDitude Magazine Webinar*, 10 October 2013. Available at www.additudemag.com/adhdblogs/29/10430.html, accessed on 31 January 2014.
6. "It's About Time." (2013) *ADDitude Magazine*, Winter 2013, p.12.
7. Banta, S. (2013) "Museum." Unpublished essay, Fall 2013.
8. "ADHD and Higher Education" (2013) *ADHD & You.* Available at www.adhdandyou.com/adhd-patient/adhd-tips-young-adult/adhd-college.aspx, accessed on 31 January 2014.
9. Kravets, M. and Wax, I. (2012) *The K&W Guide to College Programs & Services for Students with Learning Disabilities or Attention Deficit/Hyperactivity Disorder*, 11th edn. Princeton Review: College Admissions Guides. Paperback.
10. The Equality Act 2010. Available at www.legislation.gov.uk/ukpga/2010/15/section/91, accessed on 31 January 2014.
11. "Attention Deficit/Hyperactivity Disorder (ADD/ADHD) Information Pack for Students." (2012) Oxford University. Available at www.ox.ac.uk/media/global/wwwoxacuk/localsites/studentgateway/documents/disabilityadvisoryservice/ADHD.pdf, accessed on 31 January 2014.
12. Kellye, T. (2013) "ADHD Pill Faces High Hurdle in Europe as Stigma Persists." Bloomberg, 1 October 2013. Available at www.bloomberg.com/news/2013-10-01/adhd-pill-faces-high-hurdle-in-europe-as-stigma-persists.html, accessed on 30 January 2014.
13. "Succeeding in College (WWK13)." (2009) Available at www.help4adhd.org/education/college/WWK13, accessed on 30 January 2014.
14. "ADHD Coaches Organization—Promoting ADHD Coaches and Coaching Worldwide." (2005) Available at www.adhdcoaches.org, accessed on 30 January 2014.
15. International Coach Federation. (n.d.) "Need Coaching?" Available at www.coachfederation.org/need/landing.cfm?ItemNumber=980&navItemNumber=569, accessed on 30 January 2014.
16. Edge Foundation. (2014) "How a Coach Helps" Available at https://edgefoundation.org/parents/how-a-coach-helps/, accessed on 30 January 2014.
17. Scheib, M. (2006) "Finding a Good Fit: Two Students Study Abroad with ADHD." Available at www.miusa.org/ncde/stories/scheib3, accessed on 30 January 2014.

Chapter Sixteen

1. Hardie, A. (2013) "Sunday Conversation with Collier Hostler: Youngster Explains Art of Grocery Bagging." *Atlanta Journal Constitution*. Print. 3 August 2013. Available at www.ajc.com/news/news/local/sunday-conversation-with-collier-hostler-youngster/nZByZ, accessed on 30 January 2014.
2. Robinson, W. (2013) "Is This the World's Most Boring Job? Meet the Woman Who Is Actually Paid to Watch GRASS GROW." MailOnline, 21 October 2013. Available at www.dailymail.co.uk/news/article-2470107/Is-worlds-boring-job-Grass-seed-analyst-paid-watch-grow.html, accessed on 30 January 2014.
3. Blake, H. (2010) "You Really Can Be Bored to Death, Study Shows." *The Telegraph*, 8 February 2010. Available at www.telegraph.co.uk/health/healthnews/7187812/You-really-can-be-bored-to-death-study-shows.html, accessed on 30 January 2014.
4. Britton, A. and Shipley, M.J. (2010) "Bored to death?" *International Journal of Epidemiology 1–2*. Published by Oxford University Press on behalf of the International Epidemiological Association. Available at http://ije.oxfordjournals.org/content/early/2010/02/01/ije.dyp404.full.pdf, accessed on 30 January 2014.
5. "Poll: Bored at Work? Don't Worry, So is Half of America." (2013) *The Independent*, 25 June 2013. Available at www.independent.co.uk/voices/iv-drip/poll-bored-at-work-dont-worry-so-is-half-of-america-8672833.html, accessed on 30 January 2014.
6. "State of the American Workplace: Employee Engagement Insights for U.S. Business Leaders." (2013) *Gallup*. Available at www.gallup.com/strategicconsulting/163007/state-american-workplace.aspx, accessed on 30 January 2014.
7. Rothlin, P. and Werder, P. (2008) *Boreout! Overcoming Workplace Motivation*. London and Philadelphia: Kogan Page, p.4.
8. Rothlin,P. and Werder, P. (2008), p.44.
9. Smiley, S. (2013) "Dinner with the Smileys." *Parade Magazine*, 12 May, pp.6–11.
10. Mulling, E.W. (2002) *The Mulling Factor*. Sanford, FL: DC Press, a division of the Diogenes Consortium, p.116.

Chapter Seventeen

1. Csikszentmihalyi, M. (2000) *Beyond Boredom and Anxiety: Experiencing Flow in Work and Play, 25th Anniversary Edition*. First published in 1975. San Francisco: Jossey-Bass Publishers, p.206.

SUBJECT INDEX

AUTHOR INDEX